Mandate to Difference

Other books by Walter Brueggemann
from Westminster John Knox Press

Abiding Astonishment: Psalms, Modernity, and the Making of History

Cadences of Home: Preaching among Exiles

First and Second Samuel (Interpretation: A Bible Commentary for Teaching
   and Preaching)

Genesis (Interpretation: A Bible Commentary for Teaching and Preaching)

Hope for the World: Mission in a Global Context

Hope within History

An Introduction to the Old Testament: The Canon and Christian Imagination

Isaiah 1–39, Vol. 1 (Westminster Bible Companion)

Isaiah 40–66, Vol. 2 (Westminster Bible Companion)

Many Voices, One God: Being Faithful in a Pluralistic World (coedited with
   George W. Stroup)

Power, Providence, and Personality: Biblical Insight into Life and Ministry

Reverberations of Faith: A Theological Handbook of Old Testament Themes

Struggling with Scripture (with William C. Placher and Brian K. Blount)

Texts for Preaching: A Lectionary Commentary Based on the NRSV—Year A (with
   Charles B. Cousar, Beverly R. Gaventa, and James D. Newsome)

Texts for Preaching: A Lectionary Commentary Based on the NRSV—Year B (with
   Charles B. Cousar, Beverly R. Gaventa, and James D. Newsome)

Using God's Resources Wisely: Isaiah and Urban Possibility

The Vitality of Old Testament Traditions (with Hans Walter Wolff)

Mandate to Difference

An Invitation to the Contemporary Church

Walter Brueggemann

Westminster John Knox Press
LOUISVILLE • LONDON

Book design by Sharon Adams
Cover design by Eric Walljasper, Minneapolis, MN
Cover art: Bassano, Francesco (1549–1592). The Good Samaritan. *Kunsthistorisches*
   Museum, Vienna, Austria
Cover photo: Erich Lessing/Art Resource, NY

First edition
Published by Westminster John Knox Press
Louisville, Kentucky

This book is printed on acid-free paper that meets the American National Standards Institute Z39.48 standard. ∞

PRINTED IN THE UNITED STATES OF AMERICA

07 08 09 10 11 12 13 14 15 16—10 9 8 7 6 5 4 3 2 1

Library of Congress Cataloging-in-Publication Data is on file at the Library of Congress, Washington, D.C.

ISBN-13: 978-0-664-23121-7
ISBN-10: 0-664-23121-7

For
Douglas John Hall

Contents

Acknowledgments

"The Good News of Regime Change" was preached at a United Methodist Consultation on Worship, Christ United Methodist Church, New York, on May 8, 2005.

"Weeping and Hoping in Jerusalem" was presented at a Conference on Urban Ministry at the College of Preachers, National Cathedral, Washington, D.C., on June 6, 2005.

"The Sabbath Voice of the Evangel: Against Death, Denial and Despair" was preached at the Presbyterian Church (USA) Conference in Snowbird, Utah, on May 29, 2005.

"A Welcome for the Others" was presented at a North American Conference of Episcopal Bishops in Windsor, Ontario, Canada, on April 28, 2005.

"The Fearful Thirst for Dialogue" was presented at a North American Conference of Episcopal Bishops in Windsor, Ontario, Canada, on April 30, 2005.

"Can We Hope? Can Hope Be Divided?" was presented at a Jewish-Christian consultation of the Chicago Cluster of Theological Seminaries at Luther School of Theology, February 28, 2005. This paper will be included in a publication by Fortress Press along with other papers from that consultation.

"Spirit-Led Imagination: Reality Practiced in a Sub-version" was presented at a United Methodist Consultation on Worship, Christ United Methodist Church, New York, on May 6, 2005.

"You Cannot Fool Your *Nephesh*" was presented at a retreat on Sabbath at the Presbyterian Church (USA) Conference in Snowbird, Utah, on May 28, 2005.

"Just Like You . . . Forgiven!" was presented at a retreat on Sabbath at the Presbyterian Church (USA) Conference in Snowbird, Utah, on May 30, 2005.

"Bread: The Good Stuff on the Table" was preached at a Luce Consultation for the Association of Theological Schools, Pittsburgh, on October 2, 2005.

"Some Theses on the Bible in the Church" was presented at The Christian Century, Chicago, on September 29, 2005. An abridged form of this paper was published in *The Christian Century* (November 29, 2005).

Preface

Over the last year I have had the happy opportunity (and demanding assignment) to make presentations in a variety of inviting and responsive venues. The papers included in this volume are the outcome of these several oral presentations during 2005. For the most part, these opportunities specified particular themes and topics, thus directing my energy in a focused way. The result, of course, is a set of presentations that are to some extent ad hoc, with each study on its own as a self-contained exposition.

Nonetheless, there is a kind of coherence to the collection of presentations, because to each one I have brought my critical passion and conviction. The commonality in these presentations is an ecclesial insistence that the church in this demanding moment of its life must recover and re-embrace its missional identity that sets it in significant tension with major political-economic-ideological developments in U.S. society. From that, moreover, comes consideration of the shape of moral reflection and moral action that a missional community under discipline may expect to undertake. A byproduct of making the same argument with reference to a number of discrete issues is some inevitable repetition, but I do not mind my critical passions being reiterated.

I am glad to thank my several hosts who initiated and managed these occasions of the presentations. I am pleased to say that on every such occasion I enjoyed generous and thoughtful hospitality. More important, for the most part those who heard my presentations were willingly engaged and eager to respond. The conclusion I draw is that there is a profound readiness and a genuine eagerness that the church accept a bold missional stance on the great issues of the day. I am delighted that Westminster John

Knox Press has been willing to publish these interpretive efforts and so to make them more widely available.

I am grateful to Tia Foley, who has persevered in the demanding task of turning my efforts into a coherent, publishable form. I am grateful to Jon Berquist and his colleagues at Westminster John Knox Press for seeing things through to publication. I am again grateful to Chris Hooker for preparing the indexes. And beyond that, I am the recipient of support and generous critical feedback from a host of friends and colleagues without whom my work would be thinner and safer than it is.

I am glad to dedicate this book to Doug Hall, who is my ancient schoolmate from Union Seminary and my abiding friend and teacher. I am among the many who celebrate and give thanks for his wry humor, his deep brooding thought, his glad embrace of Reformed theology, and his ironic love of life. This is with my thanks and love to him and Rhoda.

Walter Brueggemann
Columbia Theological Seminary
Epiphany 2006

Chapter One

The Good News of Regime Change

You might think

- if you cringe at the boisterous, cocky new sound of religion in politics,
- if you worry about the divisiveness of "red" and "blue," and
- if you are vexed that too many people claim to be speaking directly for Christ . . .

you might think that our Christian faith is all about getting the moral issues right and leveraging others to think and act the right way, as do we. But if you think that, you are very wrong, because such contemporary loud posturing is not so much about faith as it is about anxiety and maintaining control in the world. Our faith, I propose, is not about pinning down moral certitudes. It is, rather, about *openness to wonder* and *awe in glad praise*.

Think back with me to what the church celebrates as the Ascension of Jesus, usually recognized one Sunday before Pentecost, but marked specifically on a Thursday, forty days after Easter. The ascension refers to the poetic, imaginative claim of the church that the risen Jesus has "gone up" to share power and honor and glory and majesty with God. It is a claim made in our creed that "he ascended into heaven and sitteth on the right hand of God the father almighty."

Now if you want to, you can vex about this prescientific formulation all you want. But you can also, as I do, take the claim as a majestic poetic affirmation that makes a claim for Jesus, that Jesus now is "high and lifted up" in majesty, that the one crucified and risen is now the one who shares God's power and rules over all the earth. This prescientific

1

formulation of the matter is important, because it gives us imagery of a quite concrete kind to imagine Jesus receiving power, real power in a drama not unlike Miss America when she takes the throne. It's about coming to real authority.

That poetic imagery as *ascent to power* had in the background, for New Testament narrative writers, very old liturgical poetry that is even older than the Old Testament. Our psalm for the day, Psalm 68, is one such piece of poetic imagery that likely was used in Canaanite liturgy for their God Baal and was taken over for use of YHWH the God of Israel. In liturgical project, gods are always ascending to power, always being celebrated in authority, always being acknowledged as real rulers to whom allegiance and obedience are owed.

If you listen carefully to the poetic cadences of Psalm 68, you may hear the surging of the cosmic God who is portrayed—as was Baal and as was YHWH—as the great storm God who caused thunder and rain and who used clouds as transportation. This primitive rhetoric imagines the great God riding around in the sky on a cloud, supervising, monitoring, breathing life, and giving power to the creation. In its doxology, Israel recognizes the immense power of God who celebrated in his coming:

> As smoke is driven away, so [God drives enemies] away;
>> as wax melts before the fire,
>> let the wicked perish before God.
> But let the righteous be joyful;
>> let them exult before God;
>> let them be jubilant with joy.
>
> (Ps 68:2–3)

Then Israel refers to the holy cloud-rider:

> Sing to God, sing praises to his name;
>> lift up a song to him who rides upon the clouds—
> his name is the LORD—
>> be exultant before him.
>
> (Ps 68:4)

The psalm, at the end, returns to that same imagery:

> Sing to God, O kingdoms of the earth;
>> sing praises to the Lord,
> O rider in the heavens, the ancient heavens;
>> listen, he sends out his voice, his mighty voice.

Ascribe power to God,
> whose majesty is over Israel;
> and whose power is in the skies.
> > (Ps 68:32–34)

The accent is on power before which Israel and all of the nations, and all creatures in heaven and on earth are subject in glad obedience:

> Praise God from whom all blessings flow.
> Praise him, all creatures here below.
> Praise him above, ye heavenly host.
> Praise Father, Son, and Holy Ghost.

Praise him all creatures, and that became an anthem concerning "all creatures" for Francis of Assisi.

But I want you not to miss another angle in the great doxological celebration of God's power as the one who has ascended to the throne. It is offered in verses 5–6:

> Father of *orphans* and protector of *widows*
> > is God in his holy habitation.
> God gives the desolate a home to live in;
> > he leads out the *prisoners* to prosperity,
> > but the rebellious live in a parched land.
> > > (Ps 68:5–6, emphasis added)

The song of Israel now opens for us another side of the God who reigns in power. It turns out that God's reign is not simply about power. It is about a relationship of caring fidelity, wherein God is in solidarity with the most vulnerable and most needy in society, which in ancient Israel includes

- *orphans* who lack a protector in a patriarchal society, so that God is a father for those who have no father;
- *widows* who lack a male protector in a patriarchal society, so that this God is a protector of the unprotected;
- *prisoners* who, then as now, were characteristically poor people who lacked resources or a smart lawyer. Thus God is an ally to those whom society would hold in bondage.

It turns out that the one who has ascended into power is not transcendent in remoteness, is not splendid in indifference, but is deeply in touch with the reality of the earth where money and power and social leverage and differentiation of gender, race, and class leave some dangerously exposed. This father-God to whom we pray "our father" rides the clouds not as a joy rider, but rather to be in a position to see and to know and to care and to intervene and to feed and to heal and to forgive and to reconcile and to liberate. It turns out that ascension, whereby God is celebrated in power, is a claim that the earth is ordered differently because of the one who governs it.

It is clear that in the New Testament narratives concerning the "ascent" of Jesus that this ancient poetry is in purview. Israel has taken the liturgy of the ascent of Baal and made it into an ascent of YHWH the God of Israel, and now the early church does the same. It takes the poetry of the ascent of YHWH and transforms it into the ascent of Jesus who is now the one who is elevated and celebrated with majestic sovereignty,

> who gives daily bread;
> who forgives sins;
> who rescues us from evil and makes life possible.

We may then, on this Ascent Sunday, imagine that the same Jesus who was known in the Gospel narrative is able to do on a cosmic scale what Jesus of Nazareth had done locally:

> He feeds hungry multitudes.
> He touches lepers and they are healed.
> He welcomes children who are vulnerable.
> He enjoys the company of those disapproved of by proper society.

Or as Luke puts it, everywhere Jesus goes good stuff happens:

> And he answered them, "Go and tell John what you have seen and heard: the blind receive their sight, the lame walk, the lepers are cleansed, the deaf hear, the dead are raised, the poor have good news brought to them." (Luke 7:22)

And that leaves us to answer. If we accept this particular scenario of the truth of our life, we may confess the creed: "He ascended into heaven and sitteth on the right hand of God the Father." But we may do more than confess. We may move our life into coherence with the new rule of Jesus. I suggest three urgent issues where we may take into account this regime change:

1. Jesus has come that we may have an abundant life. His feeding narratives attest that the generosity of God is assured wherever Jesus rules in the earth and we count on that generosity. And that means, does it not, that our common practices of greed, of the pursuit of consumer goods, of the frantic effort to acquire more, are both inappropriate and unnecessary. Our society hungers always for more: more body surgery, more cosmetics, more cars, more beer, more sex, more certitude, more security, more money, more power, more oil . . . whatever. This hunger for more is a true sign that we do not trust the goodness of God to supply all of our needs; we do not trust that the generous rule of Jesus who has ascended to power is in effect. But we, we are Jesus people, and therefore we are pledged and empowered to act differently, differently in the neighborhood, differently in the economy, and as citizens of the last superpower, differently in the world.

2. Jesus has given a new commandment, that *we love one another*. And then it is added,

> We love because he first loved us. Those who say, "I love God," and hate their brothers or sisters, are liars; for those who do not love a brother or sister whom they have seen, cannot love God whom they have not seen. The commandment we have from him is this: those who love God must love their brothers and sisters also. (1 John 4:19–21)

And Jesus went to great length to identify "sister and brother" as everyone, including those most unlike us, those who do not fit, those who upset us and make us uncomfortable.

What a gospel word in a society that is increasingly given over to exclusion, to hate, and to vengeance! There is an ideology at work among us that wants to make the world very small, in order to make it safe for us, and to exclude and eliminate everyone who is not like us. That attraction to hate and resentment spins off in policies concerning immigrants and capital punishment, so that our hate of the other turns to violent vengeance and all in the name of religious piety. Such a practice of hurt that is among us is a contradiction to the father of mercy who loves all the children and protects all the weak ones.

3. Jesus is the glue of the universe. Paul has written,

> in him all things hold together.
> (Col 1:17)

And Jesus said, "Therefore I tell you, do not worry about your life" (Matt 6:25). This is an assurance that God's caring sustenance is everywhere at work in creation.

As you know, we live in a fearful society that is devoured by anxiety. And we imagine in our anxiety that there are extreme "security" measures that will make us safe. But if this is God's world and if the rule of love is at work, then our mandate is not to draw into a cocoon of safety; rather, it is to be out and alive in the world in concrete acts and policies whereby the fearful anxiety among us is dispatched and adversaries can be turned to allies and to friends.

So imagine on this ascension day in poetic idiom, the ascended Lord Jesus, riding on a cloud of glory, keeping the world under caring surveillance. Imagine that the cloud is the throne room where sits the Father of all mercy. Imagine the governance of Father-Son sending out edicts, directives, and policies that concerning the earth:

Here is a press release that says,

> The newly ascended power has decreed that there is *more than enough*, and *greed* is inappropriate in this world of God's generosity.

Here is a new act of legislation from the government of God that says,

> *Perfect love* casts out hate, that we are not free for *vengeance* but must leave such matters to the wise Father.

Here is an edict from the government that says,

> Do not *fear* for *I am with you* and the world will hold.

My urge to you this day is that you go deep into the vision of the psalm concerning a new governance, a new heaven, and a new earth. And then you can decide day by day—as your lifelong vocation—to bring your life and our common life more fully in response to this regime. The claim that he ascended into heaven is not an abstract theological formula. It is, rather, an act of praise that asserts that the gospel is true. The world is under new management. Think of us under new management:

> Once you were not a people,
>   but now you are God's people;

once you had not received mercy,
    but now you have received mercy.
                (1 Pet 2:10)

Be glad, be obedient, be joyous. Pray and sing and give thanks!

Chapter Two

Weeping and Hoping in Jerusalem

The city, most especially the city of Jerusalem, occupies a complex place in biblical faith; much of the Protestant tradition has been suspicious of and resistant toward the city. Moreover, a part of the current threat of right-wing Christianity in the United States is that it opts for a suburban "family values" project that seeks to withdraw from the city, seeing it as a place of chaotic threat and hopeless evil. But we, of course, have refused to abandon the city; our faith requires us to think again about the city. I begin my articulation with general comments about the city, focus on four accents in the Old Testament, and reflect finally on some dimensions of the city in the New Testament.

Even a surface consideration indicates enormous complexity that admits of no simplistic judgment about the city. We may begin with three general comments about urban reality that we can test in terms of our own experience and in terms of biblical claims for and against the city.

1. *The city is a collage of technological achievements*, for the city characteristically enjoys a monopoly of technology. Such technology may trickle down to the rural economy, but its origin and primary exhibit are characteristically in the city. The city is almost always at the head of the state, and technological advance in the state is characteristically linked to military needs and developments. We may thus begin by seeing that the city is what it is as the producer and beneficiary of technological capacity.

Such technological capacity may function in a largely positive way for the well-being of its members. Such a positive capacity is evident, for example, in medical technology, so that the best urban hospitals are best in part because of technological advances. In a less dramatic way, the same technological capacity is evident in universities that perform in the urban

9

economy. The function and maintenance of good hospitals and good schools is most likely to be an urban matter. There is, of course, good biblical precedent for an urban monopoly of technology. In 1 Samuel 13:19–22, the Philistines controlled the flow of military technology, limiting the capacity of Israel even in its agricultural productivity:

> Now there was no smith to be found throughout all the land of Israel; for the Philistines said, "The Hebrews must not make swords or spears for themselves"; so all the Israelites went down to the Philistines to sharpen their plowshare, mattocks, axes, or sickles; The charge was two-thirds of a shekel for the plowshares and for the mattocks, and one-third of a shekel for sharpening the axes and for setting the goads. So on the day of the battle neither sword nor spear was to be found in the possession of any of the people with Saul and Jonathan.

And of course there is complete correspondence between the Philistine strategy in the narrative and that of U.S. policy concerning nuclear capacity in Iran and North Korea. Those with monopoly find ways to sustain monopoly, and it is always by way of urban management and manipulation.

2. *The city is a money economy with a concentration of power and control.* The money economy is both necessary and possible because of urbanization that includes a capacity for surplus wealth, that is, the capacity to live off the produce of others. That of course is why great cities—since the early Canaanite city-states—are filled with banks and other financial institutions and why wealth is characteristically exhibited and flaunted so that Donald Trump is only an extreme case and not an aberration. Such concentration, moreover, is contrasted with a rural economy, in which wealth is at best modest and hidden, and in which the disparity between rich and poor is not at all exaggerated; the stratification of society between the haves and the have-nots is not nearly as conspicuous in a rural economy as in the city.

That urban concentration of wealth and power is evident, moreover, in the recurring strategy of revolutionary coups in which one has mainly to seize the media (which, in a pre-urban economy, would be only the village well), and second, to seize the airport, which has no counterpart in village life. Urban dominance depends upon the control of information and the control of transportation that keeps goods and, therefore, money flowing, always to the top of the pyramid.

3. But the city is not only a monopoly of technological capacity or a monopoly of power and control. *The city is also an ongoing act of artistic imagination*, artistic in the sense that subversive alternatives are regularly rendered, whereas the rural economy tends not to know that alternatives are available, given a high commitment to conformity. The city is where the theater and music occur, from Lincoln Center to the Kennedy Center. It is the place where the orchestra performs and in which the poets congregate. It is there that actors, musicians, poets, and prophets—all the performers—give expression to alternatives in human life. Artists, at their best, are open to a live edge against the complacency of power and control. In the ancient world, the practice of alternative imagination was characteristically in the temple. To be sure, the temple—now read Cathedral—is mostly a part of the urban-political-economic establishment; this is evident in ancient times in Jerusalem with its songs of Zion (Pss 46; 48; 76; 84), and in contemporary time exemplified by President Bush's address regarding September 11, 2001, at the National Cathedral. But the temple-as-theater, even when claimed by the establishment, always carries a political edge to it; along with songs of Zion are old images of prophetic danger that still continue in the liturgy. Alongside presidential acts of ideology, there is still a playfulness in the cathedral; poets and clowns and prophets and other dissidents show up there and are given air time.

So think of the city as a place of artistic imagination as, for example, with Meg Greenfield, *Washington*, and Carl Sandberg in Chicago and "hog butcher of the world," or Walt Whitman in Brooklyn observing Manhattan, or Jeremiah weeping and hoping, or Jesus in a triumphal approach to Jerusalem that became a death watch for old ossified faith and a trial of the Roman governor.[1] These are all artistic acts that witness to the depth and complexity of the city in ways that affirm and question, celebrate and subvert, and keep the city open for possibility. That witness continues until the poets weep, but in weeping laugh and dance and sing and wait for a New Jerusalem, a newness that moves in and with and under all technological monopoly and all concentration of power. It has always been so, and the banks are always on edge with the artists; they fund them and they worry about them!

In that matrix of ambivalence we in the church have a peculiar task today and every day: to weave together an honest, complex, narrative account of the city—*narrative* because the city is still under way and the story remains to be constructed; *complex* because the city consists in many competing, conflicted voices that will not be readily harmonized; and *honest* because we are adherents to the God of all truth.

I submit that that honest, complex narrative account of the city needs to pay attention to many voices:

- voices of establishment power
- voices of dissent sounded from the margin of power
- voices of remembered pain that will not collude in a preferred amnesia of the urban establishment
- voices of hope that refuse despair about what has not yet been achieved

The Bible offers no simple narrative account of the city, nor will I propose one. Rather, in the course of this and the next chapter I cite four voices in the Old Testament on the city that need to be taken into account, and then offer two brief vignettes from the New Testament. These materials will help inform our interpretive boldness through which we will construct the narrative of the city.

A Voice of Critical Dissent: Joshua

When Israel entered the land of promise, the land was organized into "Canaanite city states," centers of economic-political power that featured a "city king" and a small, privileged urban elite that lived a life of luxury.[2] They did so because the urban establishment presided over the surrounding agricultural economy of the peasants who produced tax money through a rent economy based on agricultural produce—the peasants who grew the wealth but did not receive the benefit of their produce or labor. At the outset, the Old Testament sounds a voice on behalf of resentful peasants who regarded the urban concentration of power as a ruthless engine for economic exploitation. In this tradition, the city is regarded as a mechanism for acquisitive coveting. It features:

A division of labor, the sort the educated urban elite always enjoy, of pencil pushers and people who sweat when they work, a division that in the contemporary West now requires guest workers.

Social stratification in which every element of the population is locked into position; consequently peasants have no chance to move out of peasantry and are enduringly denied access to social power and social goods.

Surplus value in which peasants live from crop to crop or, as we say, "one paycheck away from homelessness." At the same time, the urban elite needs a strong central bank—a "Fed," so to speak—to keep, invest, grow, and enhance money that will never be needed.

A close critical reading of the literature of the books of Joshua and Judges, when seen alertly, offers evidence that these dimensions of urban-peasant reality are fully operative. One example, illuminated by the categories of James C. Scott, is the narrative of Ehud in Judges 3:12–30.[3] In the narrative account of entry into the land, Joshua becomes a representative cipher in Israel who champions Torah-covenantal faith (Josh 1:7–8; 23:6–8). As Joshua enters the land and mobilizes the peasant solidarity of Israel, he is profoundly opposed to the city, for the city is the center of Canaanite power, Canaanite religion, and Canaanite ideology that constitute a practice of commodity fetishism. The narrative account is thus a clash of ideological systems so that the "Canaanites" are not just preexisting residents in the land, but practitioners of an urban system that defeats and diminishes the peasant population with which YHWH is allied, indeed has been allied since the slave emancipation from Egypt.

In Joshua 1

At the very beginning of this counternarrative that we call "conquest," Israel used military rhetoric, but the rhetoric in detail concerns not arms but Torah obedience:

> "Be strong and courageous; for you shall put this people in possession of the land that I swore to their ancestors to give them. Only be strong and very courageous, being careful to act in accordance with all the law that my servant Moses commanded you; do not turn from it to the right hand or to the left, so that you may be successful wherever you go. This book of the law shall not depart out of your mouth; you shall meditate on it day and night, so that you may be careful to act in accordance with all that is written in it. For then you shall make your way prosperous, and then you shall be successful. I hereby command you: Be strong and courageous; do not be frightened or dismayed, for the LORD your God is with you wherever you go." (Josh 1:6–9)

The military imagery makes the movement sound like conquest, but the only "weapons" mentioned are the commandments of the book of Deuteronomy, which line out a policy and a system of covenantal neighborliness. Joshua offers covenantal neighborliness as a powerful antidote to the uncritical self-indulgence of the preexisting Canaanite urban system in the land of promise.

In Joshua 6

The old and great city of Jericho is cited in a particular narrative as a case study of Joshua's critique of the Canaanite city-state system. It is to be noticed, on the one hand, that Jericho is a place of enormous wealth:

> "But all silver and gold, and vessels of bronze and iron, are sacred to the LORD; they shall go into the treasury of the LORD." (Josh 6:19)

On the other hand, it is also noted that Joshua is to "devote" all of that community wealth to YHWH, that is, to destroy it; the reason for the destruction is that the commodities themselves have seductive power to erode commitment to neighborly covenantalism:

> "As for you, keep away from the things devoted to destruction, so as not to covet and take any of the devoted things and make the camp of Israel an object for destruction, bringing trouble upon it." . . . Joshua said to the two men who had spied out the land, "Go into the prostitute's house, and bring the woman out of it and all who belong to her, as you swore to her." (Josh 6:18, 22)

Primitive guerrilla methods of warfare on the part of Joshua were able to defeat the city:

> On the seventh day they rose early, at dawn, and marched around the city in the same manner seven times. It was only on that day that they marched around the city seven times. And at the seventh time, when the priests had blown the trumpets, Joshua said to the people, "Shout! For the LORD has given you the city." . . . So the people shouted, and the trumpets were blown. As soon as the people heard the sound of the trumpets, they raised a great shout, and the wall fell down flat; so the people charged straight ahead into the city and captured it. (Josh 6:15–16, 20)

The destruction of Jericho was, of course, an astonishing achievement made possible only because of YHWH. But then the guerrilla warfare of covenantalism has always depended upon the power and presence of the

God of covenant who acts as surreptitiously as the guerrillas. Thus, the Joshua narrative is a celebrative report on the capacity of the Torah community to counter the commodity practice of the city.

Joshua 12:7–24

In this passage we are offered a summary inventory of Joshua's military success, indicating that Joshua and the Israelites defeated thirty-one city kings. Taken at face value, the work of Joshua sounds like a bloodbath. It seems clear, however, that the point is the defeat of a system of social exploitation, a defeat that is accomplished in an alliance of Torah-committed peasants and the invisible but deeply engaged God of covenant. This defining alliance of peasants with YHWH is indicated in the remarkable poetic parallelism of Judges 5:11:

> To the sound of musicians at the watering places,
>   there they repeat the triumphs of the LORD,
>   the triumphs of his peasantry in Israel.

The last two lines of the poem hold in close parallel "the triumphs of the LORD" and "the triumphs of his peasantry in Israel." It is the same "triumphs" that are credited both to YHWH and to the peasants because the alliance in solidarity between them is total.

Joshua 2:1–21; 6:22–25

Particular attention is given in these passages to Rahab the prostitute. It is odd that she receives such narrative attention. The reason is that she is the "insider" in the guerrilla movement. She confesses YHWH as God:

> "I know that the LORD has given you the land, and that dread of you has fallen on us, and that all the inhabitants of the land melt in fear before you. For we have heard how the LORD dried up the water of the Red Sea before you when you came out of Egypt, and what you did to the two kings of the Amorites that were beyond the Jordan, to Sihon and Og, whom you utterly destroyed. As soon as we heard it, our hearts melted, and there was no courage left in any of us because of you. The LORD your God is indeed God in heaven above and on earth below." (Josh 2:9–11)

And then she acts in solidarity with the Joshua movement. Taken theologically, she is presented as a faithful adherent to YHWH. Taken sociologically, she is a devalued outsider to the urban system, one without rights or resources. Her theological identity as a woman of faith and her sociological standing as a despised outsider converge. This convergence delivers the Joshua movement from romanticism and grounds this view of the city in social reality. The Joshua movement in general and the narrative of Rahab in particular indicate that an alternative narrative of the city can be imagined because of the nervy and brave counteraction of people like Rahab. That narrative, moreover, is characterized by *ḥesed*. In Joshua 2:12, Rahab says:

> Now then, since I have dealt *kindly* with you, swear to me by the LORD that you in turn will deal *kindly* with my family. Give me a sign of good faith. (emphasis added)

And the men of Joshua respond:

> "Our life for yours! If you do not tell this business of ours, then we will deal *kindly and faithfully* with you when the LORD gives us the land." (Josh 2:14, emphasis added)

This version of urban reality does not concern power and wealth but rather fidelity. The narrative claims that such a vision of the city will prevail. In that prevailing, Joshua is indeed the new Moses. As Moses saved the slaves from Pharaoh, so Joshua saves from the Pharaoh-like Canaanites. It is no wonder his name is "Joshua" as it might have been written, "You shall call his name Joshua, for he will save his people" and make new life possible in the city (see Matt 1:21). That will happen when the city is emancipated from its overly passionate commitment to the accumulation of commodity.

An Uncritical Embrace of Anticovenantal Urbanism: Solomon

Solomon, of course, is the great patron and builder of the royal city of Jerusalem.[4] By the time of David, Joshua's antipathy toward the city and toward the system of "Canaanite city-states" was forgotten in some quarters. It was David who initiated the transition of Israel from the hill-country peasantry with hostility toward the city to a stratified symbiosis of urban elites and wealth-producing peasants. As is well known, it was under David, by Joab, that the old Canaanite city of Jebus was conquered and made into David's capital city (2 Sam 5:6–10). It is widely thought that when David seized Jebus and transposed it into Jerusalem, he bought the total package of a Canaanite city-state that he found there. It is a telling interface to think that Israel at that time was the occupant of the land of promise, children of Abraham and Sarah, aware of the gift of it all. On the other hand with David and then Solomon, it was the city of David, the city occupied and organized in a "Canaanite" way. It is often noted that Jerusalem is always the "city of David," or as we sing, "Once in royal David's city." Jerusalem is never Israel's city, but always belongs to David as property and possession, no longer gift. Thus we may juxtapose "land of promise" and "city of David" as a core tension in Israel's memory and faith. David, entrepreneur that he was, remained rooted in the old covenant, but just barely. In his new private city that he would organize as he wished,

- he borrowed governmental arrangements from neighboring bureau-cracies,
- he appropriated a cultic apparatus that has marks of Canaanite self-securing, and
- he began the practice of *ḥerem*, a practice of sexual politics seem-ing inimical to the old covenant.

By the time he finished, Jebus apparently has not much to do with the old covenantal traditions of Sinai. So now this very different urban establish-ment is put down in the midst of covenantal Israel.

The move from land of promise taken as a gift and organized covenan-tally to city of David taken as conquest and organized in Canaanite ways is begun by father David. He, however, is presented in the narrative as, at best, ambiguous about the move and still rooted in Yahwistic covenantal traditions. With son Solomon, however, the matter is very different; the transition is brutally and shrewdly accelerated until Solomon, in one generation, completely reshapes Israel in the environs of the city of Jerusalem. While father David had become king through popular accla-mation, Solomon accomplishes royal power by a ruthless and uncompro-mising coup (1 Kgs 1:11–40). Solomon knows or cares nothing for old covenantal rootage. He ostensibly prays to YHWH for a "listening heart" and "to govern justly," but in fact none of that counts. We may pause over Solomon at some length, for he seems to embody exactly the kind of city to which Joshua so vigorously and negatively responded.

I identify here six facets of the city of Jerusalem under Solomon that provide grist for theological critique of the city in the Old Testament:

1. Solomon is the master builder (after all, the founding myth of the Masons arises from his building program).[5] There can hardly be any doubt that Solomon's building program was primarily a symbolic exhibit of royal power, wealth, and grandeur; like all such urban accomplishments, the purpose is mythic and symbolic rather than functional. In 1 Kings 7:1–12, Solomon's extravagant urban redevelopment project is detailed, consisting of a series of grand buildings:

> The House of the Forest of Lebanon, no doubt featuring much cedar
> The House of Pillars
> The Hall of the Three
> The Hall of Justice
> "His own house" that was thirteen years in construction
> A palace for Solomon's daughter, suggesting that Solomon had married into an old-state ideology and a state practice of exploitative economics

As is well known, moreover, Solomon devoted great energy to the temple, a standard royal enterprise that is laden with dynastic ideology underscoring the ostensible piety of the king, and which provides powerful public evidence of divine commitment to the royal dynasty. The temple, of course, is opulent in its appointment. Its three-chambered design, moreover, witnesses to a hierarchical ordering of social power, a point not lost on the belated development of Masonic lore. The three-chambered arrangement, a standard in royally operated temples, created a system of graded holiness that, given the centrality of the cult, embodied gradations of social power and social wealth—that is, an ideological stratification of social worth. The architecture of the city attests to what is to be valued and who is to be consigned to the margins of whatever wealth their guarantees may be offered.

2. Solomon's capacity to finance such visible opulence is a consequence of his astonishing trade policies, whereby he was a trader and broker of goods from south to north and north to south. Solomon would not have believed in NAFTA and was not for free trade, for his tariff system was well developed. The basis of his trade empire was his alliance with the Phoenicians under Hiram, reinforced by his military capacity that evoked "tribute" from other dependent states. The remarkable economic success of the regime, of course, required that Solomon would have none of

Israel's traditional aversion to "Canaanite" commerce, for he readily compromised Israel's distinctiveness for the sake of trade.

First Kings 10 offers a comprehensive portrayal of the royal economy that was totally and aggressively committed to acquisitiveness. It is all about the gold!

> The weight of gold that came to Solomon in one year was six hundred sixty-six talents of gold, besides that which came from the traders and from the business of the merchants, and from all the kings of Arabia and the governors of the land. King Solomon made two hundred large shields of beaten gold; six hundred shekels of gold went into each large shield. He made three hundred shields of beaten gold; three minas of gold went into each shield; and the king put them in the House of the Forest of Lebanon. The king also made a great ivory throne, and overlaid it with the finest gold. The throne had six steps. The top of the throne was rounded in the back, and on each side of the seat were arm rests and two lions standing beside the arm rests, while twelve lions were standing, one on each end of a step on the six steps. Nothing like it was ever made in any kingdom. All King Solomon's drinking vessels were of gold, and all the vessels of the House of the Forest of Lebanon were of pure gold; none were of silver—it was not considered as anything in the days of Solomon. (1 Kgs 10:14–21)

Everyone brought tax, tribute, and bribe to the royal treasury in Jerusalem:

> Moreover, the fleet of Hiram, which carried gold from Ophir, brought from Ophir a great quantity of almug wood and precious stones. . . . Every one of them brought a present, objects of silver and gold, garments, weaponry, spices, horses, and mules, so much year by year. (1 Kgs 10:11, 25)

Solomon was an arms dealer:

> Solomon's import of horses was from Egypt and Kue, and the king's traders received them from Kue at a price. A chariot could be imported from Egypt for six hundred shekels of silver, and a horse for one hundred fifty; so through the king's traders they were exported to all the kings of the Hittites and the kings of Aram. (1 Kgs 10:28–29)

Most telling is the narrative account of the visit of the queen of Sheba to Jerusalem. This was a trade summit. People who conduct trade summits in order to enhance the urban economy are not detained by sectarian, confessional commitments. As a result one can trade with Arabs or communists or Muslims or whoever can serve the economy. The queen of Sheba herself was a huge trading partner. In the imagination of Israel, however, she is made less by Solomon. She comes to Jerusalem in deference to Solomon, who is the stronger party:

> She came to Jerusalem with a very great retinue, with camels bearing spices, and very much gold, and precious stones; and when she came to Solomon, she told him all that was on her mind. (1 Kgs 10:2)

And, we are told, Solomon took her breath away! With the term *ruah*, NRSV renders, "there was no more spirit with her" (v. 5). Solomon, having secured the agreements he wanted and needed, was generous in return to the queen:

> Meanwhile King Solomon gave to the queen of Sheba every desire that she expressed, as well as what he gave her out of Solomon's royal bounty. Then she returned to her own land, with her servants. (1 Kgs 10:13)

The city, unlike hill country peasants, fully defined all social relationships in terms of economic interest.

3. Behind Solomon's effectiveness as a demanding and aggressive trading partner, there was need for a standing army. Thus we learn that Solomon had a huge military corps in waiting:

> Solomon gathered together chariots and horses; he had fourteen hundred chariots and twelve thousand horses, which he stationed in the chariot cities and with the king in Jerusalem. (1 Kgs 10:26)

That standing army, of course, depends on tax dollars, but the urban elite does not mind because such tax for the military is essential to protect investments, and to keep guard over the disproportionate share of commodity goods that are essential to a high standard of living. The report on Solomon's tax-collecting apparatus indicates a highly organized system that produced all that was needed to sustain a strong military:

> Solomon had twelve officials over all Israel, who provided food for the king and his household; each one had to make provision for one month in the year. (1 Kgs 4:7)

The inventory of tax districts in 1 Kings 4 suggests that all subjects of Solomon, of course including the peasant producers, shared in the tax burden. While the peasants paid the taxes, the creation of a strong central government and a strong military establishment clearly did not benefit the peasants; the arrangement served the urban elites who lived at the top of the pyramid of social power.

4. The state apparatus of building, trade, military, and tax policy all depended upon cheap labor—or, more properly, forced labor whereby men are conscripted to serve the aims of the regime even when that course violated their own vested interest. Some dispute exists in the text over the extent of the Solomonic policy of forced labor, the kind of dispute we might expect given the need to defend the policy and to twist data in the defense of policy. First Kings 5:13 asserts that

> King Solomon conscripted forced labor out of all Israel; the levy numbered thirty thousand men. (1 Kgs 5:13)

But in chapter 9, the matter is qualified:

> All the people who were left of the Amorites, the Hittites, the Perizzites, the Hivites, and the Jubusites, who were not of the people of Israel—their descendants who were still left in the land, whom the Israelites were unable to destroy completely—these Solomon conscripted for slave labor, and so they are to this day. But of the Israelites Solomon made no slaves; they were the soldiers, they were his officials, his commanders, his captains, and the commanders of this chariotry and cavalry. (1 Kgs 9:20–22)

The dispute is left unsettled. In either case Solomon is remembered as the enforcer of a draft that conscripted young men and young women to the cause of the state and the urban economy. More than that, Solomon is remembered as having policies that replicated and imitated those of Pharaoh in ancient days, the Pharaoh whose belated daughter he had married. Even after the qualification of 9:22 is allowed, moreover, it may mean only that the Israelites were higher-ranking state recruits but still recruits for the acquisitive exhibitionism of the imperial corporate economy. Such a conscription would be unthinkable in old covenantal patterns. This new "Canaanite" pattern of deployment of cheap labor had of course long ago been anticipated by Samuel in his critique of the coming urban economy:

> "These will be the ways of the king who will reign over you: he will *take* your sons and appoint them to his chariots and to be his horse-men, and to run before his chariots; and he will appoint for himself commanders of thousands and commanders of fifties, and some to plow his ground and to reap his harvest, and to make his implements of war and the equipment of his chariots. He will *take* your daughters to be perfumers and cooks and bakers. (1 Sam 8:11–13, emphasis added)

It is a "taking" economy that gives only to the well connected.

5. Solomon practiced sexual politics in ways that the old tradition could not have countenanced, a practice already begun by father David. But as in all things, son Solomon moved the matter to a new scale of brazenness. I have already mentioned Pharaoh's daughter. Beyond that particular case, the pejorative verdict of Solomon is that he "loved many foreign women," a practice that caused him, so the text asserts, to love YHWH less:

> King Solomon loved many foreign women along with the daughter of Pharaoh: Moabite, Ammonite, Edomite, Sidonian, and Hittite women, from the nations concerning which the LORD had said to the Israelites, "You shall not enter into marriage with them, neither shall they with you; for they will surely incline your heart to follow their gods"; Solomon clung to these in love. Among his wives were seven hundred princesses and three hundred concubines; and his wives turned away his heart. For when Solomon was old, his wives turned away his heart after other gods; and his heart was not true to the LORD his God, as was the heart of his father David. (1 Kgs 11:1–4)

This report no doubt is homiletically exaggerated; at least I hope it is. It must not, however, be taken as an indictment of royal lust. These many alliances are political-economic arrangements whereby the dynasty in Jerusalem intertwined with trading partners and military allies. There is nothing exceptional in this, as powerful families, especially landed families, have always consolidated power and social leverage by way of marriage.

What counts for the biblical text is that "foreign wives"—that is, those not committed to the Israelite covenant—inevitably brought with them alien theological commitments that are deeply linked to alien socio-political-economic assumptions and values. Faith and social theory are inescapably linked, a linkage made clear in the later narrative of Ahab, Jezebel, and Elijah (1 Kgs 21). The common theme of all these alien theological-*cum*-socioeconomic commitments is that they commonly assume that enough power and wealth will permit self-securing for the state and for the economy, without the costliness of an inconvenient social ethic. Thus, that Solomon's heart should be turned away from YHWH also means that his heart has turned away from the neighbor, which in turn led to social policies that disregarded the neighbor. Disregard of the neighbor in the formation of policy becomes, predictably, a hallmark of urban economy, characteristically intoxicated as it is with the love of opulent grandeur and the autonomy of self-serving acquisitiveness that is never curbed by social reality.

6. The core ingredients of the new urban economy of Solomon are expansive building, acquisitive commerce, strong military apparatus, cheap labor by inscription, and sexual politics. Every aspect of this development of political economy is in sharp tension with the old covenantal assumptions that governed, according to Israel's memory, the pre-urban society of Israel. All of that—major achievement that it is, precisely because it is radically innovative in Israel—required theological legitimacy, and for that reason the building of the temple occupies the center of the Solomon narrative. Solomon is officially pious and devoted to "good works."

However, a close and careful reading of the 1 Kings narrative clearly reveals that the temple is in fact a royal chapel designed for state purposes in which the leadership and liturgical imagination are enthralled by the Solomonic apparatus (see Amos 7:13 for a like notion). State religion thus exists to maintain the status quo of aggressive acquisitiveness by the elites that is based on taxation and conscription of the peasant economy. At the center of this ambitious and shameless program of legitimacy is the God of the temple, YHWH, now portrayed as patron of the dynasty and its economic apparatus, destined to dwell benignly in Jerusalem forever (see 1 Kgs 8:12–13). The habit of religious endorsement of a greedy status quo by religious functionaries is not a new emergent in our own urban culture.

In sum, then, the Solomonic urban achievement, according to the text, constitutes a convergence of an *economic monopoly, political oligarchy*, and a *religion of equilibrium*. This emergence gave great stature to Solomon. The narrative, however, does not hide the conviction that it was, in toto, a system of aggressive exploitation and oppression that amounted to a deep contradiction of and repudiation of the covenant God of emancipation who had dreamed a dream of covenantal justice.

This Solomonic achievement was immensely generative in the imagination of Israel, three facets of which generativity are discussed here:

1. The book of Psalms contains hymns that scholars term "Songs of Zion." This includes Psalms 48, 76, and 84, and the best known, Psalm 46.[6] These psalms serve to celebrate, legitimate, and enhance Zion-Jerusalem as the epicenter of reality wherein YHWH dwells permanently in a way that guarantees the city. This presentation is, by any measure, a convergence of faith and urban culture that serves the equilibrium of the practice of inequality. Psalm 46 celebrates God's presence in Jerusalem whereby the city is made utterly safe and immune to threat or critique:

> God is our refuge and strength,
>   a very present help in trouble.
> Therefore we will not fear,
>   though the earth should change,
>   though the mountains shake in
>   the heart of the sea;
> though its waters roar and foam,
>   though the mountains tremble
>   with its tumult. . . .
> The nations are in an uproar, the kingdoms totter;
>   he utters his voice, the earth melts.
> The LORD of hosts is with us;
>   the God of Jacob is our refuge.
>   (Ps 46:1–3, 6–7)

The liturgical imagination of Solomon's temple city simply preempted the old traditions and created a city that was said and seen to be immune to the vagaries of history. This claim of absoluteness yields an immense illusion of security made possible by the convergence of God and redefined social reality.

2. But liturgy by itself does not always persuade and does not always override the facts on the ground. First, it is clear in 1 Kings 11:1–13 that the Solomonic achievement did not persuade all thinking people in Israel. Some were so grounded theologically and rooted in Mosaic tradition that they were not deceived by the surface achievements in Jerusalem. This is

evident in the indictment of chapter 11 that I have mentioned, wherein the entire urban achievement is understood as a betrayal of Yahwistic covenantalism, that is, a violation of the first commandment to love only YHWH. That indictment is built into a standard prophetic speech of judgment that is given in the narrative account by a nameless voice of critical Yahwism. The indictment against Solomon is that love of many foreign women caused violation of the first commandment and a royal heart turned away from YHWH. In identifying this failure, moreover, the indictment concerns not simply sexual politics but the entire convergence of socioeconomic practices that I have identified.

The sentence that follows the indictment is that the violation of the first commandment leads to land loss, insecurity, and a life deeply under threat:

> Then the LORD was angry with Solomon, because his heart had turned away from the LORD, the God of Israel, who had appeared to him twice, and had commanded him concerning this matter, that he should not follow other gods; but he did not observe what the LORD commanded. Therefore the LORD said to Solomon, "Since this has been your mind and you have not kept my covenant and my statutes that I have commanded you, I will surely tear the kingdom from you and give it to your servant." (1 Kgs 11:9–11)

The speech of judgment makes a daring connection that could only arise in Yahwism. A violation of covenant results in land loss and the failure of the state security system. Of course, the rest of the books of Kings is a slow, steady narrative of that loss and dismantling of the state security system until the narrative account ends in exile, displacement, and deportation (2 Kgs 24:10–25:26). The narrator is not seduced into the urban ideology of self-congratulations.

3. But the articulation of such a large theological critique is itself rather grandiose. We should not miss the fact that alongside this theological condemnation, the narrative of 1 Kings 11–12 lines out dissent and opposition of a quite concrete kind:

> On the one hand, in 1 Kings 11:29–40, it is reported that Ahijah the prophet catches up with Jeroboam, who was Solomon's secretary of forced labor. The prophet, rooted in the radical, anti-urban tradition of the ancient shrine of Shiloh, urges Jeroboam, a functionary of Solomon, to take action against the crown and seize the

throne in a prophetic movement. What a daring intervention in a
tightly supervised urban scene!

On the other hand, it is reported in 1 Kings 12:1–19 that the social
movement that led to the success of Jeroboam as a counter-king
to Solomon was a tax dispute in northern Israel in the territory that
had all along resisted Solomon. Eventually it was not a grand theology that challenged Solomon. It was rather the rawness of the
peasants in being taxed to support the grand scheme of urban militarism that became a hallmark of Solomon. I note in passing that
such a social revolution was possible because the religious legitimacy of the urban system was challenged by a countertheology of
covenant that understood that none shall be made politically or
economically subservient even to a grand urban exhibit.

Thus, the complex Solomon narrative, in its subtle way, exhibits the
city as a place where the dominant voice is the confident one of acquisitiveness that offers guaranteed equilibrium; but it is challenged by
rooted covenantal traditions. This ongoing narrative of Jerusalem in the
books of Kings indicates that a city that, in its acquisitiveness, lacks self-
awareness and a capacity for self-criticism finally cannot be sustained.
It contains its own seeds of destruction. Solomon and his ilk, of course,
are so inured to their practices that they cannot notice. The narrator,
moreover, does not comment on their lack of responsiveness but simply
tells about the force of destructiveness that is subtly and relentlessly
under way.

But there is more about the city. The story of 1 and 2 Kings—which is
essentially the story of Jerusalem—has Solomon at its beginning.

A Voice of Alternative Torah Possibility: Josiah

As we traverse 1 and 2 Kings, eventually, near the end, we come to King
Josiah (639–609 BCE). Josiah is singled out by this narrative of the city as
special and peculiar:

Before him there was no king like him. (2 Kgs 23:25a)

There was no one like him. Distinguishing Josiah from all the others is
that he loved YHWH's Torah:

> . . . who turned to the LORD with all his heart, with all his soul, and with all his might, according to all the law of Moses. Nor did any like him arise after him. (2 Kgs 23:25b)

Thus we may say that Josiah is the voice of *alternative Torah possibility* for the city. In this he is the total antithesis of Solomon, who turned away from YHWH and away from Torah. Solomon believed that urban power can and must be organized without regard to Torah, but Josiah believed that urban power could be aligned with and responsive to Torah commands.

The defining narrative in 2 Kings 22 tells that as Josiah's government was renovating the temple—an act that connects him to Solomon—they found a scroll. But when the scroll was read to Josiah, it evoked in the king an immediate and massive act of repentance:

> When the king heard the words of the book of the law, he tore his clothes. Then the king commanded the priest Hilkiah, Ahikam son of Shaphan, Achbor son of Micaiah, Shaphan the secretary, and the king's servant Asaiah, saying, "Go, inquire of the LORD for me, for the people, and for all Judah, concerning the words of this book that has been found; for great is the wrath of the LORD that is kindled against us, because our ancestors did not obey the words of this book, to do according to all that is written concerning us." (2 Kgs 22:11–13)

The first thing that Josiah did was to consult with Huldah, a prophet in Jerusalem. And Huldah, while she gave personal assurances to King Josiah for his own life, delivered a massive speech of judgment against the city and its inhabitants:

> She declared to them, "Thus says the LORD, the God of Israel: Tell the man who sent you to me, Thus says the LORD, I will indeed bring disaster on this place and on its inhabitants—all the words of the book that the king of Judah has read. Because they have abandoned me and have made offerings to other gods, so that they have provoked me to anger with all the work of their hands, therefore my wrath will be kindled against this place, and it will not be quenched." (2 Kgs 22:15–17)

Again, as in 1 Kings 11 on Solomon, it is the violation of the first commandment, "no other gods." It becomes clear that that commandment is not a thin religious mandate, but pertains to socio-political-economic practices that in systemic ways conform to or violate the character of YHWH who loves the neighbor. Josiah and the narrative believe that public life in the city can indeed be reorganized according to the will and character of the God of the covenant.

Scholars commonly believe that the scroll found in the city is a version of the book of Deuteronomy. When we look at the social vision and social alternative of that book of instruction, it is clear that obedience to covenant requires the reordering of the urban economy in neighborly ways, so that the resources of the community are available to all, which is a strong alternative to the hierarchy and acquisitive oligarchy of Solomon. I mention here only four dimensions of this vision of urban alternative from the book of Deuteronomy, though there are others that might be cited.

> The centerpiece is the year of release in Deuteronomy 15:1–18. This command provides that debts against poor people will be canceled after six years, thus subordinating the economy to the social fabric and the infrastructure of society. The command, moreover, provides that the poor will be given economic wherewithal to reenter the economy in a viable way.

> In Deuteronomy 23:15–16, with Exodus memories ringing in their ears, it is provided that escaped slaves shall be given hospitality and not return to their masters:

> Slaves who have escaped to you from their owners shall not be given back to them. They shall reside with you, in your midst, in any place they choose in any one of your towns, wherever they please; you shall not oppress them. (Deut 23:15–16)

> This provision is as radical as the exodus itself, for it intends to make slavery completely unworkable.

> In Deuteronomy 23:19, it is prohibited that interest on loans shall be charged against others in the covenant community. The tradition understands that compound interest is a harsh weapon of social leverage that characteristically widens the gap between the creditor class and the debtor class. And Torah intends that the gap should be narrowed and eventually overcome, because all belong together in covenant.

> In Deuteronomy 24:17–22, the command urges economic provision for the marginated—in this case, widows, orphans, and aliens.

Thus, droppings of wheat, olives, and grapes are to be left in the field for these resourceless neighbors. The provision is exactly part of a welfare system by which the owner class shares its produce.

These commands and others like them affirm that the economy can readily be made to serve the entire community. The ground for this mandate is a memory of the exodus, for practice of covenant is a transaction among former slaves who act on the memory of emancipation, and so organize and practice neighborly economics. There is evidence in Deuteronomy 15 of real resistance to this mandate, no doubt among former slaves who could no longer remember the burden of powerlessness or the wondrous gift of emancipation. This tradition is urgent in its conviction that the economy can be structured in a way that lets the entire population celebrate the accomplishment of urban wealth and power.

Out of this tradition King Josiah fashioned a revolutionary reform of society. He purged the temple of seductive alternative religious artifacts. He reinvigorated the Passover celebration so that the defining memory of emancipation would be dramatically available in the community. He closed rural places of worship so that the community would come under discipline. Some think that Josiah's reformist activity also had an economic dimension whereby the regime confiscated new revenues, but that is speculative. What is clear is that something different was known to be possible. It was Huldah who confirmed to the king that something alternative should have been chosen, an alternative that is theological and implicitly economic; it is very, very late for the city.

Josiah's effort, however, became only an inconvenience for royal-urban policy that proceeded on its destructive way.

A Voice of Harsh Truth and Wondrous Possibility: Jeremiah

Finally, in this Old Testament study of urban voices, I refer to Jeremiah, contemporary of Josiah, whose ancestor Abiathar had been expelled from the city by King Solomon (see 1 Kgs 2:26–27). We may mark Jeremiah as a voice of prophetic realism, an urban voice of harsh truth and wondrous possibility.

At the outset of his prophetic utterance, we are told that he received from YHWH a twofold mandate:

"See, today I appoint you over nations and over kingdoms,
to pluck up and to pull down,

to destroy and to overthrow,
to build and to plant."
                    (Jer 1:10)

Jeremiah's first mandate is to "pluck up and tear down," to give utterance to the failure, destructiveness, and death of the city, for a city organized against the covenanting will of God will surely fail:

> Jeremiah, from his ancestor Abiathar, was rooted in resentment. He is "son of Hilkiah of the priests who were in Anathoth," the very place to which his ancestor was exiled by that ancient king (Jer 1:1). Jeremiah belonged to this family that had known forever that royal David's city was engaged in a project of self-destruction, and now he had to utter it!

> Jeremiah is an advocate of Torah, the Torah of Deuteronomy. Thus, in his famous temple sermon, he issues an imperative toward social justice, and then observes the mocking of the Ten Commandments in the city:

>> For if you truly amend your ways and your doings, if you truly act justly one with another, if you do not oppress the alien, the orphan, and the widow, or shed innocent blood in this place, and if you do not go after other gods to your own hurt, then I will dwell with you in this place, in the land that I gave of old to your ancestors forever and ever. (Jer 7:5–7, 9)

> Jeremiah critiques the phony *shalom* theology of the city that in the name of YHWH pretends that all is well, when in fact the city is on its way to death:

>> For from the least to the greatest of them,
>>   everyone is greedy for unjust gain;
>> and from prophet to priest,
>>   everyone deals falsely.
>> They have treated the wound of my people carelessly,
>>   saying, "Peace, peace,"
>>   when there is no peace.
>> They acted shamefully, they committed abomination;
>>   yet they were not ashamed,
>>   they did not know how to blush.

Therefore they shall fall among those who fall;
   at the time that I punish them,
     they shall be overthrown,
       says the LORD.

              (Jer 6:13–15)

Jeremiah delivers a critique of royal power, kings who imagine that
   their opulence is a mark of royal entitlement:

Woe to him who builds his house by unrighteousness,
   and his upper rooms by injustice;
who makes his neighbors work for nothing,
   and does not give them their wages;
who says, "I will build myself a spacious house
   with large upper rooms,"
and who cuts out windows for it,
   paneling it with cedar,
   and painting it with vermillion.
Are you a king
   because you compete in cedar?

              (Jer 22:13–15a)

Jeremiah critiques in an equally direct way the urban prophets who
   echo the party line and trust religious truth in their preemptiveness:

But in the prophets of Jerusalem
   I have seen a more shocking thing:
they commit adultery and walk in lies;
   they strengthen the hands of evildoers,
   so that no one turns from wickedness;
all of them have become like Sodom to me,
   and its inhabitants like Gomorrah. . . .
I did not send the prophets,
   yet they ran;
I did not speak to them,
   yet they prophesied.
But if they had stood in my council,
   then they would have proclaimed my words to my people,
and they would have turned them from their evil way,
   and from the evil of their doings.

              (Jer 23:14, 21–22)

Jeremiah employs poetic imagery to show that infidelity toward
YHWH issues in neighborly anti-justice:

> They do not say in their hearts,
>   "Let us fear the LORD our God,
> who gives the rain in its season,
>   the autumn rain and the spring rain,
> and keeps for us
>   the weeks appointed for the harvest." . . .
> Like a cage full of birds,
>   their houses are full of treachery;
> therefore they have become great and rich,
>   they have grown fat and sleek.
> They know no limits in deeds of wickedness;
>   they do not judge with justice
> the cause of the orphan, to make it prosper,
>   and they do not defend the rights of the needy.
>   (Jer 5:24, 27–28)

Jeremiah reminds his city listeners that while they imagine security
for themselves, God operates on a broad geopolitical scope and
may summon the foreigners to attack the city that has betrayed its
proper vocation:

> Raise a standard toward Zion,
>   flee for safety, do not delay,
> for I am bringing evil from the north,
>   and a great destruction.
> A lion has gone up from its thicket,
>   a destroyer of nations has set out;
>   he has gone out from his place
> to make your land a waste;
>   your cities will be ruins
>   without inhabitant.
> Because of this put on sackcloth,
>   lament and wail:
> "The fierce anger of the LORD
>   has not turned away from us."
>   (Jer 4:6–8)

The prophet can imagine this city, so proud of itself, reduced to grief and shambles. He is convinced that if the city refuses systemic neighborliness, it is a city that will fail.

As you know, Jeremiah's prophetic imagination turned out to be correct. The city did fail. The enemy did come. The temple was torn down. The kings were "plucked up," and the city of Jerusalem ended in a long dirge of sadness for its failure to live its vocation, ending in unrelieved disappointment:

> How lonely sits the city
>   that once was full of people!
> How like a widow she has become,
>   she that was great among the nations!
> She that was a princess among the provinces
>   has become a vassal.
> She weeps bitterly in the night,
>   with tears on her cheeks;
> among all her lovers
>   she has no one to comfort her;
> all her friends have dealt treacherously with her,
>   they have become her enemies.
> Judah has gone into exile with suffering
>   and hard servitude;
> she lives now among the nations,
>   and finds no resting place;
> her pursuers have all overtaken her
>   in the midst of her distress.
> The roads to Zion mourn,
>   for no one comes to the festivals;
> all her gates are desolate,
>   her priests groan;
> her young girls grieve,
>   and her lot is bitter.
>
> (Lam 1:1–4)

But Jeremiah has a second facet to his prophetic call. He is to "plant and build." He is to imagine a new Jerusalem. He is, by his utterance, to call a new city to possibility.

He imagines that the city will make a comeback and be restored to new vitality after it suffered and is now sobered to the claim of YHWH:

> For surely I know the plans I have for you, says the LORD, plans for your welfare and not for harm, to give you a future with hope. Then when you call upon me and come and pray to me, I will hear you. When you search for me, you will find me; if you seek me with all your heart, I will let you find me, says the LORD, and I will restore your fortunes and gather you from all the nations and all the places where I have driven you, says the LORD, and I will bring you back to the place from which I sent you into exile. (Jer 29:11–14)

Jeremiah can imagine that the exile—the wilderness of failure and deportation—is exactly where YHWH's life-giving grace will yet show up:

> Thus says the LORD:
> The people who survived the sword
>   found grace in the wilderness;
> when Israel sought for rest.
>   (Jer 31:2)

Jeremiah, even in the pain of failure, can assert that YHWH has not stopped loving the city:

> The LORD appeared to him from far away.
> I have loved you with an everlasting love;
>   therefore I have continued my faithfulness to you.
> Again I will build you, and you shall be built,
>   O virgin Israel!
> Again you shall take your tambourines,
>   and go forth in the dance of the merrymakers.
> Again you shall plant vineyards
>   on the mountains of Samaria;
> the planters shall plant,
>   and shall enjoy the fruit.
> For there shall be a day when sentinels will call
>   in the hill country of Ephraim:
> "Come, let us go up to Zion,
>   to the LORD our God."
>   (Jer 31:3–6)

Jeremiah, in vivid imagination, can liken the city to a child rejected
by an angry parent. But in that anger with Jerusalem now in exile,
the father nonetheless loves and cares and will have mercy that
permits rehabilitation:

> Is Ephraim my dear son?
>   Is he the child I delight in?
> As often as I speak against him,
>   I still remember him.
> Therefore I am deeply moved for him;
>   I will surely have mercy on him,
>   says the Lord.
>   (Jer 31:20)

Jeremiah can anticipate that this failed city and its failed population
are still the beloved people of YHWH's covenant:

> But this is the covenant that I will make with the house of Israel
> after those days, says the LORD: I will put my law within them,
> and I will write it on their hearts; and I will be their God, and
> they shall be my people. No longer shall they teach one another,
> or say to each other, "Know the LORD," for they shall all know
> me, from the least of them to the greatest, says the LORD; for I
> will forgive their iniquity, and remember their sin no more. (Jer
> 31:33–34)

The newness is because of forgiveness, with sin no more remembered by
YHWH.

And then, as though to confirm his poetic imagination, Jeremiah
commits a public concrete act of hope. He buys up land that is now
worthless; he does not doubt restoration and newness:

> For thus says the LORD of hosts, the God of Israel: Houses and
> fields and vineyards shall again be bought in this land. . . . I will
> rejoice in doing good to them, and I will plant them in this land
> in faithfulness, with all my heart and all my soul. . . . Fields shall
> be bought in this land of which you are saying, It is a desolation,
> without human beings or animals; it has been given into the
> hands of the Chaldeans. Fields shall be bought for money, and
> deeds shall be signed and sealed and witnessed, in the land of
> Benjamin, in the places around Jerusalem, and in the cities of

> Judah, of the hill country, of the Shephelah, and of the Negeb;
> for I will restore their fortunes, says the LORD. (Jer 32:15, 41,
> 43–44)

Jeremiah is a voice of prophetic, critical realism. He looks the city square in the face and notices the cadences of its death march. But beyond that, he can imagine the new gift of YHWH that takes urban form so that neighborliness becomes the big urban agenda.

The Old Testament features all these voices in tension, each of which is to be taken seriously. In Christian tradition, all these voices move toward and await the coming Messiah Jesus. We wonder how he will present himself and what he will say and do in this city. In Christian interpretation, of course, Jesus has been variously made to sound like Joshua, Solomon, Josiah, or Jeremiah. But of course, in the end, none of these catch fully what he will say and do.

It is this Jesus around whom this new city revolves:

> He is the Lord of the temple and will have religious legitimization pressed into his service (Matt 21:12–17).

> He is the Lord of the Sabbath and will bend all social convention and propriety to his will for healing (Matt 2:28).

> He is the lover of a city who grieves its death wish:

> > "Jerusalem, Jerusalem, the city that kills the prophets and stones those who are sent to it! How often have I desired to gather your children together as a hen gathers her brood under her wings, and you were not willing! See, your house is left to you. And I tell you, you will not see me until the time comes when you say, 'Blessed is the one who comes in the name of the Lord.'" (Luke 13:34–35)

> > As he came near and saw the city, he wept over it, saying, "If you, even you, had only recognized on this day the things that make for peace! But now they are hidden from your eyes." (Luke 19:41–42)

The city does kill the prophets. The city refuses what makes for *shalom*. The city wants to be autonomous but in the end it will come to terms with the role of the Torah-giving, Messiah-sending God. Before he finishes, Jesus warns against the oppressive acquisitiveness of urban style that we call "coveting" that in turn produces endless anxiety. He tells a parable about a rich man who was self-indulgent, but when he thought he was alone he was addressed:

> "But God said to him, 'You fool! This very night your life is being demanded of you. And the things you have prepared, whose will they be?' So it is with those who store up treasures for themselves but are not rich toward God." (Luke 12:20–21)

The rich man in the parable sounds like the city on the make:

> "Then he said, 'I will do this: I will pull down my barns and build larger ones, and there I will store all my grain and my goods. And I will say to my soul, Soul, you have ample goods laid up for many years; relax, eat, drink, be merry.'" (Luke 12:18–19)

And then Jesus calls his disciples away from coveting and away from anxiety:

> He said to his disciples, "Therefore I tell you, do not worry about your life, what you will eat, or about your body, what you will wear. For life is more than food, and the body more than clothing. Consider the ravens: they neither sow nor reap, they have neither storehouse nor barn, and yet God feeds them. Of how much more value are you than the birds! And can any of you by worrying add a single hour to your span of life?" (Luke 12:22–25)

And then he says:

> "Yet I tell you, even Solomon in all his glory was not clothed like one of these." (Luke 12:27)

It is no accident that Jesus cites Solomon. Jesus knows that Solomon is a metaphor for aggressive urbanism. And the disciples are called to be otherwise.

I finish with a text I have not yet cited and then return to one that I have already cited.

First, I call your attention to Hebrews 11, that great chapter of faith wherein our mothers and fathers walked into the future they could not control. The chapter features father Abraham who began our pilgrimage in faith in quest of a city:

> For he looked forward to the city that has foundations, whose architect and builder is God. (Heb 11:10)

It is, as the recital says, all "by faith, by faith, by faith":

> All of these died in faith without having received the promises, but from a distance they saw and greeted them. They confessed that they were strangers and foreigners on the earth, for people who speak in this way make it clear that they are seeking a homeland. If they had been thinking of the land that they had left behind, they would have had opportunity to return. But as it is, they desire a better country, that is, a heavenly one. Therefore God is not ashamed to be called their God; indeed, he has prepared a city for them. (Heb 11:13–16)

It is all by faith toward a new city. And then the chapter ends with a bid for the new generation:

> Yet all these, though they were commended for their faith, did not receive what was promised, since God has provided something better so that they would not, apart from us, be made perfect. (Heb 11:39–40)

Everything depends on us! What they accomplish depends on our daring faith, for they are nothing "apart from us." The memory of faith is a bid for daring contemporary faith.

Finally, I return to 1 Samuel 13:19ff. You may recall I cited it because the text reports that the Philistines controlled all of the technology, especially military technology. It did so in order to make the Israelites dependent and powerless:

> So on the day of the battle neither sword nor spear was to be found in the possession of any of the people with Saul and Jonathan. (1 Sam 13:22a)

I cite this text because the work of the new city is to be done by those denied tools—except in a surreptitious footnote that is added after this verdict of no weapons, it is reported:

> But Saul and his son Jonathan had them. (1 Sam 13:22b)

They had them! We do not know how Saul and Jonathan had them. They had tools they were not permitted. They had technology about which the

Philistines did not know. They were able to do dangerously more than the Philistines ever intended. These weapons and tools are what James C. Scott calls the "weapons of the weak" that are used in acts of resistance. We need, for the sake of the city, to have such weapons. It is clear that the Church of the Savior and Gordon and Mary and Elizabeth and a host of others have had tools and weapons beyond the reckoning of city hall. For that reason we give thanks. These weapons are the ones that Paul knows about and enumerates:

> Finally, be strong in the Lord and in the strength of his power. Put on the whole armor of God, so that you may be able to stand against the wiles of the devil. For our struggle is not against enemies of blood and flesh, but against the rulers, against the authorities, against the cosmic powers of this present darkness, against the spiritual forces of evil in the heavenly places. Therefore take up the whole armor of God, so that you may be able to withstand on that evil day, and having done everything, to stand firm. Stand therefore, and fasten the belt of truth around your waist, and put on the breastplate of righteousness. As shoes for your feet put on whatever will make you ready to proclaim the gospel of peace. With all of these, take the shield of faith, with which you will be able to quench all the flaming arrows of the evil one. Take the helmet of salvation, and the sword of the Spirit, which is the word of God. (Eph 6:10–17)

For that reason we do not lose heart.

Chapter Three

The Sabbath Voice of the Evangel

Against Death, Denial, and Despair

We begin with the words of Matthew 11:25–29:

> At that time Jesus said, "I thank you, Father, Lord of heaven and earth, because you have hidden these things from the wise and the intelligent and have related them to infants; yes, Father, for such was your gracious will. All things have been handed over to me by my Father; and no one knows the Son except the Father, and no one knows the Father except the Son and anyone to whom the Son chooses to reveal him.
>
> "Come to me, all you that are weary and are carrying heavy burdens, and I will give you rest. Take my yoke upon you, and learn from me; for I am gentle and humble in heart, and you will find rest for your souls."

The one who speaks to us in this gospel text is Jesus. He speaks to us in a specific tone, "for I am gentle and humble in heart." As you know, Jesus does not always speak in that tone. But here he does, for he speaks in his sabbath voice. Humble and gentle of heart, making no demands. Here there is no coercion, no rigorous discipline, no big brick quotas. Jesus is more like the Psalmist who does "not occupy [him]self with things too great and too marvelous" (Ps 131:1), like Baruch who is not "to seek great things for [him]self" (Jer 45:5). The Jesus who speaks here, "gentle and humble in heart," is contrasted to the condemned cities in the same chapter of Matthew 11, Bethsaida and Capernaum, who engage in "deeds of power" and are condemned for those deeds of power.

41

Here Jesus claims no "deeds of power," but only issues an invitation, "Come to me." It is not an altar call. It is a call to an alternative existence, away from deeds of power, away from brick quotas, away from things "too great," away from control and domination and success. Away from the way the world wants us to be . . . into the life of well-being with Jesus who is one with the Father. What is offered in this invitation is not revealed to the wise and the intelligent, but only to "infants," to those innocent and vulnerable, the ones capable of trust and ready to receive a gift. For these moments, imagine yourself away from your wisdom, your intelligence, your capability, your drive, your effectiveness, and imagine yourself a good respondent to the one who invites, the one who is gentle and humble in heart.

The invitation has particular addressees; the ones weary who carry heavy burdens:

> "Come to me, all you that are weary and are carrying heavy burdens, and I will give you rest." (Matt 11:28)

So what is it that makes people like us weary? It is not working too hard that makes us weary. It is rather, I submit, living a life that is *against the grain of our true creatureliness*, living a ministry that is *against the grain of our true vocation*, being placed in a false position so that our day-to-day operation requires us to contradict what we know best about ourselves and what we love most about our life as children of God. Exhaustion comes from the demand that we be, in some measure, other than we truly are; such an alienation requires too much energy to navigate.

So consider this option. We are the weary ones whom Jesus invites in gentleness, because we are overly busy and overly anxious about the maintenance of our world. We are overly busy and overly anxious because we believe that one more pastoral call, one more committee meeting, one more careful preparation, one more street demonstration, one more published article, one more golf game, one more staff review, one more check to make sure the lights are out and the dishes washed and the mail answered, one more anything will make this a better place and enhance our sense of self.

But of course it is never enough, for our anxious sense of responsibility will never touch the truth of creation. For the truth of creation, without any regard for us or our need to make it right, is that God has ordained the world in its abundance; it will perform its life-giving exuberance without us, as long as we do not get in the way. Our exhaustion, I propose, is rooted in anxiety that mistrusts the abundance that God has ordained into creation and, as a result, we—like the creator on the sixth day—have our *naphshim* completely depleted. But we, unlike the creator, take no seventh day for refreshment, because, unlike the creator, we are too anxious to rest. And he says, "Come to me, all you that are weary." True creatureliness, like birds and lilies, trusts the abundance of the Father. But we imagine we know better in our wisdom and in our intelligence. We spend ourselves in the futility of trying to take the place of the life-guaranteeing God. We are weary because in the end we can guarantee the life of no one and certainly not the life of the church.

So what causes people like us to bear heavy burdens? It is because, is it not, we are coerced, driven kinds of folk, responding to the endless echoes of some Pharaoh in our present life or from our past life. Pharaoh, of course, has insatiable demands, and as long as we live in the regime of some Pharaoh, we will never make enough bricks. I notice one other element in Pharaoh's narrative. When he died, the slaves cried out in hurt. But until he died, they did not cry out. They were silenced. They kept it all in. They did not dare to speak their pain. That is how Pharaoh works and how Pharaoh works in your life and mine. As a result we dare not say what we know best, or we say it so carefully and so guardedly that we siphon off our passion. And when it gets said in that way, it has no power. The church—or surely dominant society—is pharaonic in its silencing. Such silencing gives us a visa to the realm of death. We die a little every day in silence because we know better, and yet we dare not speak.

Jesus invites people like us—the anxious weary who try to compensate for the lack of abundance that we do not trust, the silenced burdened who become zombies of denial! People like us are invited by the gentle one of humble spirit. We are invited away from our contradictions.

So how to move from weariness and being burdened to Jesus? Well, by sabbath! But not sabbath like one more day of golf, good as that might be. Rather, sabbath rest by taking a break from our contradicted lives of anxiety and our silenced life of coercion. Sabbath rest consists in bringing our daily existence into congruity with our true selves. Here is how I have experienced it that I suspect is not remote from your life in our shared demanding vocation.

Sabbath practice is to break the denial and become "truth-tellers," for the truth will make us sabbath free.

• Tell the truth, free of ideological rancor, about the pain of the world for it is the truth of pain on the cross through which the world is saved.

- Tell the truth about the pain of the ancient slaves who were reduced to silence in Egypt, and the whole history of enslavement down to the contemporary pain of economic bondage and racial shut-out and gender selfishness.
- Tell the truth about the pain of the destruction of Jerusalem through arrogant, obtuse political-military policy and the whole history of self-destruction enacted through military arrogance.
- Tell the truth of the pain of exile and displacement and grief, of the whole history of refugees and displaced persons who ache for not belonging. And then give a hint that even we are among those displaced people in our ache.
- Tell the truth about the lament Psalms and the absence of God and the indifference of God that violates the claims of the catechism, an absence and an indifference that are known everywhere in an honest church.
- Tell the truth of a green hill far away without a city wall, and when you finish telling that saving truth, you will have uttered the pain that our society so much wants to deny.
- Tell the truth and you will end the power of denial, the frantic need to make it right, the anxiety about augmenting the "inadequate" abundance of the creation.

We always stand, as did Jesus, before the governor who notoriously asked, "What is truth?" The truth withheld from the wise and given to babes is that *pain is the matrix of newness*. Tell the truth without pious protectiveness, without ideological reductionism, stay close to the text, tell the truth and you will find the weariness easing as you come clean to the one who is the truth, and the way and the life, a way of pain, a life of vulnerability. Imagine a sabbath church filled with truth-tellers that are neither red nor blue. But stay close to the one of whom we say, "And him crucified."

Take sabbath rest by taking a break from our contradicted life of silenced coercion. As you tell the truth that breaks denial, so become a "hope-teller" that breaks the spell of despair. Do you imagine, as do many, that there is no way out of our moral morass, our ideological fantasies, our burden of a world mismanaged and irreversible? Do you imagine a church so preoccupied with ideological passion that it has no energy for mission and leaves you weary and without hope? Well, take a sabbath rest and become a hope-teller, a poet of "assurance of things hoped for, the conviction of things not seen." Take a sabbath from despair by the staggering truth that Christ is risen and that creation surges with the Easter power of new life that God is now giving. Tell hope that knows that the brick quotas of fear and coercion and usurpation are about to end. Tell hope that does not depend on our conservative certitude or on our liberal self-assuredness, but only on the God who has given the Easter verdict over a new world and called it "very good":

> Tell hope in the lyric of Miriam about freedom wrought via tambourines beyond enslavement.
> Tell hope in the lyrical imagination of Israel of a new heaven and a new earth and new Jerusalem, or a more sober Jeremiah of a new covenant that in fact works via forgiveness.
> Tell hope in the laments that turn to praise for,

> > weeping may linger for the night,
> > > but joy comes with the morning.
> > > > (Ps 30:5)

> Tell hope in the Pentecostal vision of Joel about young dreams and old visions that supersede present-tense righteousness.

You tell that textual hope, and the congregation eventually comes to believe that gifts are given and that life does begin again. In the process you find the heavy burdens of coercion lifted, because you now know that Pharaoh—your particular Pharaoh—has no say in the future that has been broken open, and you end in sabbath wonder and joy.

Do you think that I exaggerate? This is what we have always known:

> The *Friday people of pain* have never given in to immobilizing anxiety, but have told the truth that makes free.
> The *Sunday people of hope* have never given in to despair, but have always known that newness breaks fresh from the word fleshed and then words on our lips.

So here is the diagnosis:

> We are weary with anxiety fed by our denial;
> we are heavy laden with coercion fed by our despair.

Here is the remedy:

> Anxiety fed by denial has no power where *truth is told*;
> coercion fed by despair has no power where *hope is told*.

Jesus, gentle and humble of spirit, invites us. It is not a free lunch. There is a yoke . . . but it is easy:

> It is not the yoke of Pharaoh's bricks or Jewish law or Roman demands or capitalist exploitation or Presbyterian rigor;
>
> It is an easy yoke of trusting discipleship. Sabbath from the hard yoke is to take the easy yoke of becoming who we are determined to be, and then living becomes easy.

There is a burden . . . but it is light:

> It is not the burden of our weariness. It is the burden of simple commands, traveling light . . . staked completely on Friday-Sunday truth and rejecting the fake schedule of the world that holds no interest for us.

Sabbath—actual, concrete, visible, regular discipleship—is a sign. It signifies an alternative life. It is an invitation to get our public performance in sync with our inner selves so that there need be no gnashing of teeth or self-hatred or sense of failure. But it is more than public and personal congruity; sabbath is an invitation to get our public performance and our personal brooding both in sync together with our true self in the Gospel:

> To come to trust in assured *abundance* that characterizes our creation;
> To embrace *freedom* that is given that our culture resists.

Taking a break from anxiety and coercion will make time available so that our life need not be lived as a victim or a citizen or a perpetrator of devouring acquisitiveness. It will not surprise you, will it, if I remind you that just after this text at the end of Matthew 11, the next texts that follow in Matthew 12 are two sabbath moments:

- In Mark 12:1–8 is the debate about working on sabbath and Jesus' assertion that he is the Lord of the sabbath.
- In Mark 12:9–14 there is a debate about healing on the sabbath.

They conspired how to destroy him, because they sensed intuitively that sabbath practice subverts the entire world of acquisitiveness. As you come to the table, expect yourself to be subverted by *abundance* and by *freedom* and by *truth* and by *hope*:

"Come to me, all you that are weary and are carrying heavy burdens, and I will give you rest. Take my yoke upon you, and learn from me; for I am gentle and humble in heart, and you will find rest for your souls. For my yoke is easy, and my burden is light." (Matt 11:28–30)

There was an old ad for Lipton iced tea. It presented a young person on a hot day falling backward, joyously, into a cool swimming pool. Be like that today and all your days as you fall back into rest. You will be held, emancipated, and embraced. You will be a happier person and a better minister. Your power will stir in your life, and you will notice. And when you notice you will give thanks . . . and dance! You will notice your true self, dancing away from denial and singing away from despair. You will dance. Others will notice. You will notice, and you will dance!

Chapter Four

A Welcome for the Others

Israel's greatest voice of hope, Second Isaiah, sounded precisely amid a community of displaced people (Isa 40–55). It is the truth of biblical faith that the God of hope is most powerfully present in seasons of hopelessness. Thus, the poetry of the book of Lamentations, a near contemporary of Second Isaiah, concedes:

> "Gone is my glory, and all that I had hoped for from the LORD." (Lam 3:18)[1]

In that very moment of the loss of hope, that poet remembers and, consequently, asserts:

> But this I call to mind,
> and therefore I have hope:
> The *steadfast love* of the LORD never ceases,
> his *mercies* never come to an end;
> they are new every morning;
> great is your *faithfulness.*
> "The LORD is my portion," says my soul,
> "therefore I will hope in him."
> (Lam 3:21–24, emphasis added)

Out of that moment of grief and loss in the exile, Second Isaiah imagined a wondrous homecoming and restoration to Jerusalem.

We pick up the story just at the edge of the city as the returning exiles moved from hope to a historical reality which is much more modest than

49

the hope of Second Isaiah. I take up these texts, dear mothers and fathers in faith, because all of us—and you in your daring offices—must think of the future of God's people. Like those ancients, you have great evangelical promises ringing in your ears, even while you face the vexed reality of the facts on the ground. Poised between hope and reality, perhaps you also vacillate, as did they, thinking variously that this is an impossible moment of difficulty or that this is a wondrous moment of possibility. The returning exiles did not know the future as they arrived back in town . . . and we do not know either.

I first consider Isaiah 56; then I reflect on the textual trajectory out of Isaiah 56; finally I add a few texts about testimony.

As they approached the future in the city, the returning Jews fresh from exile immediately entered into dispute, a contest between various notions of the future. One claim in the dispute had to do with the constitution of the community. They asked who in fact now constitutes Israel, the restored community of the people of God. And that question pressed them to ponder, "Who is in and who must be excluded?" The people who undertook that dispute, moreover, were those who returned from exile and to Persian auspices. They are the ones labeled, in current scholarship, "the urban elites" who monopolized power and who thereby had the capacity to define the community and its constituents.[2] Thus, Isaiah 56–66 is one voice in the dispute at the return, the one that I have chosen to champion for the moment.[3] I will, from this great text in Isaiah 56, suggest five accent points that we may consider in our own thinking about the future of the church.

1. The problem that the dispute addresses is the *reality of exile*, the pain of deportation, and the acute sense of displacement.[4] The deportation and displacement in the sixth century were a reality for Jews. Some were removed to Babylon or other places far from Jerusalem. Some remained in Jerusalem and experienced demanding imperial imposition. Our story concerns the ones who had been in Babylon who were cut off from the conventional props that make social life possible. Some from Babylon now had come home to Jerusalem, but they are mindful of the others who had not yet come home and they hear God make this incredible promise:[5]

> Thus says the Lord God,
>   who *gathers* the outcasts of Israel,
> I will *gather* others to them
>   besides those already *gathered*.
>   (Isa 56:8)

The God present to the dispute is the God who gathers. The term "gather," a technical term for ending exile, is used in this verse three times. It asserts,

> that some are already gathered home;
> that some are not yet gathered home; and
> that all will, by the mercy of God, be gathered home.

The statement is a disclosure of the intention of God who wills that all should be gathered home to well-being.

I submit that the experience of exile-displacement-deportation and the counteraction of gathering offer an apt characterization of the process of ministry among us. This double motif refers, in our context, to the fact that all the conventional, homegrown props of established society are now largely gone. Old institutions scarcely perform their tasks anymore, and that reality of loss generates enormous, amorphous anxiety among us.

Thus, I propose that the church is now God's agent for gathering exiles of which I can think immediately of two groups. First, there are those exiles who have been made exiles by the force of our society, those who are rejected, ostracized, and labeled as outsiders. This, of course, includes the poor, and inevitably we would also think in one way or another of gays and lesbians. We have an exile-producing culture that displaces some folk who are variously visible and vocal among us. But second, after the obviously excluded, I suggest that the category of "exile" also includes those whom the world may judge normal, conventional, establishment types. For the truth is that the large failure of old values and old institutions causes many people to experience themselves as displaced people . . . anxious, under threat, vigilant, ill at ease, and so in pursuit of safety and stability and well-being that is not on the horizons of contemporary society. It is not obvious among us how the dream of well-being can come to fruition among us.

In context, then, ministry cannot be about maintenance; it is about gathering, about embrace, about welcoming home "all sorts of and conditions" of people. Home is a place for the mother tongue, of basic soul food, of old stories told and treasured, of being at ease, known by name, belonging without qualifying for membership. The ministry of gathering is one to which this God has been committed forever. I have no doubt, moreover, that gathering is now a crucial ministry not only among the visibly excluded but among the visibly included who nonetheless know themselves to be marginated and increasingly powerless and under threat.

2. The church's place is in exile with other displaced persons, practicing the gathering that is the work of the gathering God. But that poses the urgent question: Who can be gathered? This most astonishing Isaiah 56 names the two most objectionable classes of folk to be gathered in that ancient society:

> Do not let *the foreigner* joined to the LORD say,
>   "The LORD will surely separate me from his people";
> and do not let *the eunuch* say,
>   "I am just a dry tree."
>
> (Isa 56:3, emphasis added)

Foreigners and eunuchs! People most unlike "us"! My thesis is that the church's work is the gathering of the others, not the ones that belong obviously to our social tribe or class or race.

There is more that we might learn from the two groups made explicit in the text. First, the foreigners should be included. This teaching, as scholars have noticed, is a direct and plausible interpretive challenge to the teaching of Moses in Deuteronomy 23:3–6:

> No Ammonite or Moabite shall be admitted to the assembly of the LORD. Even to the tenth generation, none of their descendants shall be admitted to the assembly of the LORD, because they did not meet you with food and water on your journey out of Egypt, and because they hired against you Balaam son of Beor, from Pethor of Mesopotamia, to curse you. (Yet the LORD your God refused to heed Balaam; the LORD your God turned the curse into a blessing for you, because the LORD your God loved you.) You shall never promote their welfare or their prosperity as long as you live.

The Mosaic theology of the book of Deuteronomy was very much on the minds of fifth-century Jews at the time of Isaiah 56. That theology was intentionally exclusionary and had not forgotten anything about previous affronts. In that Torah provision of Deuteronomy 23, there is no opening for forgiveness or reconciliation. By the turn of the fifth century, moreover, the covenantal terms of faith had been largely transposed into ethnic self-understanding, and the task was the maintenance of "holy seed," as though faith is transmitted through semen.[6] In a breathtaking utterance, our text in Isaiah 56 breaks from the commandment of Moses in an interpretive maneuver that must have been as radical as was that of Paul in Acts 15 in the welcome of Gentiles into the community of faith.

But the second category of inclusion in our text of Isaiah 56 is even more astonishing: *eunuchs!* This text as well seems to have rootage in the exclusionary teaching of Moses in Deuteronomy 23:1, a text that harshly resists people with inadequate genitals:

> No one whose testicles are crushed or whose penis is cut off shall be admitted to the assembly of the LORD.

Our text challenges that teaching of Moses. Now it will occur to you, as it has occurred to other interpreters, that the text may, in a relatively frontal way, pertain to current issues of gays and lesbians, as it is a case of reversing exclusion on the basis of sexuality.[7] That is a possible probe that I only mention here, as I do not wish to pursue it. My accent on these categories, however, concerns on two counts much broader issues.

First, the only other usage of this word for "eunuch" in Isaiah is in Isaiah 39:7 wherein the prophet Isaiah announces to King Hezekiah that his sons will be eunuchs in the Babylonian court:

> "Days are coming when all that is in your house, and that which your ancestors have stored up until this day, shall be carried to Babylon; nothing shall be left, says the LORD. Some of your own sons who are born to you shall be taken away; they shall be eunuchs in the palace of the king of Babylon." (Isa 39:6–7)

That is, the prophet anticipates royal persons becoming powerless servants in a foreign court. This textual reference in Isaiah 39 is important because it is the last chapter of "First Isaiah," Isaiah 1–39. Our text in Isaiah 56, the other mention of eunuchs in the book of Isaiah, is in the first chapter of "Third Isaiah," so that chapters 39 and 56 with their two mentions of eunuchs bracket the powerful poetry of Second Isaiah in Isaiah 40–55. This literary arrangement suggests that Isaiah 56 aims precisely at rehabilitating the princes of the Davidic house who had lost their power and their royal credentials, who had become powerless, nameless nobodies in a foreign court. They are nobodies out there, but in here, in restored Jerusalem, they are to be made welcome.

From that observation about chapters 39 and 56, I draw a second observation. There was some time ago a book on the pressure that corporations put on male employees in middle management; the book was entitled something like *Corporate Eunuchs*. These are the guys who sign their life away in the corporation, who are well cared for but who live with the relentless pressure of meeting endlessly increasing quotas for production and sales. In the process of that pressure they are robbed of their emancipated manhood in order to receive the largesse of the corporation; they end, surely predictably, with a loss of self, including in many cases, of course, the energy to maintain the sexuality of their life.

Thus, the inclusion of "eunuchs" pertains to all those, gays and lesbians, straight and successful, all those ground down to lost self in a relentless environment of production, the gains of which go to the stockholders and not to the producers. The summons of God before us, I propose, concerns *the gathering God* who will gather the scattered to a new community. That gathering concerns those so unlike us, foreigners unlike us who have no credentials, eunuchs robbed of their identity and self, all those others who are gathered who legitimately lament of their future in the words of our text as they pondered their failed, excluded life:

> Do not let the foreigner joined to the LORD say,
>   "The LORD will surely separate me from his people";
> and do not let the eunuch say, "I am just a dry tree."
>
> (Isa 56:3)

The poem knows about the despair of exclusion, loss, and fatigue. It states that reality. But then it moves to contradict that fateful reality with an offer that counters failed exclusiveness.

3. It has struck me that as we ponder the church that gathers the others, we must pay attention to the conditions of inclusion, for this is not unconditional love. There is a realistic, hard-nosed requirement of what it takes to maintain a community that is genuinely alternative. Here is the condition affirmed in the texts that I will divide into two parts:

> For thus says the LORD:
> To the eunuchs who keep my sabbaths,
>   who choose the things that please me
>   and hold fast my covenant,
>
> (Isa 56:4)

> And the foreigners who join themselves to the LORD,
>   to minister to him, to love the name of the LORD,
>   and to be his servants,
> all who keep the sabbath, and do not profane it,
>   and hold fast my covenant—
>
> (Isa 56:6)

The first and surely principal condition is that those to be included—foreigners and eunuchs—are to hold fast to covenant. (The word *ḥazaq* means to "grasp firmly"; it is perhaps interesting that from that verb "grasp" comes the name of Hezekiah, the one mentioned in Isa. 39:5–8 whose heirs will become eunuchs.) That is, to be included one must be singularly committed to the covenant. This uninflected expectation is perhaps illuminated by other phrases in this invitation:

- "Choose the things that please me."

Those to be included are to bring their lives into coherence with the inclination of YHWH;

- "To love the name of the LORD,"

which in context refers to the first commandment of exclusive loyalty.

- "To minister to him."

That phrase means to exercise worship leadership, or perhaps as laypersons to bring offerings to be publicly seen in YHWH's presence.

These three notations help some in explicating the requirement, but in fact they still provide no specific content for the matter of covenant. So let us try another way to think about "holding fast to covenant." It is more than likely that Third Isaiah—and fifth-century Judaism in general—paid particular attention to the traditions of Deuteronomy. I will accept that as a premise and pursue the thought that grasping covenant in this text means to come within the orbit of Deuteronomic covenantal theology. That theology is multifaceted, but the core of being a "holy people" in the tradition of Deuteronomy is about neighborly generosity that is an imitation of the God who has practiced neighborly generosity since the exodus. I cite three texts in Deuteronomy to that effect:

a. A most remarkable signature text reflects on obedience to covenantal Torah:

> So now, O Israel, what does the LORD your God require of you? Only to fear the LORD your God, to walk in all his ways, to love him, to serve the LORD your God with all your heart and with all your soul, and to keep the commandments of the LORD your God and his decrees that I am commanding you today, for your own well-being. (Deut 10:12–13)

This text grows doxological about YHWH, affirming both YHWH's large sovereignty and then YHWH's compassionate neighborliness:

> For the LORD your God is God of gods and Lord of lords, the great God, mighty and awesome, who is not partial and takes no bribe, who executes justice for the orphan and the widow, and who loves the strangers, providing them food and clothing. (Deut 10:17–18)

The text offers a remarkable vision of the God who presides over the great synod of all the gods and yet who is the one who does justice for widows and orphans who have no advocate in a patriarchal society, who gives attentive mercy to strangers who do not really belong, and who responds to material need for food and clothing. This is indeed an inventory of attentive generosity, and it is a characteristic of YHWH, the God of covenant. What distinguishes this God from all of the other gods is not power, but attentiveness to societal justice. YHWH is the divine agent of a welfare program for the least.

The text of Deuteronomy 10 then makes the characteristic maneuver from doxological praise of YHWH toward covenantal requirement upon Israel:

> You shall also love the stranger, for you were strangers in the land of Egypt. (Deut 10:19)

That is all. An economy that reaches out toward the disqualified is an echo of the exodus event itself, a divine reach toward the disadvantaged labor class. God does it . . . you do it, "for you were strangers in the land of Egypt."

b. The centerpiece of Deuteronomic demand is the year of release in Deuteronomy 15:1–18.[8] This commandment provides that debts within the neighborly community of covenant shall be canceled and forgiven after six years. The effect of the command is to subordinate the economy to the social fabric, so that the economy has no autonomous life in society. The intent of the command is that there shall be no permanent underclass; every member of the covenant community should be able to maintain economic and therefore human viability. The members of the community with resources are directly obligated toward their neighbors.

The rhetoric of Moses makes clear that the commandment was not an easy case in Israel. Moses warns against being "heart-hearted or tight-fisted" (v. 7) and against "a mean thought" that evokes hostility toward your needy neighbor (v. 9). Thus, the covenantal requirement is not a way of "natural" economic preference, but is an extraordinary exception to normal behavior that is definitional for Israel. The requirement, moreover, is not just cancellation of debts, but positive action whereby the poor neighbor should have economic viability so that members of the community must "give liberally and be ungrudging" (v. 10). The concluding command is:

> "Open your hand to the poor and needy neighbor in your land."
> (Deut 15:11)

Of interest in this command is the recognition that "the poor will never cease in the land" (v. 11). That, of course, is the text quoted by Jesus to very different effect (Mark 14:7). The fact that there will always be poor is what makes the command important. In verse 4, however, Moses also accents the effectiveness of the provision, "there will . . . be no one in need among you" if you do this command. And then the predictable motivation in verse 15:

> Remember that you were a slave in the land of Egypt, and the LORD your God redeemed you; for this reason I lay this command upon you today.

Covenant entails engagement for the material well-being of the community!
   c. In Deuteronomy 24:17–22, there is a series of commands that pertain to economic welfare for the disadvantaged in society:

> You shall not deprive a *resident alien* or an *orphan* of justice; you shall not take a *widow's* garment in pledge. Remember that you were a slave in Egypt and the LORD your God redeemed you from there; therefore I command you to do this.
>   When you reap your harvest in your field and forget a sheaf in the field, you shall not go back to get it; it shall be left for *the alien, the orphan*, and *the widow*, so that the LORD your God may bless you in all your undertakings. When you beat your olive trees, do not strip what is left; it shall be for *the alien, the orphan*, and *the widow*.
>   When you gather the grapes of your vineyard, do not glean what is left; it shall be for *the alien, the orphan*, and *the widow*. Remember that you were a slave in the land of Egypt; therefore I am commanding you to do this. (emphasis added)

The cadence of the text reiterates the "triangle of vulnerability," widow, orphan, immigrant.[9] The triad refers to those without a male advocate in a patriarchal society who are, for that reason, dangerously exposed to economic disadvantage. The command provides that those with prosperity and produce are obligated to devote a portion of their produce to a welfare program for needy neighbors. The series concludes, as we have seen in Deuteronomy 10:19 and Deuteronomy 15:15, with a reminder, "You were a slave in the land of Egypt," and therefore a recipient of the produce of Egypt at the behest of YHWH.

If we may take these three commands from Deuteronomy as typical of covenant keeping in the context of neighborly generosity, then we may conclude that the invitation to foreigners and eunuchs in Isaiah 56 to participate in a community of faith requires participation in a counterintuitive economic practice that is said to be at the initiative of YHWH, the original counterintuitive economist. This view of the matter is reinforced when we recall that Third Isaiah begins in 56:1 with an admonition to justice:

> Thus says the LORD:
> Maintain justice, and do what is right,
> for soon my salvation will come,
>   and my deliverance be revealed.

The foreigner and eunuch are included in the community, given their readiness to engage in covenantal practices that are odd in every social environment and urgent in this particular social environment.

4. There is a second prerequisite in this text for candidates of inclusion, namely, sabbath keeping:

> To the eunuchs who keep my sabbaths,
>   who choose the things that please me.
>   (Isa 56:4a)

. . . .

> And the foreigners who join themselves to the LORD,
>   to minister to him, to love the name of the LORD,
>   and to be his servants,
> all who keep the sabbath, and do not profane it.
>   (Isa 56:6a–d)

This particular accent, moreover, is anticipated in Isaiah 56:2, the beginning of the summons of Third Isaiah with an affirmation of sabbath:

> Happy is the mortal who does this,
>   the one who holds it fast,
> who keeps the sabbath, not profaning it,
>   and refrains from doing any evil.

This is a spectacular accent of a most specific practice. We do know that sabbath became in the fifth century of Judaism a distinguishing mark of Jews, a fact that receives underscoring in the testimony of Nehemiah:

> In those days I saw in Judah people treading wine presses on the sabbath, and bringing in heaps of grain and loading them on donkeys; and also wine, grapes, figs, and all kinds of burdens, which they brought into Jerusalem on the sabbath day; and I warned them at that time against selling food. Tyrians also, who lived in the city, brought in fish and all kinds of merchandise and sold them on the sabbath to the people of Judah, and in Jerusalem. Then I remonstrated with the nobles of Judah and said to them, "What is this evil thing that you are doing, *profaning the sabbath* day? Did not your ancestors act in this way, and did not our God bring all this disaster on us and on this city? Yet you bring more wrath on Israel by *profaning the sabbath*." (Neh 13:15–18, emphasis added)

But even given that mark for communal identification, we may still marvel at the centrality of this command among all of the commands that might have been noticed. I suggest that the reason for this particular accent is that sabbath in that society, as in our own acquisitive society, was the most radical discipline that could be practiced, made more radical in the provisions of the year of release and the jubilee, procedures that are sabbath writ large.

The reason that sabbath is a radical discipline is that it is a regular, disciplined, highly visible withdrawal from the acquisitive society of production and consumption that is shaped only by commodity. Work stoppage and rest are public statements that one's existence and the existence of one's society are not defined by the pursuit of commodity, and that human well-being is not evoked by commodity but precisely by the intentional refusal of commodity. We may imagine that this insistence, in the midst of the Persian empire, constituted a challenge to imperial economics wherein work is evaluated in terms of productivity, a challenge that if broadly taken with seriousness becomes a threat to the dominant economy.

The invitation to sabbath is all the more spectacular when it is issued to foreigners and eunuchs. The invitation to foreigners is entry into the quintessential discipline of Jewishness and thus a radical departure from whatever "home environment" the foreigners had departed. Even more daring, the invitation to eunuchs is made exactly to those who previously had signed on for productivity in foreign courts. In both cases, this imperative to sabbath was a requirement to give up the old self and its acquisitive perspective for the sake of a new self in an alternative community of neighborliness.

5. With accents on neighborliness and sabbath as alternative practices, we are scarcely ready for the phrasing of Isaiah 56:7:

> These [foreigners and eunuchs] I will bring to my holy mountain,
>   and make them joyful in my house of prayer;
> their burnt offerings and their sacrifices
>   will be accepted on my altar;
> for my house shall be called a house of prayer
>   for all peoples.

The poetry anticipates inclusive worship in the Jerusalem temple and evokes the now-familiar phrase, "a house of prayer for all peoples" (on which, of course, see the use of Jesus in Matt 21:13). We may identify three remarkable aspects of this conclusion to the poetry:

First, the culmination of this radical vision of restoration is prayer in the temple. The ultimate hope voiced here does not have to do with the economy or with the neighborhood, but with the practice of communion with God in the holy precinct. The end of life in the restored community is prayer that makes all human enterprise penultimate. The proper posture of all prayer, so Karl Barth, is petition, admission of need, and gladness in dependence.[10] The centrality of prayer constitutes a total reconfiguration of human life in the world as life is now to be lived "before God."[11]

Second, the temple is "for all peoples," specifically including the aforementioned foreigners and eunuchs. In this vigorous act of hope, the conventional practices of Jewishness are daringly transposed into a vision of astonishing inclusiveness. The vision is an echo of the initial Isaiah vision of pilgrimage to Jerusalem for Torah instruction that will in turn lead to disarmament:

In days to come
    the mountain of the Lord's house
shall be established as the highest of the mountains,
    and shall be raised above the hills;
all the nations shall stream to it.
    Many peoples shall come and say,
"Come, let us go up to the mountain of the Lord,
    to the house of the God of Jacob;
that he may teach us his ways
    and that we may walk in his paths."
For out of Zion shall go forth instruction,
    and the word of the Lord from Jerusalem.
He shall judge between the nations,
    and shall arbitrate for many peoples;
they shall beat their swords into plowshares,
    and their spears into pruning hooks;
nations shall not lift up sword against nation,
    neither shall they learn war any more.

                          (Isa 2:2–4)

That vision, moreover, is reiterated in Micah 4:1–4, but there with an even more daring conclusion:

For all the peoples walk,
    each in the name of its god,
but we will walk in the name of the Lord our God
    forever and ever.

                          (Mic 4:5)

Here, perhaps beyond even the inclusive impulse of the book of Isaiah, the "all peoples" gives enormous freedom for worship in one's own local idiom, "each in the name of its [own] god." These texts altogether, Isaiah 56:9, Isaiah 2:2–4, and Micah 4:1–5, envision a community well beyond the usual separateness that constitutes conventional reality.

Justo González has traced "the new catholicity" anticipated in the book of Revelation, that envisions a great coming together of humanity across all usual divisions:[12]

They sing a new song:

"You are worthy to take the scroll
  and to open its seals,
for you were slaughtered and by your blood you ransomed for God
  saints *from every tribe and language and people and nation.*
                                        (Rev 5:9, emphasis added)

. . . .

After this I looked, and there was a great multitude that no one could
count, from every nation, *from all tribes and peoples and languages,*standing before the throne and before the Lamb, robed in white, with palm
branches in their hands. (Rev 7:9, emphasis added)

. . . .

Also it was allowed to make war on the saints and to conquer them.
It was given authority *over every tribe and people and language and
nation.* (Rev 13:7, emphasis added)

. . . .

Then I saw another angel flying in midheaven, with an eternal gospel
to proclaim to those who live on the earth—to *every nation and tribe
and language and people.* (Rev 14:6, emphasis added)

When the poet said "all peoples," it was a breathtaking vision.

Third, we may connect our phrasing to the familiar letter to the exiles by
Jeremiah in Jeremiah 29. It is usual in the phrase, "house of prayer for all
peoples," to mean a place where all peoples come to pray, and that may be
what is intended. It is possible, however, to read it as a place where prayer
is said on behalf of all peoples, that is, petition and intercession cohere with
the inclusiveness of YHWH's rule. With that alternative reading we may consider afresh the imperative of Jeremiah to the exiles in Babylon:

But seek the welfare of the city where I have sent you into exile, and
pray to the LORD on its behalf, for in its welfare you will find your
welfare. (Jer 29:7)

The term "seek" (*drš*) may indeed refer to praying, thus, pray for *shalom.*
But then the imperative becomes more specific: "Pray to YHWH in its

behalf." Pray for the empire. Prayer for the feared, despised brutal empire for it is the seat of *shalom*, the tool of the *shalom*-making God in the world.

This configuration of texts offers an alternative vision of the world, a world in which conventional boundaries are superseded in testimony to the one governor of the whole, thus making old, trusted distinctions passé and penultimate.

I am aware, as I have lined out these elements, that they are likely commonplace. I submit, however, that they are so commonplace that we become jaded about what it is that has been entrusted to us:

1. To *live as displaced people among displaced people* who have no continuing city;
2. To *live with openness to the others*, the ones most unlike us who violate the "holy seed" of the pure church;
3. To *practice covenantal fidelity* in terms of *neighborly generosity*;
4. To *submit to the discipline of sabbath* that means relinquishment of acquisitive assumptions and practices; and
5. By *prayer to imagine a whole world together at the throne of mercy*.

These are surely the marks of an obedient church to which God is calling us.

The accent I want to make, however, is that this vision of the people of God is a distinctly countercultural one that is profoundly subversive. This poetry affirms a genuinely alternative way of being human in a way that exposes conventional culture as not only inadequate but as profoundly anti-human.

1. Dominant culture among us is rightly characterized as technological, therapeutic, military consumerism that touches every aspect of our life, public and personal, religious and secular:

- an uncritical *commitment to the technological* introduces a Promethean mind-set about what is possible among us, a Promethean commitment that is led most poignantly among us by military adventurism;
- a self-indulgent *therapeutic passion* that imagines a pain-free, death-free, inconvenience-free existence at the expense of the neighbor;
- a *military saturation* of the public consciousness so that the capacity for violent power is taken on its own terms as legitimate; and
- a fascination with and pursuit of *commodity in an acquisitive mode* as if commodity may eventually make us safe and make us happy.

This largely uncriticized pursuit of life was likely at work in the immense power of the Persian empire; it surely pertains to our society. We can, for an instant, be "king of the mount," and it seems to be a wonderful achievement. But this mode of social existence is harsh and unforgiving; it uses up people and casts them off, and even in a mode of success it nurtures alienation and cynicism that erodes the human spirit. People are, in the word of Herb Anderson, "depleted," without energy or courage or freedom to be fully themselves.

2. Or let me recharacterize this technological, therapeutic, military consumerism in terms of Isaiah 56:

- Dominant culture imagines a centered, secure, well-ordered world that permits *absolutes and certitudes*, and a deep sense of coherence about the world. This is fed and reinforced in the United States by the imperial practice of hegemony in military and economic terms that imagines security is established by having our way everywhere in the world. No displacement here!

- Dominant culture imagines a normative security of *legitimacy and conformity* that enforces norms about life, finance, the military, and sexuality and imposes a high degree of conformity on all members of the community. It is impatient with those who do not submit and conform and who practice and advocate deviation from consensus norms. This impatience is symbolized currently in a public assertion of the Ten Commandments that is accompanied by a hermeneutical innocence that is immune to complexity. No "other" here!

- Dominant culture is largely committed to *acquisitiveness and to the uncriticized centrality of the market*. Such acquisitiveness pertains not only to the economy, but to all social relationships including those of sexuality, a point indicated in characteristic soap operas, survival shows, and "comedies" that are characteristically marked by aggressive attitudes and mean-spirited interaction which is said to be "entertaining." No covenant here!

- Dominant culture is *committed to 24/7 about everything*, about work, about play and self-indulgence, about instant availability by cell phone or whatever. There is no space left for the human spirit, and attentiveness to the underneath mystery of human life is totally eroded. No sabbath here!

- Dominant culture is a culture of *assertive initiative taking* without any openness for mutuality or mood or practice of receptivity. No yielding prayer here!

Now, I understand that I may have overstated the negative aspects of current culture. I do so because I believe that the way in which our culture seduces people, most especially young people, away from humanness and then uses them up is a staggering threat among us. And if you think I have overstated, you can tone it down and still be left with enough to work with.

To help our thinking about the mission of the church in emerging society, Isaiah 56 provides us an inventory of the ways in which the church invites people to alternative humanness. I will consider that alternative through the five aspects of our text. The urgency of the alternative is in the deep conviction that evangelical conservatives and evangelical liberals share the conviction that our society, in its main accents, has lost its way and is organized against our God-given, God-led humanness.

a. The *exile* as the true character and venue of our humanness is an alternative to the dominant imagination that we live in a centered, coherent world in which we can establish security on our own terms. It matters greatly if the metaphor of exile, deportation, and displacement is an accurate characterization for the context of ministry. The claim of success and security, so powerful among us, causes us not to notice the cast out and often not to acknowledge our own displacement or anxiety about coming displacement.

b. *Openness to foreigners and eunuchs*, that is, welcome to others who are not like us, is a radical alternative to the ideology of conformity that takes all those not like ourselves to be dangerous and unacceptable deviants. The issue, of course, concerns the otherness of sexuality, but it also concerns the otherness of immigrants and those with alternative social practices. That intolerance of the others among us is even more toxic now that our society in the United States is divided into "red" and "blue," and I fear we are at the edge of red and blue clergy and red and blue parishes. And here is this poet who says, let not the foreigner or the eunuch imagine that they will be excluded or forgotten.

c. The *memory of the exodus* that leads to neighborly generosity is the primary mark of a covenantal society. That memory in practice issues in a subordination of the economy to the social fabric with focal attention to the marginated who are without social access, social power, or social advocacy. The covenant is an assertion of interdependence and an institution of mutuality that flies in the face of acquisitiveness that regards everyone else as a competitor for the same commodity or as a threat to my self-securing. The poem is an act of imagination that allows that social relationships are not necessarily cast in terms of aggressive commodity competition, for there is a more elemental belonging with and for each other that chastens such aggressiveness.

d. The *visible practice of sabbath rest* that disengages from the pursuit of commodity is an insistent assertion about the nature of being human. The pause for receptivity of holy gifts that are inscrutably given is a break in the rigor of production and consumption. Taking time to be human is a deep contrast to the drivenness of the acquisitive life that is always on the make and that ends in fatigue that has no energy for humane living.

e. The *practice of prayer* that binds us in love to God and in love to neighbor beyond our small claim is the resolve to *live life on terms other than our own.* Such yielding to the largeness of God's rule is a challenge to much of our tribalism, for our conventional tribalism limits the scope of concern and teaches us that to yield is to lose.

The conclusion I draw is that on all five issues Isaiah 56 offers a venue for rethinking and redeciding about our place in the world. It is a rethinking and a redeciding not unlike that of fifth-century Judaism and not unlike the regular subversive work of synagogue and church. The witness of this poem is not commonplace; it is, rather, profoundly countercultural, revolutionary, transformative, and subversive. I suggest that this agenda provides clues to our way to be the church in a culture that is increasingly organized against human reality.

I do not suggest that a simple move from dominant modes of reality to this alternative is an easy or obvious one. Nor do I imagine that many of us, liberal or conservative, are easily ready for such a move. One task of the church is, of course, advocacy of this alternative testimony to the coming rule of God and the profound regime change entertained in this new governance. But advocacy by itself is inadequate. Therefore, I propose that the church be a safe venue for the hosting of ambiguity about these options that may be named and identified. Most of us are exceedingly complex and ambivalent about the great issues. Dominant society wants not to honor that complexity, and so we are accustomed to many layers of denial. In our various arenas of denial, God's spirit has little chance for newness. The first break in our common denial is to give voice to ambiguity and thereby to have an awareness that alternatives are indeed available and choosable. So imagine a church of Word and sacrament making claims,

- that *exile is a choosable venue for life* as alternative to a safe, ordered coherence that is at most an ideological construct;

- that *others belong with us and for us* and are welcome as we are welcomed, an alternative so much more healthy than urging exclusivism or pretending that the others are not there;
- that *generosity to the neighbor* creates futures that self-indulgent acquisitiveness can never offer;
- that *sabbath disengagement from production* causes us not to fall behind but to redeem our lives from the frantic rat-race; and
- that *yielding and relinquishing in prayer* is a proper human mode given the Holy One who loves us.

Of course none of this is new. The option has always been there as it is now. But the covenantal embrace of this alternative in our current circumstance requires great resolve, self-awareness, and passion for the world that is imagined in this poem.

Isaiah 56 is enough for us to ponder. It culminates with the promise that God will gather all exiles. That promise, of course, is echoed in the great Eucharistic invitation, that great meal of grateful gathering:

> I tell you, many will come from east and west and will eat with Abraham and Isaac and Jacob in the kingdom of heaven. (Matt 8:11)

From that great venue of ingathering, this poet, in what follows, goes on to give detail and nuance to the coming world that will displace the tired world of dominant culture:

- In Isaiah 58 we are given an instruction on true worship:

> Is not this the fast that I choose:
>   to loose the bonds of injustice,
>   to undo the thongs of the yoke,
> to let the oppressed go free,
>   and to break every yoke?
> Is it not to share your bread with the hungry,
>   and bring the homeless poor into your house;
> when you see the naked, to cover them,
>   and not to hide yourself from your own kin?
>   (Isa 58:6–7)

It is promised in three "then" clauses that life will be different as a consequence of right worship:

Then you shall call, and the LORD will answer;
   you shall cry for help, and he will say, Here I am.
                          (Isa 58:9)

. . . .

Then your light shall rise in the darkness
   and your gloom be like the noonday.
The LORD will guide you continually,
   and satisfy your needs in parched places,
   and make your bones strong;
and you shall be like a watered garden,
   like a spring of water,
   whose waters never fail.
                    (Isa 58:10b–11)

. . . .

Then you shall take delight in the LORD,
   and I will make you ride upon the heights of the earth;
I will feed you with the heritage of your ancestor Jacob,
   for the mouth of the LORD has spoken.
                  (Isa 58:14)

• In Isaiah 61, it is anticipated that there will be a radical alternative practice of human community:

The spirit of the Lord GOD is upon me,
   because the LORD has anointed me;
he has sent me to bring good news to the oppressed,
   to bind up the brokenhearted,
to proclaim liberty to the captives,
   and release to the prisoners;
to proclaim the year of the LORD's favor,
   and the day of vengeance of our God;
to comfort all who mourn.
                 (Isa 61:1–2)

Jesus quotes this text at the synagogue in Luke 4:18–19. The text imagines a Jubilee year, and Jesus dares to claim,

"Today this scripture has been fulfilled in your hearing." (Luke 4:21)

They drive him out of their worship that echoes dominant culture, because they rightly perceive that the Jubilee would undo all dominant modes of social relationships.

- In Isaiah 60, it is anticipated that Jerusalem will become the new center of peace and prosperity, that trade will flourish, and foreigners will bring all their precious cargo for trade:

A multitude of camels shall cover you,
    the young camels of Midian and Ephah;
    all those from Sheba shall come.
They shall bring gold and frankincense,
    and shall proclaim the praise of the LORD.
(Isa 60:6)

The wealthy visitors will hurry to this Jerusalem center of *shalom* with gold and frankincense. When they arrive there belatedly with their gold and their frankincense, they will discover by inscrutable means that they must go eight miles further to Bethlehem that has become the new center of social reality. And because God will situate us anew in a healthy world, it is promised at the end of the chapter:

The sun shall no longer be your light by day,
nor for brightness shall the moon
    give light to you by night;
but the LORD will be your everlasting light,
    and your God will be your glory.
Your sun shall no more go down,
    or your moon withdraw itself;
for the LORD will be your everlasting light,
    and your days of mourning shall be ended.
Your people shall all be righteous;
    they shall possess the land forever.
They are the shoot that I planted, the work of my hands,
    so that I might be glorified.
The least of them shall become a clan,
    and the smallest one a mighty nation;
I am the LORD;
    in its time I will accomplish it quickly.
(Isa 60:19–22)

- In Isaiah 65:17–25, a new world is envisioned that offers human relationships rooted in God's presence:

> I will rejoice in Jerusalem,
>   and delight in my people;
> no more shall the sound of weeping be heard in it,
>   or the cry of distress.
> No more shall there be in it
>   an infant that lives but a few days,
>   or an old person who does not live out a lifetime;
> for one who dies at a hundred years will be considered a youth,
>   and one who falls short of a hundred will be considered accursed. . . .
> Before they call I will answer,
>   while they are yet speaking I will hear.
> The wolf and the lamb shall feed together,
>   the lion shall eat straw like the ox;
>   but the serpent—its food shall be dust!
> They shall not hurt or destroy
>   on all my holy mountain,
>   says the LORD.
>
> (Isa 65:19–20, 24–25)

All of that is only imagined. And it has not yet been given. But for those deep in denial or despair or cynicism or narcissism about dominant culture, this act of imagination that we do in Word and sacrament is a genuine alternative. It is an alternative that lives on the lips of the church. And when we engage it again, we are filled with energy and courage and generosity, enough to risk and to resist, and to wait with eager longing.

I am aware, of course, that a little Bible study changes nothing. Nonetheless, as you do your work between hard reality and flimsy promises, here is the invitation:

> *You are my witnesses*, says the LORD,
>   and my servant whom I have chosen,
> so that you may know and believe me
>   and understand that I am he.
> Before me no god was formed,
>   nor shall there be any after me.
> I, I am the LORD,
>   and besides me there is no savior.

I declared and saved and proclaimed,
  when there was no strange god among you;
  and *you are my witnesses*, says the LORD.
I am God, and also henceforth I am He;
  there is no one who can deliver from my hand;
  I work and who can hinder it?

> (Isa 43:10–13, emphasis added)

. . . .

Do not fear, or be afraid;
  have I not told you from of old and declared it?
  You are my witnesses!
Is there any god besides me?
  There is no other rock; I know not one.

> (Isa 44:8, emphasis added)

You are my witnesses. When the truth is told, a new world remains possible. Everything depends on that testimony!

Chapter Five

The Fearful Thirst for Dialogue

I find a glorious clue in the verdict of the great Jewish critic, George Steiner:

> It is the Hebraic intuition that God is capable of all speech acts except that of monologue, which has generated our acts of reply, of questioning, and counter-creation. After the Book of Job and Euripides' *Bacchae*, there *had* to be, if man was to bear his being, the means of dialogue with God, which are spelled out in our poetics, music, art.[1]

Steiner's point in his book, *Real Presences*, is that great art must be dialogic. Behind that point, however, the argument of his book is that great art is only possible if it is rooted in faith in God. And if art is to be dialogic, it must be rooted in a sense of a God who is dialogic, a holy agent who is engaged interactively with creaturely subjects in a mutuality that impinges upon both parties. I take that theological conviction as my beginning point and extrapolate from it two further convictions that the work of the church in its preoccupation with God's holiness is to bear witness to dialogic holiness and to engage in the practice of that dialogic holiness. My thesis is that the church is a venue for dialogue in the midst of a monologic culture that finds such dialogue to be an unbearable threat that must be mightily resisted. Dialogue, I shall suggest, is not merely a strategy, but it is a practice that is congruent with our deepest nature, made as we are in the image of a dialogic God.

We, in our society and in our churches, are sore tempted to monologue. Such a temptation imagines absolute certainty and sovereignty, and uncritically imagines that any one of us can speak with the voice and

73

authority of the monologic God. There can be no doubt that such a shrill voice of certitude, in any arena of life, is an act of idolatry that is characteristically tinged with ideology.

In the public arena, the military-economic hegemony of the United States exercises a monologic practice of power that by force imposes its will on others and silences voices to the contrary. The same propensity is evident in government that is now largely co-opted and controlled by wealthy interests that amount to nothing less than an oligarchy wherein voices of need can scarcely be heard.

It is not, in my judgment, very different in the churches, wherein judgments are made and positions taken that make sounds of absolute certainty without any sense either that God's own life in the world is dialogical or that there is inevitable slippage between God's will and our perception of that will.

Such monologic practice seeks to silence, and such imposed silence kills.[2] The hope of U.S. imperialism is to silence voices to the contrary, most recently even those of "old Europe." The manipulation of the media, moreover, is an effort to still the critical voice of a free press. Such silencing in the long run will kill the spirit of our democracy and create an environment of distrust and resentment that will readily issue in violence, as is already apparent in the shrillness of the right wing in its readiness to violate the law in the service of its ideology.

The same effort at silencing is alive and well in the church. So that you may know that this is not simply a critique of the "right," I report to you that in my own church, the United Church of Christ, the same silencing is done from the left, so that there is no room remaining in our national church for those who dissent from the dominant voice. Such silencing in the church, as in our society, of course does immense damage to the church, robbing it of its healing capacity and diverting its energy from missional transformation to keeping the lid of control upon the body.

A subset of such singular silence that kills occurs when individual persons arrive at absolute certainty and claim to identify their own view with the mind of God; such persons are characteristically engaged in profound denial about the complexity and conundrums that constitute the self. There can be no doubt that such repressed, denied complexity of self issues at least in alienation and at worst in violence toward neighbor or toward self. Most of us, in our season of denial, do not go so far as overt violence; but every congregation and every diocese knows about the absolute, one-dimensional selves of shrill certitude that function as profound impediments to the life and faith of the body.

My simple thesis is that the church—summoned, formed, and empowered by the God of all dialogue—has in our anxiety-driven society an opportunity to be deeply dialogical about the most important issues, dialogical in a way that keeps our judgments penultimate before the holy throne of God. It is important, in the practice of dialogue that moves against absoluteness, to see that the evidence of Scripture itself provides data for such a theological practice. I name here such obvious examples of dialogue, and then I proceed to two texts of dialogue that have preoccupied me.

1. In the remarkable text of Genesis 18:16–33, God is engaged with a plan concerning the coming destruction of Sodom. As you know, God has resolved to destroy the city, but Abraham confronts God about that decision. Of particular importance is the fact that in Genesis 18:22 the rabbis made an adjustment in the text. Our translations, following the rabbis have, "Abraham remained standing before the LORD." But before the rabbis made that theological adjustment, the text said, "YHWH remained standing before Abraham." That is, in the original form of the text Abraham is the senior partner in the dialogue and calls YHWH to account. In that narrative, Abraham bargains YHWH down to a minion of ten righteous people, a clear dialogic act of chutzpah.

2. Moses undertakes a like dialogic challenge to YHWH. In Exodus 32, YHWH is prepared to consume Israel because of the production of the golden calf. In the narrative such a harsh act of judgment is retarded, because of the intervention of Moses.

> But Moses implored the LORD his God, and said, "O LORD, why does your wrath burn hot against your people, whom you brought out of the land of Egypt with great power and with a mighty hand? Why should the Egyptians say, 'It was with evil intent that he brought them out to kill them in the mountains, and to consume them from the face of the earth'? Turn from your fierce wrath; change your mind and do not bring disaster on your people. Remember Abraham, Isaac, and Israel, your servants, how you swore to them by your own self, saying to them, 'I will multiply your descendants like the stars of heaven, and all this land that I have promised I will give to your descendants, and they shall inherit it forever.'" (Exod 32:11–13)

The narrative reports, in response to the plea of Moses, "YHWH changed his mind" (v. 14).

3. Jeremiah notoriously remonstrates with YHWH about his unbearable prophetic vocation. In his extreme prayer at the end of all of his prayers,

Jeremiah accuses YHWH of seduction; only after he has made the charge, only after he has broken his silence in accusatory fashion, does his accusation turn to confidence in YHWH:

> O LORD, you have enticed me,
>   and I was enticed;
> you have overpowered me,
>   and you have prevailed.
> I have become a laughingstock all day long;
>   everyone mocks me.
> For whenever I speak, I must cry out,
>   I must shout, "Violence and destruction!"
> For the word of the LORD has become for me
>   a reproach and derision all day long.
> If I say, "I will not mention him,
>   or speak any more in his name,"
> then within me there is something like a burning fire
>   shut up in my bones;
> I am weary with holding it in,
>   and I cannot.
> For I hear many whispering:
>   "Terror is all around!
> Denounce him! Let us denounce him!"
>   All my close friends are watching for me to stumble.
> "Perhaps he can be enticed,
>   and we can prevail against him,
>   and take our revenge on him."
> But the LORD is with me like a dread warrior;
>   therefore my persecutors will stumble,
>   and they will not prevail.
> They will be greatly shamed,
>   for they will not succeed.
> Their eternal dishonor
>   will never be forgotten.

(Jer 20:7–11)

4. And Job, likely modeled after Jeremiah, engages YHWH in the most extreme exchange in the Old Testament. As you know, the speech of the whirlwind trumps Job and seems to reduce him to silence. Except that in the end, YHWH says of Job, in contrast to the conventional predictable

friends, "You have not spoken what is right, as has my servant Job" (Job 42:7–8). The conclusion I draw is that Job's willingness to engage YHWH and challenge both conventional theology and the justice of God is welcomed by the God of daring dialogue.[3]

These four cases are examples, the most striking examples, of the dialogue of ancient Israel with God, an intensely theological undertaking. I take these texts as background, because unless with Steiner we know that God is dialogical, we will never understand that truth takes dialogical form among members of church and society in a way that precludes ready settlement. Such a theological awareness requires among us a huge unlearning of conventional monologic theology in the church. Likewise our most conventional patterns in society have assumed monologic patterns of authority. The manifestation of a dialogical God becomes the premise for dialogic human community that precludes both absolute authority and absolute submissiveness. In every case of dialogue I have cited, the human partner to the exchange exhibits enormous energy and courage to enter the zone of holy power and issue self-announcement.

And of course more generally, this same chutzpah before the throne is evident in many psalms of complaint. In the Old Testament the community of faith—and by inference the human community—has an enormous stake in dialogue that subverts the destructive combine of authoritarianism and submissiveness. The breaking of silence that makes newness possible is nicely voiced in Psalm 39:

> I said, "I will guard my ways
>   that I may not sin with my tongue;
> I will keep a muzzle on my mouth
>   as long as the wicked are in my presence."
> I was silent and still;
>   I held my peace to no avail;
> my distress grew worse,
>   my heart became hot within me.
> While I mused, the fire burned;
>   then I spoke with my tongue.
>
> (Ps 39:1–3)

Everything in faith depends on such utterance.

I want now to conduct two forays into the psalms as practices of dialogue, with the general insistence that the church in dialogue represents a transformative subversion of society in monologue and church in monologue. I intend to exhibit two cases in which dialogic practice is at the heart of our faith. Such dialogue on the one hand requires courage and energy; on the other hand, it yields newness that can never be generated through monologue.

My first case is Psalm 35. I will show in this psalm that the human person is himself/herself an ongoing internal conversation, a conversation that is conducted before God. My own experience of such conversation is that during the day when I am awake and in control, I can give expression to my life in a single voice. At night, however, when I am defenseless, all the other voices sound, and the honoring of them becomes the condition of my emerging humanness. Thus, my first example is in the direction of pastoral care and takes place amid our understanding of Freud about the healing capacity of voice and speech. Freud's modern theories clearly are deeply rooted in what he knew intuitively of Jewish interpretive practice.[4]

Psalm 35 is a fairly standard psalm of lament and complaint with the usual accents on complaint that tells God how bad and urgent the need is and petition that recruits God to be active and effective amid the voiced trouble. What interests me, however, is that this psalm, more than any other I know, includes a candid announcement of the complexity of voices that make a single integrated person a continuing work in progress. I identify four voices that constitute something of a sociogram of the life and practice of faith.

In verses 1–3, the psalm begins with a series of six imperative petitions that are addressed to YHWH. The first five are "contend," "fight," "take hold," "rise up," and "draw." The imagery mixes the judicial and the military, asking God to be both judge and warrior. But the sixth imperative is the one that interests us: "Say to my soul, 'I am your salvation.'" After the vigorous and violent petitions, this sixth imperative asks YHWH to speak, to break the silence. The ultimate yearning of the final petition in this group is that God should speak, enter into dialogue, and offer assurance. The speaker is so daring that out of the tradition of his community he proposes to YHWH what is to be said and who is to be addressed:

Address me, my soul, my *nephesh*, my life.

As with many of the psalms, this rhetoric is so familiar and conventional that we do not notice. This simple voice of petition is speaking truth to power and is requiring from YHWH a quite specific answer. The proposed answer cuts through the neglect, silence, and absence of God, and offers assurance that God is back in play—in my life—with enough power and sufficient attentiveness to change everything. The suggested response is a salvation oracle rooted in old liturgic traditions that are best known in the exile-ending proclamation of Second Isaiah:

> But you, Israel, my servant,
> > Jacob, whom I have chosen,
> > the offspring of Abraham, my friend;
> you whom I took from the ends of the earth,
> > and called from its farthest corners,
> saying to you, "You are my servant,
> > I have chosen you and not cast you off";
> *do not fear*, for I am with you,
> > do not be afraid, for I am your God;
> I will strengthen you, I will help you,
> > I will uphold you with my victorious right hand.
> > > (Isa 41:8–10, emphasis added)

. . . .

> For I, the LORD your God,
> > hold your right hand;
> it is I who say to you, "*Do not fear,*
> > I will help you."
> > > (Isa 41:13, emphasis added)

. . . .

> But now thus says the LORD,
> > he who created you, O Jacob,
> > he who formed you, O Israel:
> *Do not fear*, for I have redeemed you;
> > I have called you by name, you are mine.
> When you pass through the waters, I will be with you.
> > > (Isa 43:1–3, 5, emphasis added)

Israel—and this Psalmist—does not doubt that God's self-announcement will change everything; but the self-announcement from YHWH does not come from divine initiative as our usual Augustinian presuppositions might suggest. Rather, it is human utterance of insistence that expects, evokes, and listens for divine announcement of truthfulness that makes newness possible. Even the expected deployment of YHWH depends upon a dialogic initiative by the Psalmist.

The psalm proceeds in verses 4–8 with a wish list of imprecations, of bad things proposed to God that God should do to "my enemies." While we treat these statements as wishes of a most regressive kind, notice that in fact the speaker is instructing God on the best way to proceed.

At the end of the imperatives, verse 9 then turns to a human promise. "Then," when God has acted decisively at the point of need, then and only then, promises the Psalmist:

> Then my soul (*nephesh*) shall rejoice in the LORD,
>   exulting in his deliverance.

The "soul" that rejoices is the same "soul" to whom God was to have said, in verse 3, "I am your salvation." That same self (soul) that has listened for God's assurance is now the self that will speak. That self, "all my bones"—every part of the self that has been addressed by God—will answer back:

> All my bones shall say,
>   "O LORD, *who is like you?*
> You deliver the weak
>   from those too strong for them,
>   the weak and needy from those who despoil them."
>   (Ps 35:10, emphasis added)

YHWH is named as the subject of a "formula of incomparability." Who is like YHWH? No one! No one is like YHWH in power. No one is like YHWH in compassionate attentiveness. YHWH is committed to the weak and the needy; it is this voice of need and weakness that speaks, now a second voice in the conversation; that voice of need has turned to become a voice of gratitude.

After this doxological utterance in verses 9–10 the psalm moves in conventional fashion. On the one hand, in verses 11–14, the speaker is permitted to practice self-absorption as the poem is dominated by first-person pronouns that state need but that also state evidence of righteousness by having cared for the neighborhood. It is the speaker who, when the others were sick, engaged in rites and rituals of grief and healing.

In verse 15, the rhetoric with a disjunctive "but" turns from self-preoccupation to "they," the same "they" who are the subject of imprecations in verses 4–8:

But at my stumbling *they* gathered in glee,
    they gathered together against me;
ruffians whom I did not know
    tore at me without ceasing;
they impiously mocked more and more,
    gnashing at me with their teeth.
                    (Ps 35:15–16, emphasis added)

They gathered. They tore at me. They mocked more and more. They gnashed their teeth. The poem does not say how this happened; all we know is that they—who remain unnamed—engaged in hostile, anti-neighborly conduct. Thus, in verses 11–14 the poem is about "me"; in verses 15–16 it is about "they." There is a standoff in this urgent struggle.

But then it becomes clear that this "I-They" presentation is at the most a rhetorical strategy for what comes next in verses 17ff. Again, YHWH is named and addressed. A large imperative is issued: Rescue my *nephesh*! This is the third use of the word "*nephesh*" (self-soul), the speaking self who now depends completely upon YHWH and is without other resources. The speaker in trouble, moreover, makes a promise to YHWH that immediately upon the rescue for which he has prayed, there will be ample thanks expressed to YHWH:

Then I will thank you in the great congregation;
    in the mighty throng I will praise you.
                    (Ps 35:18, emphasis added)

The Psalmist, however, is not yet convinced that YHWH "gets it," that YHWH understands the critical urgency of the moment. Now with YHWH at attention, the speaker returns yet again to portray the enemy that threatens:

For *they* do not speak peace,
    but *they* conceive deceitful words
    against those who are quiet in the land.
They open wide their mouths against me;
    they say, "Aha, Aha,
    our eyes have seen it."
                    (Ps 35:20–21, emphasis added)

They—the enemy—is now quoted. The enemies speak. Of course they do. Because in this life-or-death conversation, all parties have opportunity to give utterance. They do not speak *shalom*. Rather, in shamelessness they mock "more and more" (see v. 16):

> "Aha, Aha,
> our eyes have seen it."

That is what they say in their dismissive scorn. The double use of "aha" is a mock that trivializes and embarrasses the Psalmist. The speaker in need now is utterly exposed and shamed. The enemies have now seen him in ways in which he did not want to be seen. They have seen him as helpless. And we may imagine, they have also seen that he is resourceless and without an advocate. They are free to bully him because he has no means to protect himself or to injure them. The dismissive utterance of the adversaries not only mocks the speaker; we infer that the enemies also mock the God of the speaker who has not come to help (see Prov 17:5). In a shame-oriented society, such voices of derision speak loudly and dangerously.

When the enemy takes part in the conversation in this way, the speaker is again driven to YHWH, who is again named in verse 22. Now follows a series of urgent petitions, imperatives addressed to the holy one:

> You have seen, O LORD; do not be silent!
>   O Lord, do not be far from me!
> Wake up! Bestir yourself for *my* defense,
>   for *my* cause, *my* God and *my* Lord!
> Vindicate me, O LORD, *my* God,
>   according to your righteousness,
>   and do not let them rejoice over me.
>   (Ps 35:22–24, emphasis added)

The address is to God, but the verses are dominated by first-person references: "My defense, my cause, my God, my Lord." Everything for the speaker is at stake in this summons issued to YHWH. Only YHWH stands as a protector against another dismissive utterance that would, if spoken, be the unbearable extremity of social humiliation:

> Do not let them say in their hearts . . .
> Do not let them say . . .

Stop this voice sounding in my life. It is a loud, threatening voice, and I cannot bear it. We can imagine the speaker turning to God while covering his ears to resist this social dismantling that is at the brink of utterance. What he fears is that the enemy will say:

"Aha,[5] we have our heart's desire."
(v. 25)

In fact this NRSV phrasing is of only one Hebrew word, "our *nephesh*." Our soul! Our self! The Psalmist dreads that his enemies will voice their own satisfied self-affirmation that will signify their triumph and his undoing. The Psalmist is afraid that they will gloat:

Do not let them say, "We have swallowed you up."
(Ps 35:25b)

The prayer continues with more imperatives and petitions. But the speaker, having said everything that could be said about adversary, now trusts a coming well-being. He knows that he will be "vindicated," that is, treated righteously. He knows this because (in the process of the psalm) he has heard the assurance of YHWH for which he prayed in verse 3. He knows because he has given full voice to the adversary and finds the adversary, through such out-loud utterance, less overwhelming than he had imagined. Thus, by verse 27 the speaker can now enjoy a sense of well-being and can imagine himself now fully and gladly resituated in his congregation. It is that congregation that will join in praise to the God who saves. The congregation will issue one of its standard doxologies:

Let those who desire my vindication
    shout for joy and be glad,
    and say evermore,
"Great is the LORD,
    who delights in the welfare of his servant."
(Ps 35:27)

This stereotypical phrasing merits close attention, because through it the worshiping congregation connects complex strands of reality. YHWH is praised as "great," but the reason greatness is acknowledged is that the congregation knows that YHWH has taken delight in the *shalom* of this particular speaker. The final voice is the speaker's resolve to put his own tongue to glad work (v. 28). The speaker's tongue will be employed—we may imagine "without ceasing"—to celebrate YHWH's righteousness,

YHWH's capacity to take an initiative to turn the world of the speaker back to life; the last word is praise all day every day. The very process of the psalm itself permits the speaker to move from *urgent need* to *glad doxology*; we who have paid attention are permitted the same glad move in our lives.

I want to ask finally, how does that transformation from need to gladness occur? My answer is that the Psalmist has constructed and given voice to a complex conversation that was inchoately present in his life as it is inescapably present in every life. I can imagine, given my own compulsive ruminations at night, that the speaker has heard and imagined and uttered all four parts of this conversation; he has done so because these voices are characteristically present to us when our faith becomes honest:

1. There is the voice of *the saving God* who will—soon or late—say to the needy one:

> "I am your salvation."
> (v. 3)

2. There is the voice of *the speaker* who anticipates that in time to come—soon, but not very soon—he will be able to make a glad affirmation:

> All my bones shall say,
>   "O LORD, who is like you?
> You deliver the weak
>   from those too strong for them,
>   the weak and needy from those who despoil them."
> (Ps 35:10)

3. There is the voice of *the adversary* that rings in our ears. Indeed, the adversary gets the most airtime for mockery. And as we anticipate an even more threatening speech that is potentially to be uttered, this is what the enemies will say that we have already heard:

> "Aha, Aha.
> Our eyes have seen it."
> (v. 21)

In addition to what they have said, this is what they might say that I cannot bear to hear:

"Aha, we have our hearts desire . . .
We have swallowed you up."
(v. 25)

4. This dread-filled exchange, however, does not happen in a vacuum.
The Psalmist can remember that he is a member of *the community*. And as
he can anticipate—with dread—what the adversary might say, so he can
anticipate—with elation—what the congregation will say in time to come:

"Great is the LORD,
who delights in the welfare of his servant."
(Ps 35:27b)

During the day, the speaker might imagine his entire life in the single,
unified, coherent, manageable self-announcement. But at night, that singular coherence falls apart into a cacophony of voices, all of which press
for airtime. The speaker finds now that his life is reconstituted as a dialogic transaction in which everything is at stake:

Here speaks *threat* that will undo;
Here speaks *holy intervention* that will rescue;
Here speaks *self in confidence*;
Here speaks *congregation* in a summation of
    God's goodness toward the speaker.

This poem is a remarkable artistic achievement. It is of course only a
poem. But it is a poem that bespeaks the contested dialogue that constitutes life in faith under stress.
1. We can imagine that this is a *liturgical articulation* in which all voices
are routinely acknowledged as commonplace in faith, for this dialogic
faith knows about the contest between YHWH and the adversary who vie
for control of our lives.
2. But we can also imagine that behind the commonplace liturgical
expression is the deep pathos of *profound personal struggle* by one haunted
with all of these voices. Newness, as we know, can come only when these
inchoate voices are given freedom of tongue. It may be that in such a
rhetorical map of turmoil, dispute, and anxiety the speaker must play all
of the parts, because these voices are all parts of the self.[6] But even if it
is only the speaker who tongues each role, each speaking part is given

different nuance and inflection because these are identifiable voices in a divided, conflicted self. Every self that pays attention to the rich internal life entrusted to us by God knows about being haunted, knows about the voices of threat, knows about the care of the congregation, knows about the holy possibility of God, and knows about the work that the self must conduct. The happy reality is that in ancient Israel, there were public and pastoral venues where all these voices could be given air time.

3. Liturgical commonplace and pathos-filled struggle of candor surely mark this psalm. Thus we may push in a psychological direction. If we do so, I suggest that this is not an exceptionally disordered life, for every attentive life is a conversation that is on its way to articulation. But I do not reduce the psalm to psychology. Let us imagine that the psalm is a *mapping out of social forces*, a field of complex power that is real in the perception of faith:

> There really is a *yearning needy self*;
> There really are voices of *dismantling threat*,
>   anciently remembered and contemporarily uttered;
> There really is a *surrounding congregation*
>   that has not lost its confidence, buoyancy, or nerve;
> And to be sure, there really is a *holy God* who waits offstage
>   to be summoned to intervene decisively.

This is the world where God has placed us, and the self is characteristically at risk among these voices. This self at risk makes its tricky way amid all these voices in a move from need to praise. The voices are real voices. The voices are parts of the self. The voices sound in nighttime moments of vulnerability. Freud, of course, already understood that to give concrete utterance to such voices is to rob the negating voices of authority. Conversely, to give utterance is to let healthy reality override the threat.

This psalm, unlike many others, is an affirmation that life is deeply contested, a dialogue in which everything is at stake. Where we fail such pastoral, liturgical articulation, we are fated, I suggest, to a monologic world of repression and denial that can host no newness but that remains in a destructive exchange that stops short of out-loud utterance and thereby has immense and recurring destructive force. The action of such recital is to see that one's life is an open venue for God's unsettled, unresolved contestation; all parts of the self, all social realities, all forces converge in the utterance that permits newness. The challenge for the teaching pastors of the church is to authorize and enact the conversation that breaks the monologic grip of dominant ideology, whether that ideology be of the military-industrial complex or of our well-meaning mothers. To break the grip is to forswear control and domination, and to enter a practice of vulnerability that is our true human habitat.

I note one other remarkable feature in this psalm, a rhetorical maneuver that occurs three times:

- In verses 4–8 the Psalmist asks God to "do" his enemies, and follows in verse 9 with "then":

  Then my soul shall rejoice in the LORD,
     exulting in his deliverance.
             (Ps 35:9, emphasis added)

- In verse 17, the Psalmist petitions God in an imperative to "rescue me from their ravages," and follows in verse 18 with a "then":

  Then I will thank you in the great congregation;
     in the mighty throng I will praise you.
             (Ps 35:18, emphasis added)

- In verse 27, the Psalmist describes the praising congregation, and follows in verse 28 with a "then":

  Then my tongue shall tell of your righteousness
     and of your praise all day long.
             (Ps 35:28, emphasis added)

These three uses of "then" are in each case a promise to praise God and to give God thanks.[7] But the "then" indicates that the promised celebration and affirmation of God are held in abeyance until God acts to deliver. Indeed, praise of God is consequent to and dependent upon God's action of rescue.

I cite this rhetorical maneuver because it indicates that the Psalmist, as the lesser party to the dialogue, has nerve and entitlement to hold his ground in a Job-like fashion and to make demands on the senior party to the dialogue. This means, does it not, that the dialogue is not cheap or easy or facile; rather it consists in a struggle for mutual validation with the outcome held in abeyance for the future. But that, of course, is the character of dialogue that refuses premature conclusion or closure. Dialogic partners wait together, even if not comfortably, for newness to emerge in the process between them, a newness that might to some extent satisfy both parties. In this case, that expected emergent satisfaction will be *rescue* for the Psalmist and *praise* for God; both parties may thus be enhanced in the eyes of their mutual adversary.

The second facet of dialogic life in a monologic environment I will deal with more briefly. It is the capacity of the Psalms—Israel's script for worship and faithful imagination—to move from the most intent concrete personal experience to the great public agenda of the congregation. It is the interface of personal and public that concerns us here, that puts the one and the many into a conversation of mutuality. I suggest that this characteristic maneuver in the congregation is an important antidote to both the privatization of much of the life of the church and the loud moral indignation of the church without the specificities of pathos and hope. The interaction between the personal and the public is by way of testimony, the offer of specific evidence in the congregation of both need and healing, giving account of individual drama that funds and energizes the work of the active congregation.

We have seen this motif at work in Psalm 35 in two references. In verse 18, after the anticipated rescue by God the Psalmist says:

> Then I will thank you in the great congregation;
>   in the mighty throng I will praise you.
>   (Ps 35:18)

The thanks is an individual matter in which the speaker runs the course of need and the concreteness of divine intervention.[8] But that specific thanks is in "the great congregation," so that we may imagine members of the community gathered around giving praise for miracles that are never evoked, never acknowledged, never celebrated, and never publicly owned in a world of monologic control. The same motif, less directly expressed, is evident in verse 27:

> Let those who desire my vindication
>   shout for joy and be glad,
>   and say evermore,
> "Great is the LORD,
>   who delights in the welfare of his servant."
>   (Ps 35:27)

The congregation consists in those who "desire my vindication," who are pleased at God's righteous action on my behalf. The speaker can imagine, even in great need, that the congregation is filled with members who care, who are praying for and pulling for, and who are cheering God with reference to a concrete rescue.

When one pays attention to the Psalter, it is clear that even the most personal of prayers are in the horizon of the congregation. Indeed, Fredrik Lindström has vigorously argued that the Psalter is all about temple theology, about a place of centered divine presence, power, and attentiveness.[9] This communal sense of the individual is of immense importance in a society that is increasingly organized to resist any notion of the public and to isolate individuals so as to leave us all disconnected and at the mercy of market forces. The effort of the Bush administration to dismantle Social Security may be taken as a metaphor for the work of monologic society in its effort to preclude the true human functioning of society for which the Christian congregation may be a microcosm. The congregation is not simply a unit of finance or of power or of tradition. It is the defining unit of human existence whenever we become aware that genuine security is inescapably social, and the privatization of society, taken theologically, is a decision to be insecure. This dialogic alternative to monologue is a call to be "members one of another."

I will cite two clear cases of the move from personal to public whereby the claim of personal miracle evokes public thanks and praise, whereby individual thanksgiving funds the imagination and energy of the entire public.

Psalm 30 is a pure song of individual thanksgiving. At the center of the Psalm, the speaker narrates the dramatic experience of:

(a) initial well-being:

> As for me, I said in my prosperity,
>   "I shall never be moved."
> By your favor, O LORD,
>   you had established me as a strong mountain.
>   (Ps 30:6–7ab)

(b) devastating disruption:

> you hid your face;
>   I was dismayed.
>   (Ps 30:7cd)

(c) petition and bargaining with God:

> To you, O LORD, I cried,
>   and to the LORD I made supplication:

> "What profit is there in my death,
>   if I go down to the Pit?
> Will the dust praise you?
>   Will it tell of your faithfulness?"
>   (Ps 30:8–10)

(d) resolution and well-being:

> You have turned my mourning into dancing;
>   you have taken off my sackcloth
>   and clothed me with joy.
>   (Ps 30:11)

That drama is intensely personal. It culminates, moreover, in the resolve of the recipient of God's mercy to praise and give thanks forever. The speaker refuses silence and joins the practice of utterance, an utterance that goes all the way through trouble to the divine gift of well-being:

> So that my soul may praise you and not be silent.
>   O Lord my God, I will give thanks to you forever.
>   (Ps 30:12)

The speaker is totally focused on the journey of the self at the behest of God.

The psalm begins in verses 1–3 in a quite intimate, personal testimony:

> I will extol you, O Lord, for you have drawn me up,
>   and did not let my foes rejoice over me.
> O Lord my God, I cried to you for help,
>   and you have healed me.
> O Lord, you brought up my soul from Sheol,
>   restored me to life from among those gone down to the Pit.
>   (Ps 30:1–3)

But then, the Psalmist moves beyond self in verses 4 and 5. He knows that the joy and elation at his new life is too much for him to celebrate alone. He appeals to his community and recruits others to join in the celebration:

> Sing praises to the Lord, O you his faithful ones,
>   and give thanks to his holy name.
>   (Ps 30:4)

The summons is to "his faithful ones," the ones who are steadfast and keep covenant. They are the ones who are schooled in the dialogic practice of fidelity, for they will of course understand the dramatic turn in his life. They not only will fully appreciate that turn, but they will know whom to credit with it and how best to acknowledge it. Indeed, it is the work of the faithful ones, the congregation, to take up individual cases and magnify and enhance them by full public coverage. The reason for communal exuberance is that the community knows that divine love outdistances divine neglect or anger. These are the ones who know about the hardness and sadness of the night that seems interminable when the haunting voice of death stalks our beds. They are the ones who have learned, amid these voices of the night, that the powerful threats of the night must flee and yield when God gives the sun:

> For his anger is but for a moment;
>> his favor is for a lifetime.
> Weeping may linger for the night,
>> but joy comes with the morning.
>> (Ps 30:5)

The congregation consists in those who have been there before us and before this speaker. They know of case after case after case of suffering turned to well-being and death turned to life, anger to grace, and weeping to joy.

Indeed Israel's self-understanding is rooted in that characteristic transformative act. The overarching awareness in ancient Israel is, of course, the exile, that harsh moment of displacement. In that context, the poetry of Second Isaiah sounds, on God's lips, a recognition very like our verse 5:

> For a brief moment I abandoned you,
>> but with great compassion I will gather you.
> In overflowing wrath for a moment
>> I hid my face from you,
> but with everlasting love I will have compassion on you,
>> says the LORD, your Redeemer.
>> (Isa 54:7–8)

This is what the congregation knows. It knows, as God here concedes, that there really are moments of divine abandonment when we must honestly say, "My God, my God, why have you forsaken me?" They know, as does the speaker in verse 7 of the psalm, about the hidden face of absence. But they are also able to trust and anticipate that as the sun rises, so the great compassion and everlasting love of the redeemer God are beyond such abandonment.

If we ask, how does the congregation so confidently know this, the answer is, by many, many individual testimonies to which this one in Psalm 30 is now added. The truth of miracle is not from above in some theoretical imposition. Rather, the truth of miracle is from below, from wonders that are daily, concrete, material, and specific. The congregation is a collection of those who know about miracles, from which it draws deep resilient doxology. And the speaker joins the song because no one can celebrate the miracle alone. This security is indeed social without at all minimizing the first-person-singular articulation.

The same dynamic practice occurs in the more familiar Psalm 22. The first familiar part of the psalm is quite intimate and personal, and of course struggles with the reality of divine abandonment (vv. 1–21a). The psalm turns in the middle of verse 21 with the abrupt, inexplicable affirmation:

> From the horns of the wild oxen you have answered me.

That simple utterance is affirmation that the prayer of petition in the foregoing verses has been effective. The petition has moved God to overcome abandonment and to answer, that is, to be dialogically present in a context of profound need.

But then the speaker, now rescued, affirmed, and addressed, must find a way to give voice to newness that is commensurate with a need that has been previously expressed. Immediately the speaker knows that he cannot do this task of acknowledgment by himself, but must recruit his companions into the task. He knows how to proceed:

> I will tell of your name to my brothers and sisters;
>   in the midst of the congregation I will praise you.
> (Ps 22:22)

It is a telling, a narrating, a bearing witness. The first hearers of his resurrection experience are "brothers," that is, fellow members of the covenant who inhabit the congregation. No privatism here! That verse 22 is followed by a much larger invitation to share the joy:

> You who fear the LORD, praise him!
>   All you offspring of Jacob, glorify him;
>   stand in awe of him, all you offspring of Israel!
> (Ps 22:23)

All celebrate the truth that God hears, answers, and thereby transforms. Ellen Davis has shown how the summons to praise moves in concentric circles until all imaginable human reality is recruited into the task.[10] The Bible characteristically moves from particular embodied truth to the larger communal acclamation as all are drawn into the utterance of joy.

In verse 25 the reference to the congregation in verse 22 is now expanded to be "the great congregation," the same phrase we have seen in 35:18:

> From you comes my praise in the great congregation.
> (Ps 22:25a)

Perhaps the move from "congregation" to "great congregation" is from local sanctuary to temple. But the circle expands even more. After that in verse 27, it is "all the ends of the earth" and "all the families of the nations," all of whom celebrate the rule of YHWH over all nations:

> All the ends of the earth shall remember
>   and turn to the LORD;
> and all the families of the nations
>   shall worship before him.
> For dominion belongs to the LORD,
>   and he rules over the nations.
> (Ps 22:27–28)

In verse 28, the psalm clearly employs rhetoric that moves out from the personal to the great public affirmation about the rule of God over the nation-states. The psalm accomplishes this transition easily and readily, for both the personal and the public have to do with overcoming alienation for the sake of *shalom*.

In a final leap of inclusiveness, the psalm now refers to praise among the deceased who are now only remembered, along with the ones only hoped for and not yet born:

> To him, indeed, shall all who sleep in the earth bow down;
>   before him shall bow all who go down to the dust,
>   and I shall live for him.
> Posterity will serve him;
>   future generations will be told about the Lord,
> and proclaim his deliverance to a people yet unborn,
>   saying that he has done it.
> (Ps 22:29–31)

The whole of creation is gathered around this one speaker. That speaker initiated the process by telling the truth of divine abandonment. The deep reality of divine abandonment, however, did not lead to silence and resignation. Rather, it led to vigorous protest, accusation, and petition that eventuated in divine attentiveness. And if we wonder why abandonment led to speech, it is because everything in this dialogic community leads to speech. Israel knows, and after Israel, Sigmund Freud and Martin Luther King and many others, that utterance produces newness. Utterance enlivens social possibility, but it enlivens social possibility because we—all of us—are in the image of the dialogic God. Praise, the alternative voice of this community, is not easy speech; it arises only after the hard trouble is told, truth that is hard on all powerful ears, including the ears of the powerful God.

So imagine, the bishops and priests of the church presiding over and empowering communities of utterance who tell truth that leads to newness. We have the script and we have the venue. It is a ministry of Word. It is a ministry of Word and sacrament, because the sacrament enacts bodily what our words dare say. And every time the bishop or the priest empowers a community of utterance, we commit a subversive act that intends to overthrow the powers of silence. I do not know our way ahead in North American society. But I do know that we live in a silencing culture, growing more silent amid electronic prattle. The empire depends on quiescent taxpayers. The market depends on isolated shoppers. As we grow quiescent and isolated, the human spirit withers and options for newness grow jaded in fatigue. And then this utterance of truth and possibility, dangerous and welcome, so dangerous as to be not very welcome, but nonetheless urgent.

I finish with the narrative of Bartimaeus. When Bartimaeus heard that it was Jesus of Nazareth, he shouted out, "Jesus, son of David, have mercy on me." Mark reports:

> Many sternly ordered him to be quiet, but he cried out even more loudly, "Son of David, have mercy on me!" (Mark 10:48)

And the rest, as we say, is history. The world is filled with librarian-like people who infuse silence into our common life. But the cry breaks that open:

> Weeping may linger for the night,
>   but joy comes with the morning.
>   (Ps 30:5b)

All these words have been entrusted to us by the word come flesh, full of grace and truth.

Chapter Six

Can We Hope? Can Hope Be Divided?

This chapter began with a series of events in 2004:

1. Michael Lerner, editor at *Tikkun*, wrote to ask if I would write about hope. *Tikkun* is, of course, preoccupied with the Israeli-Palestinian conflict, where it is clear that the missing ingredient on all sides is enough hope to think beyond present arrangements.

2. Yoko Ono Lennon, on August 30, 2004, had a full-page ad in *The New York Times* with only two large words—very large words—"Imagine Peace." The juxtaposition of "peace" and "imagine" is a recognition that peace will not come by thinking inside the box, but only by pushing beyond presently available reality to a newness that is given at the edge of the human spirit.

3. The 9/11 Commission concluded, along with a general critique of bureaucratic dysfunction, that the primary "intelligence" failure was a "failure of imagination." The commission, of course, was constituted by "hard men," so that the "imagination" that is in their purview missing was an imagination of power and control; nonetheless, their judgment reflects an awareness that technical management of power resources cannot by itself secure a livable future.

These three moments together suggest to me the theme of hope. Given that, I have made a decision that a reflection on the way in which Jews and Christians have between themselves contested texts—given Jewish particularity and recurring Christian hegemony—is not very interesting or very helpful. I reflect here, then, rather upon the ways in which Jews and Christians share a common inheritance of hope, albeit with elements of contestation, a common inheritance that makes its way in and against a dominant culture that is, by design and conviction, a venue for hopelessness and a despair. Thus, my topic is based on two convictions. First, that Jews and Christians constitute together, in common grounding, communities of hope. Second, that that shared inheritance of hope is all the more noticeable, more spectacular, and more urgent when set down in a societal context of despair. I do not want to gloss over defining distinctions and long-standing tensions between Jews and Christians, but I think that these distinctions and tensions, while theologically rooted, are massively exaggerated and problematized by a sociopolitical history of control and abuse that ought not to be defining for our future interaction.

Thus I take my lead from Hebrews 11:1:

> Now faith is the assurance of things hoped for, the conviction of things not seen. (Heb 11:1)

This, as you know, is a Christian text; it is, however, a Christian text that is preoccupied with the history of ancient Israel and in fact makes only a passing christological claim. The inventory of hopers that constitute this recited history are people in Israel who could imagine beyond present circumstance to "things not seen." I submit that it is a present task of Jews and Christians together to focus on "things not seen" but promised, in a context that is mired in and mesmerized by present power arrangements. It goes without saying, of course, that such unseen things are not otherworldly, but pertain precisely to the gifts and tasks presently in our midst.

I begin by asking about the common inheritances of hope shared by Jews and Christians by identifying four necessary components for the practice of hope:

1. Hope requires a *Source and Agent of newness* who is, in inscrutable ways, generative, who is not imprisoned in old habits or present-tense commitments. That, of course, is a theological statement about the character of God that Jews and Christians commonly confess. Thus, I begin with the affirmation that hope is theologically grounded, which of course stacks the cards at the outset. But the alternative to such an agency that stands outside present arrangements is to find ground for hope within present life arrangements themselves, a strategy that inescapably produces the absolutizing of some power arrangement that soon or late becomes idolatrous and self-destructive. The Exodus narrative is a clear assertion of hope introduced into the slave community from outside the Pharaonic system of abuse and exploitation. In Christian tradition, Calvin's great hymn makes a Moses-like affirmation, "My hope is in none other, save in thee alone."

2. Hope requires a *community of faith and action* that is open to newness that will be given as a gift. Hope is indeed a communal activity, for none can fully hope alone. The intention of Holy Agency is to form communities of obedient action that rely upon and respond to divine intention. The formation and maintenance of such a community is always problematic because the many narratives of despair are, on the face of it, more impressive and more reassuring than the narratives of hope. The community of faith and action formed around Moses struggled for fidelity and sought immediately to return to Egypt for guaranteed food (Num 14:6); and when cut free from Egypt, that community promptly made for itself images that would witness against the free generativity of YHWH (Exod 32:4). It is not different, moreover, in Jesus' formation of a community of disciples who are characteristically fearful, obtuse, and unresponsive. The community of faithful obedience is thus always in jeopardy; in its jeopardy, however, it manages over time to make enough of a response to divine generativity to make its way in the world.

3. Hope requires *a text* that mediates between *holy generativity* and *communal obedience*. Jews and Christians share such a text that is grounded in oracular assurances and that provides an account of narrative possibility that continues to be available amid the vagaries of lived reality. This mediating text that is a primal connection between holy generativity and communal obedience is perforce an odd text, or in the words of Karl Barth, always "strange and new."[1] Over time, there are many strategies to try to make manageable what is strange and to make commonplace what is new; such strategies, however, cannot in the long run succeed, because of the character of the text itself and because of the Character who occupies the text. That is why, on the one hand, there are endless quarrels about the text and why, on the other hand, the interpretive protagonists agree in a rough way that the text is revelatory, offering glimpses of that which remains hidden from us.

4. As the text mediates between holy generativity and communal obedience, hope requires a *community of interpretation* that is emancipated, emancipatory, generative, and daring in its interpretation. Both the Jewish and Christian communities of interpretation have had such an interpretive energy to move between contemporary circumstance and ancient text with hermeneutical agility, as Gerhard von Rad has seen so well in the tradition of Deuteronomy.[2] These communities at the same time, however, have found ways to resist the generative force of interpretation, whether by fundamentalist reductionism or by critical explanation, for both reductionism and explanation inescapably curb the dangerous subversive force of a text that witnesses to hidden holy mystery.

Thus, my beginning point about hope as a ground for imaginative reconciliation of the world is to focus on what Jews and Christians share of the mystery of God, the derivative mystery of community, the revelatory power of a text, and a culture of interpretation. Old violences between these communities, of course almost completely from the Christian side, have tended to obscure that which is common between us.

Jews and Christians are practitioners of hope amid a culture of despair. While despair is no doubt a recurring human condition, here I want to consider the particular shape of despair in dominant Western society to which these two communities of hope are able to respond in transformative ways. I identify five components of contemporary despair:

1. The *maintenance of a "national security state"* creates an environment that is inimical to dissent and that believes that all questions can be solved by power and control. Such an environment leads to a sense of self-sufficiency that relies on the capacity to control the global economy, and consequently a readiness to engage in violence and an equal readiness to collude in the violence of others, all in the self-justifying name of security.

2. The silencing of dissent in the interest of security requires a *closed ideology* that depends upon a cooperative, accommodating religion for legitimacy. The closed ideology that is offered in the name of the holy through policies of exploitative violence is incapable of self-criticism, incapable of moral reflection, and incapable of entertaining any alternative to present power arrangements. The only project that remains is to ensure that present power arrangements are sustained and made even more absolute, and this in the name of the holy.

3. One tool for such self-securing that is legitimated by a closed ideology in the name of the holy is *uncriticized technology* that would seem to deliver a capacity for limitless power and control.[3] The practical cost of such technology in terms of the human infrastructure is characteristically unrecognized and kept invisible, so that huge investments in technologies of control are made to seem both normal and moral, as well as inescapable.

4. The convergence of ideology and technology produces a *shameless kind of certitude* that closes off the future and shrivels the human spirit. It is clear, nonetheless, that such shameless certitude is only a veneer that conceals depths of anxiety that feed back into a quest for greater certitude. Because the human spirit finally must have something other than such a shutdown, no amount of technology-*cum*-ideology can satisfy such longing. Thus, the system of security makes us even more insecure.

5. The surface antidote to such undeniable anxiety is that we do our best to remain *smitten by commodities*, for commodities not only keep the

economy growing in ways that fund the technology, but soothe the human spirit into "happiness." The consequence, of course, is that as the security system leaves us insecure, so the happiness system leaves us unhappy.

The primary commitments of our culture to *security, ideology, technology, certitude,* and *commodity* constitute a system of hopelessness. But it was ever thus, from Pharaoh to Nebuchadnezzar to Caesar and on until now. Dominant culture—even with its myth of progress—is characteristically a culture of despair. It becomes so, because it regards itself as ultimate and can countenance no suggestion of its own penultimacy. It becomes so, because it banishes the power of the holy and in an imitation of the holy cannot recognize its own profanation. It becomes so, because it lives by control and can entertain no openness for gift. And so despair yields a culture of death . . . and violence . . . and brutality that is mostly unnoticed by the shoppers, attended only by an occasional poet who is either misunderstood or dismissed as a celebrity. It is in that matrix that Jews have forever been Jews. It is in that matrix that Christians have been placed, certainly since the book of Acts; the faithful are called before the authorities to give an alternative account of reality, an alternative consisting in imaginative leaps beyond the given, imaginative leaps that at best are gifts of God's own spirit.

The question that concerns Jews and Christians is "Can we hope?" Just as I worked on the question, I was pointed by my colleague George Stroup to some pages of Karl Barth on "Ending Time." In that closely, intensely argued chapter, Barth makes three points that provide an answer to our question of hope in a despairing culture of death:

1. Death is a defining reality of human life that constitutes divine judgment before which all are afraid:

> The inevitability of death means that this threat overshadows and dominates our whole life. It cannot be gainsaid or defied. It might well be, indeed it is necessarily the case, that the ultimate truth about man, which dominates every prior truth, is that he stands under this threat which is not to be gainsaid or defied. Less than this we cannot say. Death, as it meets us, can be understood only as a sign of God's judgment. For when it meets us, as it undoubtedly does, it meets us as sinful and guilty men with whom God cannot finally do anything but whom He can only regret having made. For man has failed as His creature. He has not used the previous freedom in which he was privileged to exist before God. He has squandered it away in the most incredible manner. He can hope for nothing better than to be hewn

down and cast into the fire. . . . There has never been a man who was not afraid of death. It is possible to stifle this fear. But in so doing, we only show that we have it none the less. Man lives in fear for his life. But this fear in all its forms, even that of Stoic resignation, is basically the fear of death which we cannot talk ourselves out of.[4]

It takes no imagination at all to see that the elements of a despairing culture cited above, most especially the national security state with all its accoutrements, are evidence of the force of death.

2. The reality of God presides over and transcends that threat of death:

It is not merely death but God Himself who awaits us. Basically and properly it is not that enemy but God who is to be feared. In death we are not to fear death itself but God. . . . But the God who awaits us in death and as the Lord of death is the gracious God. He is the God who is for man. Other gods who are not gracious and not for man are idols. . . . Death is our frontier. But our God is the frontier even of our death. For He does not perish with us. He does not die or decay. As our God He is always the same. Even in death He is still our Helper and Deliverer.[5]

3. The assurance of God's rule beyond the threat of death is known fully in the Old Testament, to which the New Testament and the witness of Jesus add concreteness, but not anything not already known:

The God of whom we do not say too much when we view our lives wholly and utterly in the light of His existence as our Helper and Deliverer, and therefore wholly and utterly on the other side of death, and conversely the God of whom we do not say too little when we seek and find our own being out of and above death wholly and utterly and exclusively in Him, is the God of the New Testament revelation and perception. But this God is the same as that of the Old Testament. Hence there is no need to retract or correct anything we have said. But as the same God, as the Lord of death and our gracious God, and therefore as the infinitely saving but exclusive frontier beyond death, He is revealed and perceptible to us according to the New Testament in such a way that all inquiry concerning Him necessarily carries a positive answer, and the positive answer which we grasp in Him necessarily leads us to genuine inquiry concerning Him.

*We learn nothing materially new when we formally enter New Testa-
ment ground.* We are again concerned with our God as the limit of
our death: with the One who is the Lord of death and therefore alone
is to be feared in death; with our gracious God and consolation, our
Helper and Deliverer in the midst of death, so that in hope in Him
death is already behind and under us. . . . The material unity of the
Old and New Testament revelation and perception is clear and con-
vincing at this point. God is always the One concerning whom we
must ask exclusively when it is a matter of our preservation from
death and victory over it. It is the fact that this exclusiveness is now
made concrete that the suggestion concerning Him becomes mean-
ingful and relevant.[6]

Barth of course has more to say about the full disclosure of God as the
God of life in the event of Jesus Christ. For our purposes, however, it is
enough to see that even Barth, given his christological accent, affirms that
Christians stand alongside Jews. Or better, Christians stand after Jews and
are instructed by them; or perhaps better, both Judaism and Christianity
stand after ancient Israel in its practice of hope. We Christians give different nuance to that hope because of the claim of Jesus Christ, and Barth
of course is unambiguous on this claim:

For it summons us to gather around Jesus Christ, to believe in Him
alone and resolutely to refuse all other offers. Without Him we
should not only be under the sign of God's judgment in death. We
should be under the judgment itself and irretrievably lost. In Him
alone God is our gracious God. If our sin and guilt were not laid upon
Him, they would still rest upon us, and it could be no real consolation to us to meet our God in our death. In Him alone is God our
Helper and Deliverer. For in His death alone our deliverance from
sin and guilt and therefore our liberation from death is accomplished.
In Him alone death has not merely been endured but overcome. In
Him alone it is really for us a defeated foe. In Him alone we may and
must seriously reckon with the fact that God is the boundary of the
death which bounds us. In Him alone that menacing no man's land
is stripped of its menace, and invading chaos repulsed. In Him alone
rests our hope, namely, that we may expect everything from God
even in and beyond our death when we shall be no more. If we cannot fix our hopes too high when they are set on Him, we cannot be

too reserved or cautious or critical in respect of all expectations which are not directed to Him and Him alone. It cannot and should not be too small a thing for us that He and He only is our hope, our future, our victory, our resurrection and our life. Nor should we regret that we have to gather around Him, concentrate wholly upon Him, wholly and utterly believe on Him as God's positive answer to us, allow God's Word of help and deliverance to be spoken to us wholly and exclusively in His person, in His death and resurrection.[7]

I will comment more on that; but for now, it is this third point of Barth that I accent, that is, that we hope together in the God who opposes death. For that reason, all derivative seductions of despair—including the ones I have identified as *security, ideology, technology, certitude,* and *commodity*—are fruits of the realm of death against which we hope, hope from the God of life, hope toward the neighbor.

Barth avers, "We learn nothing materially new when we formally enter New Testament ground."[8] From this awareness, our theme invites Christians to inquire again, without triumphal smugness, to see how we have learned hope—against the kingdom of death—from Jews who are before us and alongside us. The evidence from Judaism as a ground for hope after the manner of ancient Israel is rich and complex, and we Christians are able to be practitioners of that same hope as children of the same God. Here I mention four aspects of that practice of hope before considering some texts with more specificity:

1. One might begin at many points on the counter-practice of hope, and I will return to Genesis later. But for now, perhaps the classic text on hope is in the enigmatic formulation of Exodus 3:14, that is translated something like, "I will be who I will be," or "I will cause to be that which will be." The enigmatic quality of the statement in YHWH's mouth is to be reckoned as crucial, for the God of hope is profoundly elusive. This is an elusiveness that resists precise, idolatrous formulation. The God who speaks to Moses is the God of the ancestors who long ago made promises. But now the presence is an abiding presence. Martin Buber finally judges:

> This promise is given unconditional validity in the first part of the statement: "I shall be present", not merely, as previously and subsequently, "with you, with your mouth", but absolutely, "I shall be present". Placed as the phrase is between two utterances of so concrete a kind that clearly means: I am and remain present. . . . This is followed in the second part by: "That I shall be present", or "As which

I shall be present". In this way the sentence is reminiscent of the later statement of the God to Moses: "I shall be merciful to him to whom I shall be merciful". But in it the future character is more strongly stressed. YHWH indeed states that he will always be present, but at any given moment as the one as whom he then, in that given moment, will be present. He who promises his steady presence, his steady assistance, refuses to restrict himself to definite forms of manifestation.[9]

What begins with the burning bush culminates later in Israel and in the church as "Emmanuel." Samuel Terrien agrees with Buber about presence, but notes its enigmatic, free quality:

> The God of biblical faith, even in the midst of a theophany, is at once *Deus revelatus atque absconditus*. He is known as unknown. The semantics of the phrase "I shall be whoever I shall be" prepares the syntactically similar saying of the third Sinai theophany, "I shall grace whomever I shall grace and I shall be merciful with whomever I shall be merciful" (Exod. 33:19). . . . He wanted religious certainty. He wished to see with his own power of perception. He intended to comprehend. Yahweh's disclosure of his name was both an answer and the denial of a request. Such an ambivalence was to remain "forever" (vs. 15*b*) the mark of the Hebraic theology of presence.[10]

What counts the most, of course, is that the name of the promise maker who speaks here is disclosed amidst Pharaonic slavery. The disclosure is a counter to Pharaonic presence that was as oppressive as it was palpable in the slave community. The declaration of YHWH's presence has an emancipatory intention, providing a better future for a community that is on the move (see Heb 11:15–16).

2. The divine disclosure sets in motion a community on the way. Indeed, the purpose of the divine self-disclosure is to be on the way to a new place and to a new history. The word that counters Pharaonic decree is a generative, emancipatory word that moves the community along from slavery to well-being, and eventually from exile back to the land. To be sure, there is each time a rear-guard action of despair; the "National Security State" of Pharaoh and then of Nebuchadnezzar has a deep grip upon Israel's imagination. Thus in Exodus 16, just after the departure from Egypt, some want to return to oppressive security. And in Babylon, some shrank from departure from the Babylonian empire, being sure that YHWH's hand is too short (Isa 50:2) and that Israel's way is hid from the

Lord (Isa 40:27). Such timid collusion, of course, will not prevail in the community of hope, for the God of Hope comes to occupy the life of the hopers.

3. The God of Hope did indeed accompany the hopers. The signs of that accompaniment were *fire* and *cloud* and *name* and *glory* and *ark*. If, however, we think of praxis, we may imagine that the presence was in singing, singing that eventually became text, and thus the God of textual presence. Singing as praxis is the way hopers regularly defy Pharaonic power, even when frightened and anxious. And so we may notice that the promise as *song-become-text* was on the lips of Miriam and the other women with tambourines:

> And Miriam sang to them:
> "Sing to the LORD, for he has triumphed gloriously;
> horse and rider he has thrown into the sea."
> (Exod 15:21)

They sang in defiance and in fear, but surely against fear.

It must not have been different, moreover, in the second departure, the one from Babylon, for that poet understands the entry to the future via song-become-text:

> For you shall go out in joy,
>   and be led back in peace;
> the mountains and the hills before you
>   shall burst into song,
>   and all the trees of the field shall clap their hands.
> (Isa 55:12)

The hopers sing a defiant echo of Miriam, defiance in sixth-century Babylon, and then in Selma and in Pretoria and wherever hope defies the national security system and other manifestations of the kingdom of death.

4. The singers generated songs. The songs become text. And the text was to be read and reread, heard and reheard, interpreted and reinterpreted. It is a community of equilibrium that can confine texts to one meaning. By contrast a community of hope has texts that always "mean" afresh; hopers engaged inescapably in the juggling act of interpretation that defiantly moves between acquiescence to present arrangements and

risk that opens through many layers of imagination and polyvalence. Such layered interpretation refuses closure, for the closure of the text would only bespeak the closure of the empire and, before that, the closure of the brickyard. James C. Scott has chronicled surreptitious defiance on the part of peasants in Malaysia and in other cultures that are attuned to the defiance of hope.[11] Hope is always such an act of defiance; in these communities of hope it is done through reiterated text that traces the presence and power of the One who is sung.

The texts of hope make YHWH palpably present in a way that saturates the imagination of Judaism and Christianity, and that empowers emancipatory courage against the kingdom of death.

1. At the outset of this matrix of hope is *the initial promise to Abraham and Sarah*:

> Now the Lord said to Abram, "Go from your country and your kindred and your father's house to the land that I will show you. I will make of you a great nation, and I will bless you, and make your name great, so that you will be a blessing." (Gen 12:1–2)

As long ago as Albrecht Alt and subsequently Gerhard von Rad and Jürgen Moltmann, this initiatory utterance of promise has been seen as the ground of biblical hope.[12] In Genesis 12:3, moreover, that articulation of hope looks through and beyond the Abraham community to the nations:

> "I will bless those who bless you, and the one who curses you I will curse; and in you all the families of the earth shall be blessed." (Gen 12:3)

Genesis 12:3, with its reference to the nations, surely looks back to the great promise of Genesis 9:8–17:

> "I will remember my covenant that is between me and you and every living creature of all flesh; and the waters shall never again become a flood to destroy all flesh. When the bow is in the clouds, I will see it and remember the everlasting covenant between God and every living creature of all flesh that is on the earth." (Gen 9:15–16)

2. The initial ground of hope in Genesis 12:1–3 is strangely matched late in the Hebrew Bible by that text that has long occupied Christians, namely, concerning the one "coming with the clouds of heaven":

As I watched in the night visions,
 I saw one like a human being
  coming with the clouds of heaven.
 And he came to the Ancient One
  and was presented before him.
 To him was given dominion
  and glory and kingship,
 that all peoples, nations, and languages
  should serve him.
 His dominion is an everlasting dominion
  that shall not pass away,
 and his kingship is one
  that shall never be destroyed.
                                    (Dan 7:13–14)

This text and others like it of course opened faith, for both Judaism and Christianity, to apocalyptic that is perhaps the extreme mode of hope, an extremity now so grossly misconstrued among us.[13] The opening toward cosmic vision later in the Old Testament kept the community from excessive focus upon itself and its present circumstance as the aim of hope.

   3. Between Genesis 12:1–3 that focuses on the community of Israel and Daniel 7 that is cosmic in scope, I focus upon the great exilic prophetic promises that imagine and wait for a newness from YHWH that would override the defilement of deportation and make a worldly newness available to the people of God. The outcome of such prophetic promise is, in the first instance, Judaism, an outcome not fully commensurate with the lyric anticipation of the poets, but then Jews and Christians together live with visible outcomes that are, for the most part, short of expectant rhetoric.

   Judaism and Christianity share texts of promise that are, to be sure, contested between them about the goal and outcome of such promises. As case studies in contestation, I will consider three texts, one from each of the three major prophets:

   1. In the tradition of Isaiah, the promise in exile is dramatically and authoritatively voiced in Isaiah 43:16–21:

Thus says the LORD,
 who makes a way in the sea,
 a path in the mighty waters,

who brings out chariot and horse,
army and warrior;
they lie down, they cannot rise,
they are extinguished,
quenched like a wick:
Do not remember the former things,
or consider the things of old.
I am about to do a new thing;
now it springs forth, do you not perceive it?
I will make a way in the wilderness
and rivers in the desert.
The wild animals will honor me,
the jackals and the ostriches;
for I give water in the wilderness,
rivers in the desert,
to give drink to my chosen people,
the people whom I formed for myself
so that they might declare my praise.

Taken as best we are able on historical-critical grounds, the text anticipates a return from exile for deported Jews. The imagery appeals to the remembered exodus and then imagines that this restoration to Jerusalem is so wondrous and so glorious that it displaces the remembered exodus in the faith of the community. The imagery concerns a general restoration, including a restoration of creation. The purpose of new "rivers in the desert," however, is clearly for the sake of "my chosen people, the people whom I found for myself." This anticipated restoration, of course, took the form of returned exiles that caused a newly formulated Judaism in Babylon to be resituated in Jerusalem, eventually under the leadership of Ezra.

Christians of a historical-critical variety have not interpreted the promise of Isaiah 43:16–21 differently, and have seen in it the emergence of Judaism. But of course Christian interpretation is not satisfied with such a reading; it must, as it is able, always draw the text closer to Jesus.[14] When this text is drawn toward the Christian gospel, it concerns the work of Christ and the community that He has founded which constitute the "new thing." So the New Testament specialized in the word "new"—*new* wineskins, *new* covenant, *new* commandment. Christian interpretation does not bother to assess the "plain meaning" of Isaiah's utterance, because it historically has had no interest in such a newness, but reads promptly and programmatically beyond that to the newness of Jesus. Indeed, Walter

Moberly has made the argument, with reference to Genesis and Exodus, that in the Old Testament itself the text regularly moves from an *old* meaning to a *new*.[15] Consequently, the displacement of sixth-century newness by first-century christological newness is consistent with the hermeneutical maneuvers already evident in the Old Testament itself, except, of course, that this potential supersessionism from Judaism to Christianity has been historically a power move as well as an interpretive move, so that the transformation and transposition of memory are not merely reinterpretation but characteristically a powerful preemption.

2. The same move is surely the case in the more familiar text from Jeremiah 31:31–34:

> The days are surely coming, says the LORD, when I will make a new covenant with the house of Israel and the house of Judah. It will not be like the covenant that I made with their ancestors when I took them by the hand to bring them out of the land of Egypt—a covenant that they broke, though I was their husband, says the LORD. But this is the covenant that I will make with the house of Israel after those days, says the LORD: I will put my law within them, and I will write it on their hearts; and I will be their God, and they shall be my people. No longer shall they teach one another, or say to each other, "Know the LORD," for they shall all know me, from the least of them to the greatest, says the LORD; for I will forgive their iniquity, and remember their sin no more. (Jer 31:31–34)

That text, in the book of Jeremiah, characteristically understands that the exile is a consequence of the covenant "which they broke." That is, exile is God's punishment upon recalcitrant Israel.

The hope for the new covenant is that it is grounded in unconditional divine forgiveness, permitting a reengagement with YHWH (see Jer 33:8 as well). That is, the future of Judaism as YHWH's covenant people is grounded in divine grace and forgiveness. In that way, the oracle anticipates full reassertion of covenant with Torah provisions but without lingering over merited covenant punishment.

This text, as it is quoted in Hebrews 8:8–12, is utilized in one of the most remarkable texts in the New Testament, a text traditionally read in Christian tradition as supersessionist. The text of Jeremiah is quoted in full; then a verdict is given over that old covenant now displaced:

> In speaking of "a new covenant," he has made the first one obsolete. And what is obsolete and growing old will soon disappear. (Heb 8:13)

The text is often taken as a dismissal of God's covenant with Israel that is regarded as old and obsolete, and that is soon to disappear. This judgment is theological and not historical, but that makes the statement no less problematic. We can see here, as clearly as anywhere, that not only does Christian interpretation sometimes preempt texts from Judaism, but does so in an aggressively exclusionary way that dismisses the legitimacy of Jewish claim and Jewish community.[16]

3. In Ezekiel 47:1–12, the Priestly tradition anticipates a new future that is grounded in a restored temple so that the river of life that had flowed from the Garden of Eden (Gen 2:10–14) now flows from beneath the threshold of the temple. Jerusalem has now replaced Eden as the generative rootage for the source of life. The rebuilt temple, of course, is in the service of a restored Judaism, so that the holy place of YHWH and the holy place of Jews are expected to be the source of life for all of creation.

The usage of this text in Christian formulation of Revelation 21:22 is closely reminiscent of Ezekiel. Thus there is an anticipation of a new holy city, a new Jerusalem (Rev 21:2). As in Ezekiel, the "water of life" flows from the throne of God:

> Then the angel showed me the river of the water of life, bright as crystal, flowing from the throne of God and of the Lamb through the middle of the street of the city. (Rev 22:1–2a)

But instead of the temple that is absent in this vision, the reference is to "the throne of God" which can be the temple in Jerusalem. The distinguishing feature of the rhetoric, however, concerns "the lamb." As a result, the vision now pertains to Jesus, the one crucified as "the slain lamb," but the lamb that rules in power. The temple in Jewish tradition is thus transposed in Christian discourse to be not a place, but a person, the Christ who rules with God.

There is nothing terribly surprising or exceptional in these interpretative moves made in these three texts in Christian interpretation. In each case, a historical-critical judgment in Christian perspective surely coheres in the main with Jewish hope that is invested in restored Judaism, Judaism as the *new thing*, the *new covenant*, and the *new temple*. In each case the text is drawn, in Christian teaching, toward Jesus who is *the new thing*, the giver of *the new covenant*, and *the new presence of God* in crucified form. Nothing of this is exceptional and is commonly taken for granted among us.

This capacity for the transposition of the text is congruent with the nature of the text itself, for these are indeed figurative texts that do not have precise meanings but are verbal acts of hope that perforce must be open-ended. Because the texts are acts of hope and not prediction or predetermination, there is an openness to more than one meaning. The risky point of such contestation is not that the texts in Christian purview have a different meaning from their meaning in Judaism, but that the different meaning in Christian form is taken as exclusionary so that the text can mean this and only this, "this" being Christian claim that perforce excludes Jewish reading.

Thus, the matter to note in textual contestation is not that the texts have a second, different meaning for the second, belated community, but that the new meaning is characteristically claimed as the *only* meaning, a claim that all too often has been supported by political leverage. This contestation about text between Christians and Jews takes place with recognition that texts have variable meanings and no single meaning is adequate to the text. Judaism has been characteristically open to polyvalence in the text. The problem is that Christian interpretation has not, for the most part, allowed for polyvalence, but has insisted on single meanings—specifically, a single meaning that serves Christian hegemony and that regards Jewish reading as inadequate and now superseded.

On the basis of these texts, hope is indeed possible in these twinned communities. But when that hope, rooted in text, is reduced to an intolerant confessional position, then hope is shot through with ideology and is no longer hope that hopes in God. Such exclusionary exposition characteristically produces partisan and self-serving interpretation. Such exclusionary practice is not necessarily willfully self-serving. It is rather a confessional zeal that by intention and by default eliminates "the other" as a valid interpreter. There is no doubt that supersessionist interpretation has functioned to eliminate "the other" of Judaism. My point is that alternative readings per se do not require such exclusionary claims; that requirement arises rather from the exclusionary presupposition that texts have only one meaning and only one legitimate interpretation. Such an exclusionary presupposition is rooted in a failure to understand the nature of the text and a further failure to appreciate the nature of Jewish interpretation. Thus, I answer my first question, "Can we hope?" by answering, "Yes, Judaism and Christianity are communities that hope"; but the exclusionary dismissal of "the other" runs the ready risk that hope devolves into ideology.

The church over the centuries has found many ways to practice exclusionary interpretation that imagines its appropriation of texts as the only possible reading:

1. *Sectarianism* seeks to exclude reading by the "other" within the community of faith under a tight exclusionary discipline.
2. *Hegemony* seeks to comprehend all other readings, even those outside the community of faith in the larger culture.
3. So-called *canonical reading*, if pressed to its logical extremity, turns out to be hegemonic and regards all other readings as illegitimate or at least as preliminary readings.
4. In a very different way, *historical-critical reading* has served to foster an exclusionary reading from a modernist perspective, with an implied if not stated dismissal of readings that reflect confessional perspective, either Jewish or Christian.

In sum, the Western church, perhaps especially in Protestant traditions, has been an institution of closure that has practiced a certain form of hope, but a form of hope that has been tightly bound in preemptive modes.

Thus, I would answer, yes, we can hope, even in an environment of the national security state. But that leads to my second question, "Can hope be divided?" I understand the hope of these confessing communities, Jewish and Christian, to be expectation of "a better country . . . a [city prepared] for them" (Heb 11:16); or put differently, the promised coming of the rule of the creator-redeemer God in the earth as it is already established in heaven. That is why we pray for the coming of the kingdom on earth. Or as David Novak concludes his telling book: "Beginning with creation and nurtured by our respective revelations, Jews and Christians can and do hope for the future. From creation and revelation comes our faith that God has not and will not abandon us or the world, that the promised redemption is surely yet to come."[17]

That is our hope. And yes, Jews and Christians have the necessary gifts and prerequisites for such hope in the God whom we jointly confess, hope for the world that is jointly entrusted to us along with all humanity.

But then, as I reflected on the purpose of this conference and our long history of abuse and alienation, I wondered if that hope could be parceled out as we have done it. My judgment is that when hope is divided among our communities of interpretation, it is likely that our hope is lodged with an idol who cannot keep promises; it follows that hope in the promises of the true God can only be practiced as we hope together, and that in spite of all our differentiations.

1. Jews and Christians may hope together, and that given our different defining communities . . . for Jews the promises are rooted in Abraham but shaped by Sinai . . . for Christians hope is given a trace of fulfillment

in Jesus of Nazareth. These specificities place Christians and Jews very differently about a shared hope and cause us to read texts differently, such texts as "new things" in Isaiah 43, as "new covenant" in Jeremiah 31, and as "rivers of life" in Ezekiel 47. None of that is to be minimized. But because what Novak calls "the all mysterious end" is larger, more sweeping, more glorious, and more hidden than any of us in our distinct communities can yet know, we may hope beyond the confines of our own confessional passions.

2. When I ponder this title, "Can hope be divided?" I have in mind precisely Jewish-Christian practices of hope. But then came the incredible religious polarizing of the churches in the United States with the election of 2004. In that context I take this question back toward the church and ask again, "Can hope be divided?" The issue of "already and not yet" is an immensely acute one among Christians just now. Between Christians and Jews it is also acute, for Christians are wont to overstate the "already" in Jesus Christ whereas Jews wait for Messiah who has not yet come. But of course, both Christians and Jews who stand together in the "not yet" could not do so without an "already." The "already" of Christians is explicit in Jesus of Nazareth; but Jews are also able to hope because of the "already" of Sinai and the "already" of the promises already kept to Jews and to the world.

But now concerning "already and not yet," I ask about the church. The current accent on "dispensationalism" and the coming rapture and the *Left Behind* series—a movement that is particularly committed to the security of the state of Israel—are all about "not yet."[18] Conversely, so-called mainline churches that tend to have weak eschatology focus on the "already" of Jesus Christ, not so much in the form of the "realized eschatology," but in an easy confession that the big matters have been settled in the Christ event.

It is clear, however, is it not, that the settlement of the tension of "already/not yet"—either by a futuristic hope that despairs of present life or an "already" that expects to be barely interrupted—is a betrayal, in one direction or the other, of the in-betweenness of the life of faith that lives by a revelation and that awaits a full disclosure. The political fallout of such division of hope among us Christians is in its own way as disastrous as the way in which Jews and Christians have divided hope.

3. Reflecting on "already and not yet," there is then a third way in which we have divided hope, namely, "red" and "blue." Red hope is, in current discussion, privatized and individualized without any sense of the public.

Blue hope, in much of its articulation, is public and social, but without attentiveness to the personal conviction concerning the God of all promises that is so palpable, for example, in the Psalms of lament and in the Songs of Thanksgiving.

On all three of these issues, hope requires a repentance of our divisions of hope:

- *Jews and Christians* hope for the reign of God that maintains a special but modest place for chosenness, but the rule of God is surely beyond hope for Israel or hope for the church. Perhaps the most stunning text for hope beyond these divisions is the oracle in Isaiah 19:24–25, wherein in time to come God will have many chosen peoples:

  > On that day Israel will be the third with Egypt and Assyria, a blessing in the midst of the earth, whom the LORD of hosts has blessed, saying, "Blessed be Egypt my people, and Assyria the work of my hands, and Israel my heritage." (Isa 19:24–25)

  In the days to come, there will be many chosen peoples, each named by one of YHWH's pet names for the beloved.
- Christians maintain the *"already and not yet"* without collapse in another direction; this tension is nicely articulated in Paul's familiar summation of the Eucharistic tradition. On the one hand, "in remembrance"; on the other hand, "you proclaim the Lord's death until he comes" (1 Cor 11:25–26).
- *Red and blue Christians* together recognize that there is no way that hope in faith can be only private or only public. The promises are to the community and to each member of the community for whom a particular blessing is given.

Christians then have a common vocation with Jews to hope; indeed, Christians can only hope with Jews:

1. Christian rootage for the future hope is inescapably related to the Friday-Saturday-Sunday *triduum*. That dramatic narrative has been given sacramental force in the Eucharistic formulation:

> Christ has died;
> Christ has risen;
> Christ will come again.

The third element in this formulation looks beyond Easter to the complete victory for God's new life in the world. It is, however, the case that the large completeness of the drama does not leave Friday behind. Clear to the end, hope continues to keep the memory and the reality of failure, deficit, and emptiness at the center of awareness.

2. What is missed in the Eucharistic formula, however, is the long stretch of Saturday where the world is mostly lodged. This accent barely made it into the creed. There is no better exegesis for the world's Saturday than that of Allen Lewis in his book *Between Cross and Resurrection*, which offers a reflection on Auschwitz, Hiroshima, Chernobyl, plus the ending of his own life.[19] And George Steiner, in his characteristic eloquence, speaks of the "immensity of waiting" that is "the long day's journey of the Saturday."[20] An immense pause over Saturday will save the church from triumphalism that rings false amid barbarism of the world all around in which we ourselves are so deeply implicated. Such a pause, moreover, may curb the shrill triumphalist voice of Christian supersessionism in the presence of Jews.

3. Hope that moves beyond a claim of privilege requires an emptying of an exclusionary posture that is linked to absolutist readings. Because Jews have lived characteristically on turf other than their own, Christians may be instructed by Jews about textual readings that are not absolute and about faith claims that are not exclusionary. And, of course, Jews and Christians together may be alerted to the emptiness of hope mixed with power when we see that some forms of Israelite Zionism now practice the same absolutist claims that have been the hallmark of so much Christian hegemony. Hope that is possessed and administered in such a way is not hope but "sight." It is known among us, moreover, that we shall never enter the future by sight, but only by faith.

4. Psalm 73 is a narrative articulation that I believe provides a clear account of the seduction of hopelessness. After a conventional affirmation that God is good to Israel and to the pure in heart (v. 1), the Psalmist tells of the seduction of a life of commodity that can be learned from the self-sufficient and replicated (vv. 2–14). Only at the last instant in some kind of liturgical moment (v. 17), the Psalmist pulls back from that seduction and comes to realize that communion with God is the only real hope for life:

> Whom have I in heaven but you?
>   And there is nothing on earth that I desire other than you.
> My flesh and my heart may fail,
>   but God is the strength of my heart and my portion forever.
>   (Ps 73:25–26)

In the end, it is nearness to God that counts and nothing matters beyond that.

Thus:

1. *Can we hope?* Only if we have interpretive practices that are open beyond our habitual exclusionary commitments.
2. *Can hope be divided?* Hope in God cannot be divided
   • between Jews and Christians;
   • between "already and not yet";
   • between "red" and "blue."

When hope is divided, it is a practice of hope that appeals to an idol who cannot deliver. The alternative to such idolatrous practice is trust of the future to the God who remakes creation for good, only not on our terms,

   • not on Jewish or Christian terms,
   • not on our treasured "already" or our passionate "not yet,"
   • not "red" or "blue," but in many colors in the sky that remind God of the post-flood covenant with all flesh, many colors beyond our particular shade of preference.

In terms of contestation, we will give the penultimate word to Karl Barth as it is mediated through the exposition of Eberhard Busch:

In Barth's thinking there were two additional prerequisites for being able to talk to each other in the church of Christ, and these two are inextricably linked. First, such a dialogue between Christians, even if it has the form of an argument with each other, occurs in the brackets of the assumption that both are in the church of Christ. This gives the discussion its true seriousness but also marks the clear boundaries of the argument. Barth once said that the person we should drop completely could "only be an arch-heretic who is totally lost to the invisible church as well." But he adds, "We do not have the ability to ascertain such lost arch-heresy, we do not have this ability even in the case of Christians who are perhaps under strong suspicion." Barth concludes that this is true of two theologians with whom he especially took issue: "For me, Schleiermacher also belongs (in the community of the saints) and Bultmann does too; there is no question about that." This approach has some immediate specific consequences. As a Christian I can criticize other Christians only if I am also in solidarity with them. Furthermore, when I criticize others I can distance myself from them not on a tone of harsh indignation but only in a tone of sad dismay at a threat that had somehow turned into a temptation for me as well. And finally, believing that Israel's shepherd does not slumber or sleep even in the church, I have to keep myself open to the possibility not only that the "favorite voices" I like to hear testify to the truth of God in the church, but "that we need . . . totally unexpected voices even though these voices may at first be quite unwelcome."

The other prerequisite for talking to each other and having an argument with each other is this: Even when I boldly stand up for my understanding of the truth, I can do so only by paying attention to the boundary that is drawn by the fact that God's truth and my understanding of it are always two completely different things. At the very moment I forget this border, it will shift, and the border between my understanding of God's truth and other Christians' understanding of it will become absolute. At that very moment the other person and I no longer stand before our common judge, rather I become the judge of the other.[21]

What Barth and Busch say about Christians in dialogue of course applies to Jews and Christians in dialogue. Dialogue occurs on the assumption that both communities are communities chosen beloved of God and sent in missions of obedience and hope. The call to repentance, to move beyond our chosenness, is a call common to our two communities; in this company it is important to accent that it has been the Christian community that has been tempted to an exclusionary posture that works against the largeness of hope rooted in the promise of God that is always well beyond our own inclination.

Chapter Seven

Spirit-Led Imagination

Reality Practiced in a Sub-Version

The practice of faithful worship is more odd than we often take it to be, familiar as it is to us. In recent time much of that oddness has been relinquished in the church, in a seductive attempt to be current, popular, alternative, or entertaining. It is, I submit, a major task of the church to receive, acknowledge, and respond to the oddness of our odd holy partner. In these comments, I would like to delineate something of that oddness that matters for the missional call of the church and that ultimately matters for the well-being of the world.

Worship is an act of poetic imagination that aims to reconstrue the world. It is an act of imagination, by which I mean it presents lived reality in images, figures, and metaphors that defy our conventional structures of plausibility and that host alternative scenarios of reality that cut beyond our conventional perceptual field. This act of imagination that offers an alternative world is, perforce, a poetic act; that is, it is given us in playful traces and hints that come at us sideways and that do not conform to any of our usual categories of understanding or explanation. The practice of such poetic imagination that invites us playfully to alternative reality is deeply rooted in old texts, old memories, and old practices; it nonetheless requires contemporary, disciplined, informed imagination to sustain alternative vision.

I will cite at some length three mighty acts of poetic imagination in the Old Testament that are characteristic acts of worship to which the community returns again and again.

In Exodus 15:21, surely one of the oldest poems in the Old Testament, Miriam and the other women, as they departed Egypt and began the journey into the wilderness and eventually to the land of promise, with tambourines sang:

117

"Sing to the LORD, for he has triumphed gloriously;
horse and rider he has thrown into the sea."

(Exod 15:21)

This brief hymn is a characteristic example of the way in which Israel does praise. It invites the community to sing to YHWH. It does not explain, because everyone knows. Everyone knows we have just witnessed an inexplicable triumphant act in the world, and everyone knows that it must be referred to the holy God who is creator of heaven and earth. Everyone knows, moreover, that the only fitting response to such an awesome turn in the world is to sing, to offer deep-throated, lyrical, pre-rational exuberance to the giver of life. Miriam and the other women knew before the Wesleys what the Wesleys exhibited so well: that worship is a full, unqualified sense of glad abandonment of our life toward the giver of all life.

This little hymn gives reason for exuberance. YHWH has won a great victory. YHWH has destroyed Egyptian armaments and has overthrown the mighty imperial superpower. Miriam does not know how this has happened and has no mandate to explain. Indeed, Miriam's testimony is not a mechanical response that is connected to what happened. It is, rather, an act of deep imagination, for the overthrow of Pharaoh could be explained, as it has been by critical studies, on other grounds . . . there was a mighty wind, this was an escape of slaves, there was a lapse in state security, there was a dismissal of surplus labor. All that is of course possible, but no, says this worship leader Miriam. She has imagined and construed the wonder differently and at worship we will not pause over trivializing explanation. The event is miracle with marks of holy awe, and it must not be reduced to explanation. It is miracle that invites exuberance and dismay, whereas explanation invites control and management and no doubt another layer of committees.[1]

Well, as you might imagine, the hymnal committee (chaired by a man) took up the spontaneous outburst of Miriam and the other women and transposed that originary poetic act into a longer, more stable poem. The outcome of such a canonizing process is the so-called Song of Moses in Exodus 15:1–18. That poetry begins with the attestation of Miriam in Exodus 15:1:

Then Moses and the Israelites sang this song to the LORD:
"I will sing to the LORD, for he has triumphed gloriously;
horse and rider he has thrown into the sea."

(Exod 15:1)

It continues, by way of extrapolation, in verses 2–3 with more hymnic introduction. And then in verses 4–10, it offers poetic imagination to provide a narrative scenario of the death of Pharaoh. The community of emancipated slaves in generation after generation sing the song and celebrate the overthrow of whoever is the current pharaoh. We watch as the writers imagined the deathly power of Pharaoh and settled on a way to characterize the God of the wind who put tyranny to death:

> "Pharaoh's chariots and his army he cast into the sea;
>   his picked officers were sunk in the Red Sea.
> The floods covered them;
>   they went down into the depths like a stone.
> Your right hand, O Lord, glorious in power—
>   your right hand, O Lord, shattered the enemy.
> In the greatness of your majesty you overthrew your adversaries;
>   you sent out your fury, it consumed them like stubble.
> At the blast of your nostrils the waters piled up,
>   the floods stood up in a heap;
>   the deeps congealed in the heart of the sea.
> The enemy said, 'I will pursue, I will overtake,
>   I will divide the spoil, my desire shall have its fill of them.
>   I will draw my sword, my hand shall destroy them.'
> You blew with your wind, the sea covered them;
>   they sank like lead in the mighty waters."
>
> (Exod 15:4–10)

Nothing is explained. Everything stays hidden except the outcome. The outcome to which the narrative leads is that everything has been transformed!

The hymnal committee of course took liberties with Miriam's little verse. They added verses. In canonical form it is not enough to cross the waters, a wonder of which Miriam had sung. The whole narrative must be told, because the narrative is the screen memory for all of faith in Israel. The slaves not only go out. They go in . . . to the land of promise. Thus in verses 13–17, these ex-slaves are led "in your steadfast love," led through dangerous valleys of death amid Edomites and Moabites and Ammonites, all those who did not subscribe to this act of imagination. In the song, the children of the exodus arrive safely in the land of promise:

> "You brought them in and planted them on the mountain of your own possession,

> the place, O LORD, that you made your abode,
> the sanctuary, O LORD, that your hands have established."
> (Exod 15:17)

It was a long journey, and Israel would have many stories to tell of that journey. But the skeletal structure of Israel's imagination is now in place. The narrative that scripts this imagination is from slavery to safety, from death to life, from oppression to freedom—the story that has countless variations that is endlessly sung and then sung again, because the imaginative drama is always required yet again in new circumstance.

The poem of Exodus 15:1–18 is symmetrical: verses 4–10 concern the death of Pharaoh, who can be any face of brutalizing power; verses 13–17 tell of the arrival at well-being. In between these two units, in verses 11–12, we are offered a formula of incomparability, for no other god has been so allied with slaves:

> "Who is like you, O LORD, among the gods?
> Who is like you, majestic in holiness,
> awesome in splendor, doing wonders?"
> (Exod 15:11)

It is YHWH, directly, immediately, whose great spirit of power has turned the world. The song can for that reason culminate in verse 18 with a great mantra of enthronement:

> The LORD will reign forever and ever.
> (Exod 15:18)

There has been regime change. A new king is among us, a new king who has no brick quotas and no imperial palaces based on forced labor, a new king who offers a world covenantally arranged. It is no wonder that the men joined the women singing, precisely because "he shall reign forever and ever and ever."

So sang Miriam and so echoed Moses. They did not need to say it as they did. But they said it in this particular way, and their way of saying it in this way has become our way of speaking of a new rule of God in the earth, the realm of well-being that we regularly enact in worship. We regularly enact it in hope, in defiance, and in resolve. The song is an act of imagination that hopes an alternative, because the data is all against the song. The data indicates old management by alienating superpowers with brick quotas. But for this one moment, over and over, we refuse the data. We enter another zone of reality that must be expressed—not precisely, not didactically—but in raw exuberance about large nostrils of wind and kings sinking like lead, and populations seized with dread and then settlement and peace. We sing it over and over again against the data of the day. We refuse to give in to the data of the day because we, like them, "desire a better country," a city that has been prepared for us (Heb 11:16).

❧ ❧ ❧ ❧ ❧ ❧ ❧ ❧

Of course, the lyrical rawness that is so indispensable for Miriam and for Moses is not everywhere sustained. When the hymnal committee completed its work, the raw specificity from the beginning point is reshaped into a more urbane poetry. Now the specificity is rounded out to a fuller picture; but the tenacity of fidelity is fully sustained. So consider a third script of praise, the astonishing litany of Psalm 136.

This litany begins in 1–3 with a threefold invitation to "give thanks to YHWH." It knows that the proper stance of Israel before God is one of gratitude, because YHWH is the generous giver of life for Israel and for all of creation. Such thanks in Israel is liturgically constituted by material offerings accompanied by appropriate words.[2] Here we have only the words; thanks is constituted by public testimony that acknowledges YHWH as the giver of gifts and Israel as recipient. The psalm concludes in verse 26 with a like invitation to thank, only now YHWH is not named but is identified as "the God of heaven," that is, the presiding sovereign of all creatures and all gods.

Thus the psalm is framed in verses 1–3 and verse 26 by thanks. Between these two calls of thanks, the body of the psalm in verses 4–25 provides specific grounds of thanks as it recites YHWH's engagement in the world and on behalf of Israel. It turns out that every part of Israel's life, which it can remember or imagine, evokes Israel's thanks. The reason is that in the interpretative imagination of Israel, everything that happens is read as a sign and signal of YHWH's abiding fidelity (*ḥesed*); the world and its historical processes are known to be saturated with divine constancy and stability. Thus the litany proceeds so that the response to every line, a reprise surely uttered by the community at worship, concerns YHWH's fidelity.

The body of the psalm begins in verses 1–9 with reference to YHWH's great work in creation:

> who alone does great wonders,
> > for his steadfast love endures forever;

> who by understanding made the heavens,
>   for his steadfast love endures forever;
> who spread out the earth on the waters,
>   for his steadfast love endures forever;
> who made the great lights;
>   for his steadfast love endures forever;
> the sun to rule over the day,
>   for his steadfast love endures forever;
> the moon and stars to rule over the night,
>   for his steadfast love endures forever.
>   (Ps 136:4–9)

This is followed by a long litany concerning the exodus deliverance in a song not unlike Exodus 15 (vv. 4–15), followed by the conventional sequence of wilderness sojourn and entry into the land (vv. 16–23). The main body of the psalm concludes with a wondrous summary statement in three parts:

> It is he who remembered us in our low estate,
>   for his steadfast love endures forever;
> and rescued us from our foes,
>   for his steadfast love endures forever;
> who gives good to all flesh,
>   for his steadfast love endures forever.
>   (Ps 136:23–25)

In this conclusion, Israel can remember its abasement, surely a reference to exodus slavery, and offers an acknowledgment of divine rescue (vv. 23–24). Surprisingly this is followed in verse 25 with a reference to creation and the reliable food chain of creation:

> who gives food to all flesh,
>   for his steadfast love endures forever.
>   (Ps 136:25)

We are able to see that this Psalmic imagination reflects a larger body of poetry. Thus, the reference to "low estate" readily recalls Psalm 123, which reflects on YHWH's transformative mercy that addresses YHWH's context of contempt:

As the eyes of servants
    look to the hand of their master,
as the eyes of a maid
    to the hand of her mistress,
so our eyes look to the LORD our God,
    until he has mercy upon us.
Have mercy upon us, O LORD, have mercy upon us,
    for we have had more than enough of contempt.
Our soul has had more than its fill
    of the scorn of those who are at ease,
    of the contempt of the proud.
                                        (Ps 123:2–4)

Verse 25 with its reference to "food to all flesh," moreover, is reminiscent of the great creation hymns that celebrate the abundance of food:

These all look to you
    to give them their food in due season;
when you give to them, they gather it up;
    when you open your hand, they are filled with good things.
                                        (Ps 104:27–28)

. . . .

The eyes of all look to you,
    and you give them their food in due season.
You open your hand,
    satisfying the desire of every living thing.
                                        (Ps 145:15–16)

All creation is pulsing with YHWH's faithfulness.

This act of liturgic imagination may strike us as routine. It does not, however, need to be so. The world can indeed be imagined differently. It can be imagined with Thomas Hobbes as a war of each against all. It can be imagined with Henry Kissinger as a world in which might makes right. It can be imagined with Milton Friedman as a place of scarcity where we compete for limited goods. It can be imagined with Tom Ridge as a place of chaos and threat and risk. All such construals are possible and frequently enacted. But not in Israel. Not in this world of worship. Israel reads and imagines and celebrates otherwise, by appeal to its own remembered narrative, a narrative of constant fidelity, such constancy that evokes assured and unanxious gratitude. (There are, to be sure, testimonies in Israel that construe differently, but in this canonical recital the point is clear.) It is evident that out of the materials of its experience and observation, Israel is engaged in world making so that Israel ends the psalm in a safe place where gratitude is the appropriate response.

※※※※※※※※

As Exodus 15 narrates the raw reality of victory and Psalm 136 stylizes that victory into a collage of stylized affirmations, so my third example, Psalm 107, at the same time (a) moves from grand communal affirmation to concrete lived experience, and (b) goes underneath glad doxology to the vexations that mark every life in God's world.

Psalm 107 begins in verses 1–3 with a summons to thank, not unlike Psalm 136. The specific ground of thanks is that YHWH is "good" and that, as in Psalm 136, his steadfast love endures forever. This is the baseline of faith and the ground of gratitude:

> O give thanks to the LORD, for he is good,
>   for his steadfast love endures forever.
>   (Ps 107:1)

But this psalm goes further. It not only summons to thanks, but it identifies those who most readily and appropriately will give thanks:

> Let the redeemed of the LORD say so,
>   those he redeemed from trouble
> and gathered in from the lands,
>   from the east and from the west,
>   from the north and from the south.
>   (Ps 107:2–3)

The ones who can make gestures of gratitude are the ones who have been "redeemed from trouble." The reference could be to the oppression of Egypt, but the body of the psalm will make clear that the invitation is to all sorts of human persons. And the parallel refers to all those "gathered," that is, returned from exile and displacement. The rhetoric of verse 3 is inclusive and pertains to all Jews who have been brought home, and to all who had lived through God's generous homecoming.

The four-directional inclusion recalls Isaiah 43:6 wherein YHWH seeks out the scattered:

> I will say to the north, "Give them up,"
>   and to the south, "Do not withhold;
> bring my sons from far away
>   and my daughters from the end of the earth—
> everyone who is called by my name,
>   whom I created for my glory,
>   whom I formed and made."
>
>   (Isa 43:6–7)

That rhetorical maneuver acknowledges the God of all gathering:

> Thus says the Lord GOD,
>   who gathers the outcasts of Israel,
> I will gather others to them
>   besides those already gathered.
>   (Isa 56:8)

These are the ones who are to give thanks to YHWH, because they are the ones who know YHWH's *hesed* firsthand.

The psalm then lines out, in four case studies, some particular examples of those who have been alienated and restored. The substance of verses 4–38 is remarkable because of its capacity to remember, recall, and characterize specific situations of distress.

The first case, characteristic of the fourfold stylized report, describes a situation of wanderers that are lost in the wilderness without resources:

> Some wandered in desert wastes,
>   finding no way to an inhabited town;
> hungry and thirsty,
>   their soul fainted within them.
>   (Ps 107:4–5)

But they, Israelites that they are, know that a petition addressed to YHWH is the appropriate antidote to such dismay:

> Then they cried to the LORD in their trouble.
>   (Ps 107:6a)

The remarkable movement of the rhetoric indicates that without pause or pondering of any kind, the deliverance of YHWH follows promptly upon petition:

> and he delivered them from their distress;
> he led them by a straight way,
> until they reached an inhabited town.
> (Ps 107:6b–7)

These two rhetorical elements state the substance of Israel's most elemental worship, namely, *cry in need* and divine *response of rescue*. While it will not be true in two subsequent cases I will mention, here the crisis in which the faithful are located has nothing to do with guilt. What counts is not guilt but need. Israel, it is attested liturgically, knew exactly what to do about desperate need, namely, to recognize one's own inadequacy and to turn to the fully adequate Lord.

In a complex and extensive discussion, Karl Barth has asserted that prayer in Christian tradition is "simply asking."[3] Barth continues to say that asking God is "the most genuine act of praise and thanksgiving and therefore worship." More than that, so Barth, "God does not act in the same way whether we pray or not." Prayer "exerts an influence upon God's action, even upon his existence."

For that reason it is no surprise that the cry of the wilderness wanderers in their hunger and thirst is promptly answered with divine deliverance. This is a God who hears and who decisively responds to the need of Israel. Indeed, as Claus Westermann has shown, this structure of "cry-answer" or "cry-save" is the core plot of biblical faith and therefore the core claim of worship.[4] From the finite verbs "deliver" and "lead," Israel at worship—because of countless cases of concrete testimony—can generalize about God's *ḥesed*. The generalizing affirmation about YHWH, moreover, introduces the crucial term *"niphel'ôth"* (wonderful acts), acts of transformation that defy our explanation that belong in the peculiar category of miracle. It is no wonder that this tightly drawn rhetoric concludes with a summons to thanks. The final verse of the unit returns to the beginning and reiterates the initial need, only now it is need satisfied:

> For he satisfies the thirsty,
> and the hungry he fills with good things.
> (Ps 107:9)

Now the governing verbs are of a different sort: "satisfy," "fill." These terms, bespeaking the abundance of creation, are very different from the verbs of verses 6–7—"deliver," "lead"—that attest historical activity. The four verbs together thus witness both to YHWH's disruptive rescue as redeemer and to YHWH's generous sustenance as creator.

The plot line of Psalm 107:4–9 provides a sketch of Israel's faith and surely a sequence of right worship:

need
cry
rescue
thanks

That same plot line is reiterated in three additional case studies.

- In Psalm 107:10–16, the stylized sequence goes this way:
  need:

  > Some sat in darkness and in gloom,
  >   prisoners in misery and in irons,
  > for they had rebelled against the words of God,
  >   and spurned the counsel of the Most High.
  > Their hearts were bowed down with hard labor;
  >   they fell down, with no one to help.
  >   (vv. 10–12)

  cry:

  > Then they cried to the LORD in their trouble.
  >   (v. 13a)

  rescue:

  > and he saved them from their distress;
  > he brought them out of darkness and gloom,
  >   and broke their bonds asunder.
  >   (vv. 13b–14)

  a response of thanks:

  > Let them thank the LORD for his steadfast love,
  >   for his wonderful works to humankind.
  >   (v. 15)

a reprise of need resolved:

> For he shatters the doors of bronze,
>   and cuts in two the bars of iron.
>
> (v. 16)

In the response of YHWH, the governing verbs are "save," "bring out," "break." And in the reprise it is "shatter," "cut," all verbs of forceful action. These verbs in sum constitute a "wonderful work" (miracle) that is sure to evoke thanks for the inexplicable gift of new life.

- In verses 17–22, the plot is now familiar:

need:

> Some were sick through their sinful ways,
>   and because of their iniquities endured affliction;
> they loathed any kind of food,
>   and they drew near to the gates of death.
>
> (vv. 17–18)

cry:

> Then they cried to the LORD in their trouble.
>
> (v. 19a)

rescue:

>   and he saved them from their distress;
> he sent out his word and healed them,
>   and delivered them from destruction.
>
> (vv. 19b–20)

thanks:

> Let them thank the LORD for his steadfast love,
>   for his wonderful works to humankind.
> And let them offer thanksgiving sacrifices,
>   and tell of his deeds with songs of joy.
>
> (vv. 21–22)

In the rescue, the verbs are now "save," "send," "heal," "deliver"—thus a more extensive cluster of terms. The response of thanks is now more extended, having displaced any reprise that is absent in this episode.

Verse 21 reiterates the familiar formula of thanks for *ḥesed* and *niphel'ôth*. Verse 22 indicates the enactment of thanks in cultic form. Now the thanks is not only verbal, but includes a thank offering, a gift of material significance; and the material gift is matched by telling, that is, by narrating the rescue from the crisis described in verses 17–19. Thus verse 22 reflects precisely a combination of "Word and sacrament."

- The fourth case in verses 23–32 is quite extended but by now in a quite familiar pattern:

need:

> they saw the deeds of the LORD,
>> his wondrous works in the deep.
> For he commanded and raised the stormy wind,
>> which lifted up the waves of the sea.
> They mounted up to heaven, they went down to the depths;
>> their courage melted away in their calamity;
> they reeled and staggered like drunkards,
>> and were at their wits' end.
>
>> (vv. 24–27)

cry:

> Then they cried to the LORD in their trouble.
>> (v. 28a)

rescue:

> and he brought them out from their distress;
> he made the storm be still,
>> and the waves of the sea were hushed.
> Then they were glad because they had quiet,
>> and he brought them to their desired haven.
>> (vv. 28b–30)

thanks:

> Let them thank the LORD for his steadfast love,
>> for his wonderful works to humankind.
>> (vv. 31–32)

In this sequence, the crisis is credited directly to YHWH; the storm that causes the trouble is a *niphel'ôth* wrought by YHWH's command. The verbs of rescue here include "bring out," "made still." The element of thanks is again extended in verse 22 to include extolment and praise in the midst of the congregation. It is clear in all these cases that the moment of miracle has now been transposed into a stylized narrative, the purpose of which is to instruct, summon, and empower the congregation to participate in this world of miracles, a world of decisively answered prayer.

The psalm concludes with two more generalized affirmations, more or less derivative from these case studies. In verses 33–38, YHWH as creator is celebrated as the one who turns rivers to deserts and fruitful land to waste, and who blesses those who are hungry with all the fruitfulness of creation. The rhetoric is reminiscent of Genesis 1. In Psalm 107:39–41, the rhetoric concerns social transformation in a way reflective of the Song of Hannah and anticipatory of the later Song of Mary:

> When they are diminished and brought low
> > through oppression, trouble, and sorrow,
> he pours contempt on princes
> > and makes them wander in trackless wastes;
> but he raises up the needy out of distress,
> > and makes their families like flocks.

Nature is imagined as "creation," and history is imagined as an arena for YHWH's revolutionary activity. The psalm concludes in verse 43 with an invitation to wise discernment of this Yahwistic reality, the neglect of which leads to trouble; the final phrase, yet one more time, concerns the *ḥesed* of YHWH. All of these case studies attest concretely to the divine fidelity that is voiced in the liturgy of Psalm 136.

I have taken extended time—perhaps too much—to consider three songs in ancient Israel:

- Exodus 15, voiced alternatively by Miriam and by Moses, is a *victory* song that plots Israel's way from slavery to the land of promise;
- Psalm 136 is a hymn that attests to *YHWH's fidelity* in every sphere of life; and
- Psalm 107 is a song of thanksgiving that brings the fidelity of YHWH close to *concrete lived human experience.*

I have suggested that three highly stylized, self-aware poems are accomplishments of daring imagination that read out of and read into lived experience. Given a Yahwistic assumption, every experience that is reported in Israel is understood with reference to YHWH without whom the event would not be the event that it is. I cite these cases to insist that Christian worship is an act of human imagination that voices, advocates, and insists upon a gospel perception of all lived reality. The substance of worship is to tell the story in the form of many smaller stories, all of them featuring YHWH as the key character. The purpose of such reportage on past events of miracle is precisely so that the contemporary congregation, many seasons later, may participate as directly as possible in a world of miraculous fidelity to which the text attests and which YHWH decisively inhabits.

I have deliberately used the term "imagination" because I want to insist that such stylized narrative account is indeed a human construction. The poets put the words together in this particular way. The poets utilized this pattern of worship in order to reiterate and reenact this advocacy. It happens over and over; every time a pastor and a choir director get together to pick hymns, the work is one of constructive imagination designed to lead the congregation in turn to imagine the world in a certain way. Much worship is informed by tradition and conventional practice, but those who construct such worship must each time commit an act of imagination in order to determine what is to be accented and to adapt the advocacy to the specificity of context.

Having said that worship features our humanly constructed acts of imagination designed to advocate a perspective, we inescapably must ask if it is all "made up," for the term "imagination" is a tricky one. But of course in the community of faith, to "imagine" does not mean to "make up." It means, rather, to receive, entertain, and host images of reality that are outside the accepted given. If, however, we say "receive" images, then we may ask, "receive from whom?" Or "receive for whom?" The answer we give is that what the Psalmists and liturgists imagine and shape and offer is given by God's spirit, for it is the spirit who bears witness. It is the spirit that has given Israel freedom to recognize and acknowledge YHWH as savior from slavery. It is the spirit that gives us eyes to see and selves to notice the recurring and constant fidelity of God. It is the spirit that cries out with us that lets us cry out and receive God's rescue. It is the spirit that moves in the faith of the community and in the artistry of the poet to give voice to the odd truth of our common life.

Or it may be put differently. When Peter confessed Jesus to be the Messiah, Jesus blesses Peter for his confession:

> And Jesus answered him, "Blessed are you, Simon son of Jonah! For flesh and blood has not revealed this to you, but my Father in heaven." (Matt 16:17)

So it is with all the great liturgic claims of the church and with the text from which these liturgic claims arise. It is not "flesh and blood" that has let us see these matters. It is not human insight or imagination. It is rather the self-disclosing God who has let Israel and the church see that the drama of fidelity is God's own act. Thus the God who is the subject of our testimony and of our worship is also the God who discloses what we know of that truth. It is God—we may say "father" as in Matthew 16:17 or we may say "spirit"—who is the subject of our worship and the source of our knowing. That spirit, moreover, has been present not only in the originary event and at the point of initiation. That same spirit is present in our own contemporary appropriation of the tradition, present in our interpretation, and present in the imagination that makes contemporaneity possible. We may indeed say that worship is indeed an act of spirit-led imagination.

But notice what is implied in this notion of spirit-led imagination. Insofar as our worship is an act of spirit-led imagination that permits us to see and live differently, it is very upstream, against the grain of dominant reality. Worship does not happen in a vacuum, but always in response to context.

I submit that in the context of the North American church, worship that is spirit-led imagination is powerfully over and against dominant reality. One way to consider this interface is to consider the three texts that I have considered and to ask what the contrary may be to each of them:

1. In Exodus 15:21, and derivatively in Exodus 15:1–18, we have seen the joyous celebration of the overthrow of Pharaoh by the God who is incomparable in compassion and power. In the long stretch of the Bible, "Pharaoh" is not only a historical person, but has become a metaphor and symbol for all established power that seeks to organize the world against covenantal freedom, justice, and neighborliness.

But imagine the world of Pharaoh without this poem. Imagine this world without the incomparable God of freedom and justice and neighborliness who is attested in this song. Imagine that Pharaoh had never been overthrown, could not be challenged, and was never placed in jeopardy. Without this dangerous poetic imagination of worship, we have a world in which entrenched, oppressive power is guaranteed to last to perpetuity. Take away the poem and its worshiping practitioners, and the slaves are fated forever to brick quotas, reduced to silence without ever a moan or a groan of self-announcement. Take away the tambourines of Miriam and we are left with an unchanging world of unbearable despair.

But of course that is the world that the dominant narrative of our time offers us. It believes that technological capacity, economic monopoly, and military mastery can keep the world the way it is forever. It believes that control of finance means that wealth and poverty are to be kept as they are, which places most social pathologies beyond redress. Once given that narrative of despair, it is likely that oppressive interpersonal relationships are fated to last, because a heavy dose of authoritarianism maintains equilibrium and yields no change. At best we are left with shopping and entertainment in a world that is closed and fixed, stable without a chance for hope.

And then imagine . . . imagine . . . that the congregation, in the wake of Miriam, begins to sing and dance and remember the overthrow of power. It could have been Pharaoh overthrown. Or it could have been Nebuchadnezzar when we left exile:

> When the LORD restored the fortunes of Zion,
>   we were like those who dream.
> Then our mouth was filled with laughter,
>   and our tongue with shouts of joy;
> then it was said among the nations,
>   "The LORD has done great things for them."
> The LORD has done great things for us,
>   and we rejoiced.
>   (Ps 126:1–3)

Or it could have been the power of death when the church joined the Easter laugh, and signed on with the Lord of the Dance, the one who has led the dance since the days of Miriam.

2. Psalm 136, that highly stylized liturgy, offers a community of remembering that is able to recall in some grandeur and some close detail the wonders of creation and the dazzlement of exodus, sure that the incomparable God of freedom, justice, and neighborliness is directly at work among us. And from this acute remembering, our singing community has continued with what we take to be the long-term truth of God, that YHWH's fidelity is very, very long-term. This inventory of miracles shows God's fidelity to be concrete and accessible, and so the recital is sandwiched in the psalm by thanks, thanks to YHWH for his goodness, thanks to YHWH who is the Lord of Lords, thanks to YHWH who is the God of Gods, thanks to the God of heaven whose miracles enfold all lived reality. Israel yields

itself in gratitude, aware and glad to acknowledge that the decisive features of its life of well-being are all a gift:

> It is he who remembered us in our low estate,
>   for his steadfast love endures forever;
> and rescued us from our foes,
>   for his steadfast love endures forever;
> who gives food to all flesh,
>   for his steadfast love endures forever.
>   (Ps 136:23–25)

But imagine a world without this psalm and without the God attested there. Imagine a group of people who no longer meet to sing and dance and remember fidelity. In that world:

- Memory is lost and amnesia is the order of the day, forgetfulness that assumes that we are the ones and only ones, none before us, none to come after us, only us, free to use up all of creation . . . and its oil!—in our own extravagant way. Moses, of course, knows all about this; he knows that affluence breeds amnesia and the loss of a grounding memory:

  > When you have eaten your fill and have built fine houses and live in them, and when your herds and flocks have multiplied, and your silver and gold is multiplied, and all that you have is multiplied, then do not exalt yourself, forgetting the LORD your God, who brought you out of the land of Egypt, out of the house of slavery. . . . Do not say to yourself, "My power and the might of my own hand have gotten me this wealth." But remember the LORD your God, for it is he who gives you power to get wealth, so that he may confirm his covenant that he swore to your ancestors, as he is doing today. (Deut 8:12–14, 17–18)

Eat, enjoy, be full enough, forget enough, until we arrive at a place where we no longer say, "This do in remembrance of me," because the "me" of God has been overwhelmed in a vacuum.

- Fidelity disappears in a large binge of self-indulgence. We no longer remember the faithful God; we no longer remember to imitate God in faithfulness; we no longer remember that fidelity is the coin of humanness. In place of fidelity come power and greed, cunning manipulation, and anxiety, because covenants are reduced to contracts and promises are only conveniences. And our humanness erodes.

- Where memory fails before amnesia and where fidelity gives way to self-indulgence, in that world there will be no thanks, no acknowledgment that life is a gift; we are free to imagine it to be an achievement or a possession. Where there is no gratitude, there will be no thank-offering, no giving of self, no Eucharist, that great meal of thanks. And where there is no sacrament that dramatizes the world as a mystery of abundance, life becomes sheer commodity and human transactions are reduced to market transactions. Matters we have traditionally understood as social goods—medical care and education for example—now become only tools of leverage in the service of greed.

The dominant culture all around is one of self-indulgence without fidelity, manipulation without gratitude.

And then comes this little body of singers breaking out in Psalm 136. The loud narrative of acquisitiveness is shattered and shown to be false. The powers of manipulation and monopoly are broken. The singing itself is a dangerous protest of dissent from the dominant culture that does not sing, for everything is reduced to formulae; but then this body sings its spirit-led alternative.

3. In Psalm 107 we have considered four cases of human disaster and misery, lost in the wilderness, abandoned in prison, sick and without appetite, nearly lost at sea. In that highly stylized account, we have seen that every troubled person becomes a person able to cry out in need and address pain to God. It turns out to be no surprise that God in fidelity answers, reassures, and makes transformation possible. But the trigger in each case is the cry, the capacity to find voice, the sense of entitlement that pain may speak to power and insist upon the redress. For that reason, our worship must not be too happy, too well ordered, or too symmetrically serene, for at the heart of our worship is asking in need, being answered, and being taken seriously.

But imagine a world without Psalm 107. What if there were no one to sing this great song of thanks, no acknowledgment of rescue grounded in fidelity, no communal awareness that life consists in situations of distress, and above all no recognition of the cry of distress that sets in motion the divine mystery of rescue? Imagine a world without cry, without the public processing of pain, without the insistent sense of entitlement that we deserve better than this. Imagine a world that has grown silent and cold of human pain. Imagine a world totally silenced, no prayers uttered, no hopes voiced, no hosting of the human condition and, consequently, no miracles of newness or healing.

The dominant culture and its narrative account of reality go a long way toward such silence. Just suck it up and get on with your life! If you are in trouble, it is your fault, so get with the program. At most, those in deep need become only a forgotten statistic; "compassionate conservatism" becomes a retaliatory regression with no answering of human community and no compassionate turn toward those in need, but only slanderous impatience toward those without power to save themselves.

And then, right in the midst of such systemic silencing, the congregation breaks out in Psalm 107. It recalls disasters, remembers rescues, and gives thanks. In the center of that recall and remembering is the cry, the urge and energy and authority of out-loud pain that causes the world to regroup in new ways.[5] The congregation gives voice to old distresses resolved by the mercy of God; in giving voice to old distresses that have been solved, it invites those in present distress to find voice and hope that may yet again move God to act.

The dominant narrative of anti-neighborly late capitalism moves along without these great texts. The dominant version of reality:

- goes *without Exodus 15*, and so imagines that oppressive power is forever
- goes *without Psalm 136*, with nothing of fidelity and so gives no thanks
- goes *without Psalm 107*, and ends in silence that crushes the human spirit

We, all of us, are to some extent practitioners of that dominant version of reality. It comes at us in many forms; if we conform to that dominant voice of reality, we may receive its surface gifts of well-being and security for a while. There is enough truth in the dominant version of reality for it to maintain its credibility, but only for a while![6]

There is, however, a counter-truth that surfaces in Christian worship. It is a small counterpoint without great voice or muscle. It has been a minority perspective for a very long time. The ones who practice the counterpoint know very well that ours is not and will not be a dominant voice. It is a sub-version of reality, one that sounds beneath the loud sounds of the dominant version, one that flies low beneath the radar surveillance of the dominant version.

This evangelical sub-version of reality lives in delicate tension with the dominant version. It sometimes has aspiration to become the dominant version of reality, as in many of the psalms that make sweeping liturgical claims for the God featured in this sub-version. Thus, Psalm 117 can imagine all nations celebrating this compassionate sovereign:

> Praise the LORD, all you nations!
>   Extol him, all you peoples!
> (Ps 117:1)

Or Psalm 96 can line out a message of assurance to all nations in the name of this monarch newly come to power:

> Say among the nations, "The LORD is king!
>   The world is firmly established; it shall never be moved.
>   He will judge the peoples with equity."
> (Ps 96:10)

But in fact the sub-version is a poetic, elusive, delicate alternative even while the dominant voice of reality prevails in its facts on the ground. Our liturgical practice acknowledges the resilience of the dominant version of reality, but in the meeting we reiterate yet again the sub-version in the liturgy as a viable, credible, choosable alternative. Thus, the community:

- *offers Exodus 15* as an alternative to the claim that oppressive power is forever
- *offers Psalm 136* as an alternative of fidelity to a social vision of comparative greed
- *offers Psalm 107* as an alternative cry to a social coercion of enforced silence

In every such liturgical utterance, act, and gesture, this sub-version of reality intends to subvert dominant versions, to expose them as inadequate if not false, and to empower the community to re-engage reality according to this sub-version.

This delicate tension between dominant version and sub-version, I believe, is the true character of worship. The claims made in the sub-version, claims such as "Christ is risen," are a deeply felt, eagerly offered truth. And yet in its very utterance the community at worship knows that the facts on the ground, the data at hand, contradict this and give evidence that the odor of death is still very much in play. It will not do for the church to become cynical and give in to the dominant vision. But it also will not do for the church to become excessively romantic about its sub-version and so to imagine its dominance. Rather, I believe that the worshiping community must live knowingly and elusively in this tension, not cynical, not romantic, but wise and innocent (Matt 10:16), always engaged in negotiation between sub-claim and the world the way we find it.

The task and goal of worship, accompanied by education and pastoral care, is to move our lives from the dominant version of reality to the sub-version, finally that our old certitudes will have been subverted by the work of the spirit. Judged by the dominant version, life in the sub-version is vulnerable and foolish and exposed. But the sub-version in the end cannot be judged by the dominant version. In the end, it is judged by the truth of the gospel, by the reality of God whom we attest, and by the truth of our own lives in the image of that God. We are endlessly seduced out of that truth by the dominant version, and so we return again to worship to recite and receive this sub-version that is the truth of our life and the truth of the world.

In the Old Testament, the psalms vigorously and without apology line out that sub-version and make a claim against the data at hand. Psalm 23 is one familiar presentation of the sub-version that is contradicted by dominant views, but for all of that no less true:

> The LORD is my shepherd, I shall not want.
>   He makes me lie down in green pastures;
> he leads me beside still waters;
>   he restores my soul.
> He leads me in right paths
>   for his name's sake.
> Even though I walk through the darkest valley,
>   I fear no evil;
> for you are with me;
>   your rod and your staff
>   —they comfort me.
> You prepare a table before me
>   in the presence of my enemies;
> you anoint my head with oil;
>   my cup overflows.

Surely goodness and mercy shall follow me
  all the days of my life,
and I shall dwell in the house of the LORD
  my whole life long.

(Ps 23)

And in the New Testament, none more eloquently lined out the truth of the sub-version than did Paul:

For the message about the cross is foolishness to those who are perishing, but to us who are being saved it is the power of God. For it is written,

"I will destroy the wisdom of the wise,
  and the discernment of the discerning I will thwart."

Where is the one who is wise? Where is the scribe? Where is the debater of this age? Has not God made foolish the wisdom of the world? For since, in the wisdom of God, the world did not know God through wisdom, God decided, through the foolishness of our proclamation, to save those who believe. For Jews demand signs and Greeks desire wisdom, but we proclaim Christ crucified, a stumbling block to Jews and foolishness to Gentiles, but to those who are the called, both Jews and Greeks, Christ the power of God and the wisdom of God. For God's foolishness is wiser than human wisdom, and God's weakness is stronger than human strength. (1 Cor 1:18–25)

. . . .

Consider your own call, brothers and sisters: not many of you were wise by human standards, not many were powerful, not many were of noble birth. But God chose what is foolish in the world to shame the wise; God chose what is weak in the world to shame the strong; God chose what is low and despised in the world, things that are not, to reduce to nothing things that are, so that no one might boast in the presence of God. He is the source of your life in Christ Jesus, who became for us wisdom from God, and righteousness and sanctification and redemption, in order that, as it is written, "Let the one who boasts, boast in the Lord." (1 Cor 1:26–31)

. . . .

For this reason it depends on faith, in order that the promise may rest on grace and be guaranteed to all his descendants, not only to the adherents of the law but also to those who share the faith of Abraham (for he is the father of all of us, as it is written, "I have made you the father of many nations")—in the presence of the God in whom he believed, who gives life to the dead and calls into existence the things that do not exist. (Rom 4:16–17)

. . . .

No, in all these things we are more than conquerors through him who loved us. For I am convinced that neither death, nor life, nor angels, nor rulers, nor things present, nor things to come, nor powers, nor height, nor depth, nor anything else in all creation, will be able to separate us from the love of God in Christ Jesus our Lord. (Rom 8:37–39)

We leave the hearing and speaking of the sub-version and reenter the world that has not yet come to this alternative. We make our way in compromise and timidity, in fear and trembling. But then we enter gladly into the voice of the sub-version, yet again, very sure of our true home and our real identity:

O come, let us sing to the LORD;
    let us make a joyful noise to the rock of our salvation!
Let us come into his presence with thanksgiving;
    let us make a joyful noise to him with songs of praise!
For the LORD is a great God,
    and a great King above all gods.
In his hand are the depths of the earth;
    the heights of the mountains are his also.
The sea is his, for he made it,
    and the dry land, which his hands have formed.

O come, let us worship and bow down,
    let us kneel before the LORD, our Maker!
For he is our God,
    and we are the people of his pasture.

                                (Ps 95:1–7a)

Chapter Eight

You Cannot Fool Your *Nephesh*

In the books of the Torah, all paths lead to Sinai. The Israelites had escaped Egyptian slavery, though they remembered Pharaoh's Egypt wistfully as a place of adequate food. They had traversed the "stony road" of wilderness, been contentious, and received "wonder bread" from the sky. Then they approached the mountain. It was an awesome, dread-filled place that signaled divine presence that was in no sense user-friendly. As they approached that dread mountain, Moses reminded them of the heavy cost of life with YHWH. They would have to obey:

> "Now therefore, if you obey my voice and keep my covenant, you shall be my treasured possession out of all the peoples. Indeed, the whole earth is mine, but you shall be for me a priestly kingdom and a holy nation. These are the words that you shall speak to the Israelites." (Exod 19:5–6)

The mountain was an offer of a new identity, of life in covenant with YHWH. That is all Moses said. He gave them no detail. But Israel, in its eagerness, answered quickly and without reservation:

> The people all answered as one: "Everything that the LORD has spoken we will do." Moses reported the words of the people to the LORD. (Exod 19:8)

They answered with promptness and eagerness even though they did not know the particulars. I imagine, would you not, that the reason for their ready affirmation is that they knew that whatever YHWH required would

141

be less than Pharaoh required. They were prepared to try the new "boss" who would surely be better than the exploitative brutality of the old boss.

So they approached the mountain. As they approached, the mountain shook and trembled with smoke and fire. The mountain surged and shrieked with divine presence. This is the hidden, inscrutable, savage God who inhabits the mountain and who, like a fairytale ogre, threatens all who approach.

And then, only this one time, the God of the mountain spoke. This was a strange God whom they did not know. First off, this God tells his name. This name, however we are to take it, is a set of consonants with ill-fitting vowels. Christian scholars say "YHWH"; Jews refuse to say it. The name is an enigma, except the utterance fills out the inscrutable name, ". . . who brought you out of the land of Egypt, out of the house of bondage." Surprise! The God they had already known as their great advocate and emancipator turns out to be the God of the mountain. This is the God who, on their behalf, outmatched and outmuscled Pharaoh, terminated the brick quota, and ended the hot, demanding brickyards. That is the God who speaks, who now offers a charter for an alternative existence outside the categories of Pharaoh.

As you know, this mountain God of freedom speaks ten times, only ten, and then not again at Sinai, for after that everything comes via Moses. These ten utterances constitute the only direct speech of YHWH. As he spoke ten times, he spoke three times about the *love of God*, "love" being a covenant word for honoring treaty commitments. You know them, no rival gods, no manufactured replicas as fetishes, and no words that reduce God to a means. A pause . . . and then he spoke six times about *love of neighbor*, "love" being a covenant word for honoring treaty commitments. You know these six about parents and killing and committing adultery and stealing and giving false witness and coveting. Three for God and six for neighbor—nine altogether, love of God and love of neighbor, the two great commands. And then this emancipatory voice circled back and pressed the "insert" button on his computer; YHWH inserted between the three on *love of God* and six on *love of neighbor*, the longest of all commands. The command on sabbath occupies a central position, because it looks back to the first three and the God of restfulness and it looks forward to the last six concerning the neighbor who needs restfulness. Right at the center of this charter for freedom, the great God of freedom has placed the central provision for freedom that rings always and now in the years of the faithful:

Remember the sabbath day, and keep it holy. Six days you shall labor and do all your work. But the seventh day is a sabbath to the LORD your God; you shall not do any work—you, your son or your daughter, your male or female slave, your livestock, or the alien resident in your towns. For in six days the LORD made heaven and earth, the sea, and all that is in them, but rested the seventh day; therefore the LORD blessed the sabbath day and consecrated it. (Exod 20:8–11)

This command stands at the center of the decalogue and dominates the horizon of commands at Sinai:[1]

- The seventh day is holy, that is, it is devoted unreservedly to the reality and purpose of YHWH, thus requiring a disengagement from the way we devote our other days to ourselves.
- The seventh day is for work stoppage. There is very little evidence in the Old Testament connecting sabbath to worship. The accent is acknowledgment of God not in worship but in desisting from the common enterprises of production.
- The requirement of work stoppage is comprehensive. It includes everyone who is under the supervision of the male head of the house to which the commandment is addressed; thus, the command pertains to family, to workforce, to nonhuman animals, and to immigrants who do not really belong, but who are under the aegis of the landowner.
- But it is the motivation for work stoppage that is important for us (v. 11). The grounding of this dramatic work stoppage is that creation itself culminated in work stoppage for the creator after six days of creation. As a consequence, this day, which is unlike every other day, is blessed, invested with power for life and healing, devoted to the mystery of God's own life.
- From the eternal foundation of the world, the reality of God is not invested in perpetually "continuing creation," and so the ones in God's image are not invested in perpetual productivity. Work stoppage characterizes the way in which the creator relates to creation.

At the end of the decalogue, in Exodus 20:18–21, it is clear that the thundering God of the mountain would say no more, because everything important has now been said. At that point, a mediator, Moses, is introduced into the process of communication; Israel is now aware that direct communication with God is much too hazardous. From now on Moses will speak, and the rest, as we say, is exegesis. Israel now knows all that is to be known of God's intention for its life in covenant.

The meeting of Sinai culminates in Exodus 24:3, 7 which are oaths of allegiance and obedience:

> "All that the LORD has spoken we will do, and we will be obedient."
> (Exod 24:7)

Israel signs on gladly and quickly and without reservation to the demands of YHWH. The rabbis have long noticed that the sequence of verbs is "do and hear" (*shema'* = obey). We might expect the reverse, "hear and do," but Israel acts first and then knows what has been commanded. Israel knew from the outset that the commands of YHWH are better than the commands of Pharaoh. In Exodus 5, we are given a rendition of Pharaoh's commands:

> But the king of Egypt said to them, "Moses and Aaron, why are you taking the people away from their work? Get to your labors!" Pharaoh continued, "Now they are more numerous than the people of the land and yet you want them to stop working!" That same day Pharaoh commanded the taskmasters of the people, as well as their supervisors, "You shall no longer give the people straw to make bricks, as before; let them go and gather straw for themselves. But you shall require of them the same quantity of bricks as they have made previously; do not diminish it, for they are lazy; that is why they cry, 'Let us go and offer sacrifice to our God.' Let heavier work be laid on them; then they will labor at it and pay no attention to deceptive words."
>
> So the taskmasters and the supervisors of the people went out and said to the people, "Thus says Pharaoh, 'I will not give you straw. Go and get straw yourselves, wherever you can find it; but your work will not be lessened in the least.'" So the people scattered throughout the land of Egypt, to gather stubble for straw. The taskmasters were urgent, saying, "Complete your work, the same daily assignment as when you were given straw." And the supervisors of the Israelites, whom Pharaoh's taskmasters had set over them, were beaten, and were asked, "Why did you not finish the required quantity of bricks yesterday and today, as you did before?" (Exod 5:4–14)

The Israelite supervisors of labor who have been co-opted by Pharaoh to make the system work issue a protest to the crown:

"No straw is given to your servants, yet they say to us, 'Make bricks!' Look how your servants are beaten! You are unjust to your own people." (Exod 5:16)

But Pharaoh, the voice of the imperial production system, is relentless:

He said, "You are lazy, lazy; that is why you say, 'Let us go and sacrifice to the LORD.' Go now, and work; for no straw shall be given you, but you shall still deliver the same number of bricks." (Exod 5:17–18)

And the supervisors were quick to issue the new ferocious demands to the slave community:

The Israelite supervisors saw that they were in trouble when they were told, "You shall not lessen your daily number of bricks." (Exod 5:19)

The memory of Israel that it repeats at Passover is of an irrepressible brick quota and an impossible production schedule. And like any driven production system, the quotas keep increasing. Every success generated more rigorous demands. You may be sure that there was no work stoppage under Pharaoh because the production apparatus was at work 24/7. You may be sure that there was no seventh day, no sabbath, no day blessed and made rich with vitality, no holy day devoted to YHWH, the Lord of the sabbath. Seen in this way, the eagerness of Israel for the Sinai commands is easy to understand. The Sinai offer was an alternative to the quota system of the empire. Now the production system would be interrupted and shut down every seventh day. Israel would rest as it never did in Egypt, because YHWH, unlike the Egyptian gods, is a God of restfulness.

It is clear that the fourth command at Sinai in Exodus 20:8–11 refers to the litany of creation in Genesis 1:1–2:4a. That account of reality is in a symmetrical order with a repeated verdict of "good." The human couple, female and male, is charged with supervisory management of the fruitfulness system, to care, to maximize its fruitfulness, and to be sure that the generativity of the creator is reflected in the abundance of creation.

The creator God, the litany attests, is a God of blessing, capable of assigning life and well-being to every aspect of creation. When the Creator had arrived on the scene, the already extant chaotic matter of "Tohu-wa-Bohu" was distinctively unblessed and incapable of life. By word and by act, the creator God transposed that seething chaotic matter into an ordered, coherent life-support system. The blessing-giving God transposes reality by three times blessing the creation:

- The first blessing is toward sea monsters and winged creatures:

  God blessed them, saying, "Be fruitful and multiply and fill the waters in the seas, and let birds multiply on the earth." (Gen 1:22)

- The second blessing is toward the human couple:

  God blessed them, and God said to them, "Be fruitful and multiply, and fill the earth and subdue it; and have dominion over the fish of the sea and over the birds of the air and over every living thing that moves upon the earth." (Gen 1:28)

- The third blessing is of the seventh day now made holy:

  So God blessed the seventh day and hallowed it, because on it God rested from all the work that he had done in creation. (Gen 2:3)

The blessing, the infusion of the life force of God, is in turn to (a) non-human creatures, especially sea monsters—thus, a witness that God has ordered even chaotic waters; (b) humans as God's regents in the maintenance of an order of abundance; and (c) a day of rest intrinsic to the structure of the created order of fruitfulness.

And God rested! God had done enough. God was tired. It was the weariness of a kingly ruler who had spent a week issuing orders and edicts. It is a weariness of a caregiver who has been using energy to infuse creation with the energy of life. The fatigue of God is replicated by Jesus in the narrative of the woman who has hemorrhaged for twelve years:

  Immediately aware that power had gone forth from him, Jesus turned about in the crowd and said, "Who touched my clothes?" And his disciples said to him, "You see the crowd pressing in on you; how can you say, 'Who touched me?'" He looked all around to see who had done it. But the woman, knowing what had happened to her, came in fear and trembling, fell down before him, and told him the whole truth. (Mark 5:30–33)

Being a healer is costly to the one who heals. Being a creator is costly in the extension of blessing. Being a caregiver is costly, as every caregiver notices, because it entails the transmission of the self to the other.

But imagine: *God rested*! God rested because God was weary. This, of course, does not fit with the God of the catechism who is beyond all

such pathos in omniscience, omnipresence, and omnipotence. Such a God
never rests:

> He will not let your foot be moved;
>   he who keeps you will not slumber.
> He who keeps Israel
>   will neither slumber nor sleep.
>   (Ps 121:3–4)

Such a God is never depleted, never spent, never needs a day off, because
such a God is not intimately and intrinsically linked to needy creation.
And then, of course, it is only a small step to be made in the direction of
the Promethean God of classical theology who never rests. So the pastor,
caregiver, in the image of the Promethean divine caregiver, never rests,
never is depleted, never is needy, is alert 24/7 in piety and devotion and
self-giving because the church needs such a pastor. And we act with a theology of incessant availability.

But not this God! This God rests! This God so rests that Israel in its
poetic imagination can entertain the thought of YHWH's dormancy. Indeed
Israel can issue a wake-up call to God:

> Awake, awake, put on strength,
>   O arm of the LORD!
> Awake, as in days of old,
>   the generations of long ago!
> Was it not you who cut Rahab in pieces,
>   who pierced the dragon?
>   (Isa 51:9)

The summons in Isaiah 51 is to the creator God, the one who had in ancient
times dealt with evil sea monsters. God rests because the world will work,
because the tasks of creation have been delegated, and because creation,
blessed as it is, knows the will and energy of the Creator and does not need
constant attention. God rests, because God engages in self-care and because
God has complete confidence in the sustaining energy of creation. And
there came a silence over heaven and earth and the radishes said to the porcupines, "Shhh—be quiet because 'Himself' is resting, and we must tiptoe
until Sunday morning when we will arise after rest to new life." The rest of
the Creator causes serenity in creation. The creatures, like the Creator, are
competent and trusting and unhasting. The world works and all is well.

It is, of course, to be noticed that in the creation of liturgy there is no sabbath rest declared for the human creatures in their supervisory capacity. Are they to work 24/7 in order that creation may function properly? We may only infer. The human creature, in God-like responsibility, is in the image of God. It belongs to the image of this God—not the Promethean God of self-sufficiency as offered in too much theology—to be weary, to be depleted, to need rest, to be secure and confident about the working of creation. It belongs to the image to reflect the sabbath of the Creator, and where it is not so reflected, the image is violated and distorted.

A third text that may strike a reader as odd is the instruction that God gives to Moses in Exodus 25–31 about the construction of the tabernacle, a holy place for the in-dwelling of God. This text reflects the tedious punctiliousness of priestly perception that sounds like a building committee or a hardworking hymnal committee. This long instruction, moreover, is answered in Exodus 35–40, which is largely repetition, reporting that Moses implemented in careful detail the instructions for the holy place given at Sinai.

The text concerns us for a simple, single reason. Scholars have in recent time noticed that the long text of Exodus 25–31 is all YHWH addressed to Moses, but in seven speeches:[2]

> The LORD said to Moses. (Exod 25:1)
> The LORD spoke to Moses. (Exod 30:11)
> The LORD spoke to Moses. (Exod 30:17)
> The LORD spoke to Moses. (Exod 30:22)
> The LORD said to Moses. (Exod 30:34)
> The LORD spoke to Moses. (Exod 31:1)
> The LORD said to Moses. (Exod 31:12)

(The variation between "spoke" and "said" is the variation of *davar* and *'amar*, but the variation is scarcely significant.) When we notice the number seven, we pay attention. The first six speeches of YHWH to Moses are instructions about holy place and holy ordination. Not surprisingly, it is the seventh speech of Exodus 31:12–17 that interests us. That text is no longer interested in either space or ordination; rather, the priestly imagination culminates, yet again, as in Genesis 2:1–4a, in holy time:

> You yourself are to speak to the Israelites: "You shall keep my sabbaths, for this is a sign between me and you throughout your gener-

ations, given in order that you may know that I, the LORD, sanctify you. You shall keep the sabbath, because it is holy for you; everyone who profanes it shall be put to death; whoever does any work on it shall be cut off from among the people. Six days shall work be done, but the seventh day is a sabbath of solemn rest, holy to the LORD; whoever does any work on the sabbath day shall be put to death." (Exod 31:13–15)

Given seven speeches that culminate in sabbath, scholars draw the inescapable conclusion that this long text is an intentional play on Genesis 1. Only now the work of creation is not cosmic; rather it is the holy place where YHWH is assured a locus of dignity and order that contradicts the disorder of chaos all around in the exile, the likely time of the formation of the text. If the text means to signify reliable God-given order, it means that the priests offer an imaginative construction of a creation as holy place that is a contradiction to the disorder of creation. A new imaginative construct culminates with the sabbath, for the sabbath is a regular work stoppage, and acting out of confidence that the world works and does not depend upon our frantic ceaseless activity, sabbath is a sign of the effective governance of the creator God.

This seventh speech culminates with reference to the divine sabbath:

"It is a sign forever between me and the people of Israel that in six days the LORD made heaven and earth, and on the seventh day he rested." (Exod 31:17)

And then, in a quirky conclusion, the text adds, no longer remembering that it is cast as God's own speech, "and was refreshed."

This is a stunning theological statement! The Hebrew uses the term *nephesh*, which occurs often in the Old Testament as a noun meaning "self" and often rendered as "soul," as in "bless the Lord O my soul." But here the term *nephesh* is a verb in the reflexive niphal; YHWH "was *nepheshed*." This odd sort of usage occurs only in two other places in the biblical text. It is used in a parallel kind of way in Exodus 23:12 with reference to the sabbath:

Six days you shall do your work, but on the seventh day you shall rest, so that your ox and your donkey may have relief, and your homeborn slave and the resident alien may *be refreshed*. (Exod 23:12)

Here the verb *nephesh*, in the reflexive, pertains to "you and your ox and your donkey and your slave and your resident alien." The list is comprehensive and inclusive. Sabbath is for all parts of the household. All shall rest, for all are depleted. And in the sabbath all—slaves, immigrants, oxen, and asses—all *recover their nephesh*. All are *re-nepheshed* back to full, glad creatureliness. The other usage of the verbal form is in 2 Samuel 16:14, now more related to quotidian life and not something as high-powered as sabbath. David is fleeing for his life from his son Absalom. He retreats to the Jordan valley:

> The king and all the people who were with him arrived weary at the Jordan; and there *he refreshed himself*. (2 Sam 16:14)

David and his company are depleted by fear, by anxiety, by haste, by insecurity. They are weary with a deep dread, exhausted by having lost their secure grip on a secure world. And now they are *re-nepheshed*, perhaps by cool bathing and being in a safe place, no doubt finding food. The image is important because it suggests that our *naphshim* ("selves"), our inmost identity, is on a spectrum of refreshment and exhaustion, of life and death. We regularly have our *nephesh* diminished and then recovered, and it requires pause from anxiety in order to recover the full self.

Sabbath is a time for being *re-nepheshed*, for recovery of full self by withdrawal from all that drains and exhausts and depletes. And so for God. Because of God's own life and God's own time and God's own experience, God has ordered, in the very fabric of creation, that there are limits to the demands and expectations that are to be placed on our *naphshim*.

Thus, sabbath is about recovered *nephesh*, and *nephesh* is not a "religious idea," no "soul," but self in all of its complex social existence. That is why I entitled this presentation, "You Cannot Fool Your *Nephesh*." We say often, "You can't fool your body." Of course not, but the *nephesh* more so, for *nephesh* is that intertwined complexity of all things, spiritual, moral, mental, bodily, and material, the whole self, the true self. And it will not be lied to. There are limits because we are in the image of the God who is limited to six days of energy. We are often depleted like God and just like the ox and just like the donkey and just like a slave and just like an immigrant, we must pause. Pushed beyond that limit, the *nephesh* evaporates and creation fails. And so we must pause.

For this day ponder your *nephesh* in its wholeness, its complexity, its social location, and imagine the voices and tasks that deplete and the voices and tasks that restore. And rest! If you need a guide for *nephesh*-pondering, try Psalm 35:

Say to *my soul*,
   "I am your salvation."
(Ps 35:3b, emphasis added)

. . . .

Then *my soul* shall rejoice in the LORD,
   exulting in his deliverance.
All my bones shall say,
   "O LORD, who is like you?
You deliver the weak from those too strong for them,
   the weak and needy from those who despoil them."
                                        (Ps 35:9–10)

. . . .

How long, O LORD, will you look on?
   Rescue me from their ravages,
   my life from the lions!
            (Ps 35:17. emphasis added)

These three uses of *nephesh* in Psalm 35 disclose a life—a *nephesh*—that is in jeopardy but that is fully referred to YHWH, the one who first breathed life on our clay and the one who moment by moment sustains us. In turn the Psalmist refers to his *nephesh* in order

- to seek God's promise of salvation
- to anticipate praise and thanks toward God
- to petition for rescue of life from the lions

These uses altogether suggest a life—this life, every life, my life, your life—complex and at risk, jostled, threatened, unappreciated, in jeopardy, returning to the creator redeemer God who is the only source of solace or protection. So imagine your *nephesh*, the one weary every Sunday, the one assaulted nearly every day, the one celebrated and adored at birth, the one commuting regularly between hurt and well-being, imagine this *nephesh* depleted. In our depletion our *nephesh* is like the *nephesh* of God, and we must rest!

What a piece of literary architecture, that Exodus 25–31 imagines and construes a safe, ordered place where the holiness of God can touch down without pollution or disturbance. Except that at the last moment, in the seventh speech, the promise of space, in characteristic Jewish fashion, is converted to a safe, ordered time for rehabilitation. In this regard, the tabernacle-to-sabbath sequence is exactly parallel to Genesis 1 that ponders fruitful space for six days and at the last moment turns to holy time.

On the follow-up obedience of Exodus 35–40 where Moses constructs what God has commanded, the work is completed. The space and the time are in order, and the narrator reports:

> In this way all the work of the tabernacle of the tent of meeting was *finished*; the Israelites had done everything just as the LORD had commanded Moses. (Exod 39:32, emphasis added)

> . . . .

> He set up the court around the tabernacle and the altar, and put up the screen at the gate of the court. So Moses *finished* the work. (Exod 40:33, emphasis added)

It is finished! It is constituted! Holy zone where God dwells! Holy time where *nephesh* sets down! Holy space and holy time, holy life devoted to the presence of God and healing, and a vision of God's glory come among us—full of grace and truth—God's glory which we are to practice and enjoy. This space is unlike any other space. This time is unlike any other time. This life is unlike any other life. It is this space and this time and this life that stand as the wellness center of creation. There is no substitute, no reasonable facsimile, no adequate tradeoff or compensation. An act of restful restoration engages the character of the Creator, even as it is engraved in the life of the creation; imagine, moreover, that we are made in that image to turn from busyness to restfulness and so back to full joyous creatureliness, the kind intended by the Creator, the kind intended by good parents by whom we were first fondled. It is the truth of our life that we are meant for restful restoration.

The Creator promises and guarantees abundance, and sabbath is the day we luxuriate in that abundance as a gift which we do not need to perform or possess or acquire or achieve . . . because it is a gift! But of course, we do not keep sabbath, and so violate the inviolate reality of our God-given *naphshim*. And why? Well, I propose: we violate sabbath and so diminish and deplete our *naphshim* because *we do not believe in, trust in, or count on God's abundance.* We do not think that creation is abundant, and we do not trust the guarantee of the Creator. The outcome of such distrust, I propose, is a devouring anxiety . . . just as sabbath is a total antidote to anxiety. For what remains of my comments, I juxtapose sabbath and anxiety. Note well "anxiety" . . . not "sin" or "guilt"!

When we do not trust in guaranteed abundance, we must supply the deficiencies out of our own limited resources. We scramble to move from our sense of scarcity to an abundance that we imagine that we ourselves can supply, all the while frantically anxious that we won't quite make it:

- Not enough to be loved
- Not enough to be well liked
- Not enough to advance
- Not enough to secure my family
- Not enough members
- Not enough dollars
- Not enough published articles
- Not enough new clothes, new cars, new houses
- Not enough bombs
- Not enough stocks and bonds
- Not enough freedom
- Not enough purity
- Not enough of our kind of people

It is necessary to erode the holy time of sabbath for the sake of productivity, given our sense of scarcity grounded in distrust. In my discussion of anxiety as alternative to sabbath, I cite four texts and make one contemporary foray.

In Genesis 41:14–36, Pharaoh, the Egyptian god who presided over the resources of the superpower, had a bad dream. In the midst of his limitless abundance that is the gift of the Nile, he had a nightmare about scarcity. You know the dream of thin cows and thin years of grain, seven years of famine to come. But do you know the policy that arose from the nightmare of scarcity, as policies are always arising from our nightmares? In Genesis 47, Joseph son of Israel, child of the abundant creator God, signed on for the Pharaonic nightmare of scarcity. He went to work for the interests of corporate acquisitiveness, organized an imperial monopoly, and over a three-year period seized, in the interest of the corporate economy, the money of the peasants, the cattle of the peasants, the land of the peasants, and eventually the life of the peasants who were reduced to slavery. This achievement was all accomplished by a true son of Israel who was seduced, as we often are, into the nightmare of scarcity. You may be sure that in this anxiety over the coming famine there was no rest in the surge of confiscation, no time off, no sabbath. The machinery of acquisitiveness worked 24/7 until Pharaoh, by the genius of Joseph, achieved total monopoly. That is how our people, by the book of Exodus, ended in slavery; one among us believed excessively in the nightmare of scarcity that contradicted the abundance of the creator God. Thus, Genesis 47 stands as a prelude to the exodus narrative and indicates that a mistrust of creation's abundance created the crisis of the exodus narrative. Pharaoh's nightmare of scarcity disrupted creation and eventually evoked the plagues that constitute creation performing like chaos, a massive threat to order and abundance.

Exodus 16 is just after the departure from Egypt in chapter 15. In chapter 16, the Israelites cross the water, landing in the wilderness in a place without a viable infrastructure where the assurances of an abundant creation manifestly did not pertain. You know how the story goes. First, the desperate people of the wilderness, sensing their scarcity, yearned to return to Egypt:

> The Israelites said to them, "If only we had died by the hand of the LORD in the land of Egypt, when we sat by the fleshpots and ate our fill of bread." (Exod 16:3a)

They could not remember that the alleged abundance of Egypt had come at a very high price. Second, they accused Moses of lethal leadership:

> "For you have brought us out into this wilderness to kill this whole assembly with hunger." (Exod 16:3b)

The good news is that the complaint evokes the abundance of the creator God. The abundance of God overrides the scarcity of the wilderness. And we are told, in anticipation of a later Eucharist, bread was given in abundance:

> "I have heard the complaining of the Israelites; say to them, 'At twilight you shall eat meat, and in the morning you shall have your fill of bread; then you shall know that I am the LORD your God.'"
> In the evening quails came up and covered the camp; and in the morning there was a layer of dew around the camp. When the layer of dew lifted, there on the surface of the wilderness was a fine flaky substance, as fine as frost on the ground. When the Israelites saw it,

they said to one another, "What is it?" For they did not know what it was. Moses said to them, "It is the bread that the LORD has given you to eat." (Exod 16:12–15)

The narrative does not explain the abundance that fell from the sky. Indeed, God's abundance always outruns our expectations and our categories of explanation. But of course the abundance of the Creator is given on the terms of the Creator, as it was even in the first act of creation:

"This is what the LORD has commanded: 'Gather as much of it as each of you needs, an omer to a person according to the number of persons, all providing for those in their own tents.'" The Israelites did so, some gathering more, some less. (Exod 16:16–17)

Moses warns his people, even as he feeds them, against acquisitiveness, as their perceived scarcity drove them to acquisitiveness even in the face of divine abundance:

And Moses said to them, "Let no one leave any of it over until morning." But they did not listen to Moses; some left part of it until morning, and it bred worms and became foul. And Moses was angry with them. (Exod 16:19–20)

They gathered in their anxiety, but their anxiety was a contradiction of God's abundance. A surplus of anything gathered in anxiety will contradict God's abundance.

Now the reason I tell this story is because of a little-known footnote at the end of the narrative:

He said to them, "This is what the LORD has commanded: 'Tomorrow is a day of solemn rest, a holy sabbath to the LORD; bake what you want to bake and boil what you want to boil, and all that is left over put aside to be kept until morning.'" So they put it aside until morning, as Moses commanded them; and it did not become foul, and there were no worms in it. Moses said, "Eat it today, for today is a sabbath to the LORD; today you will not find it in the field. Six days you shall gather it; but on the seventh day, which is a sabbath, there will be none." (Exod 16:23–26)

Manna is daily bread for the day only. Only for the day, *except for a sabbath special*; provision is made because God intends and provides that normal bread gathering is unnecessary on the sabbath and it is prohibited. It is a day of pure gift in which no energy is to be given to meeting our deficits or our deficiencies. Sabbath requires confidence in God's provision; only the anxious who mistrust violate the day.

These two scenarios of Pharaoh and Joseph in Genesis 47 and Israel and Moses in Exodus 16 are two texts that bracket the exodus narrative, both portraying the nightmare of anxiety that violates God's abundance. The first case is external to Israel as it concerns Pharaoh, except that Joseph the Israelite signs on for imperial acquisitiveness and arranges an economy in which there is no sabbath. The second case is internal to Israel, but exhibits anxious acquisitiveness that violates the way of nourishment by the bread of heaven.

These two narrative crises have pointed me, for contemporary connection, to a remarkable article by Mark Slouka in *Harper's Magazine*.[3] The title of the article refers to the fact that Sherwood Anderson was a paint factory manager, and one day he just walked away from his work and became a well-known writer. Slouka develops his argument by referring to "the God of Work," and "the Church of work," the all-anxious commitment to busyness, work, the virtue of needing little sleep, and the passion for affluence that arises from much work. He turns in the article from work to leisure, and observes that the "Church of Work" is all for leisure, as long as it is organized and expensive and socially chic:

> Open almost any magazine in America today and there they are: The ubiquitous tanned-and-toned twenty-somethings driving the $70,000 fruits of their labor; the moneyed-looking men and women in their healthy sixties (to give the young something to aspire to) tossing Frisbees to Irish setters or tying on flies in midstream or watching sunsets from their Adirondack chairs.[4]

But then Slouka contrasts leisure that is approved with idleness that is harshly disapproved in contemporary society . . . time to ponder, time to consider options, time to reflect, time to develop an internal life of freedom. He asserts that such idleness is an elemental requirement in a democratic society, so that free citizens can indeed exercise free political reflection.

And then he moves to the life pattern of George W. Bush who rides and cuts brush, but who never pauses to reflect critically or think or ponder or read. He concludes that President Bush is a metaphor—"his shallowness, his bustle, his obvious suspicion of nuance"—is linked to "to the spirit of fascism."[5] The outcome is:

A man untroubled by the imagination, or by an awareness of human frailty. A leader wonderfully attuned (though one doubted he could ever articulate it) to "today's swift pace"; to the necessity of forging a new patriotism; to the idea of war as "the necessary and bloody test of a people's force"; to the all-conquering beauty of Business.[6]

I cite the article to observe that the absence of sabbath—read "idleness"—is a deep pathology in our society. It surely besets church members, and it undoubtedly infects U.S. clergy who thrive on overextended work habits to the neglect of a critical internal life. One cannot imagine Pharaoh in Genesis 47 taking time to ponder; one cannot imagine anxious people in the wilderness pondering the generosity of creation. Indeed, their anxiety that caused acquisitiveness surely made sabbath unthinkable.

I finish with two well-known New Testament texts. In Matthew 6:25–33, Jesus teaches his disciples:

> "Therefore, I tell you, do not worry about your life, what you will eat or what you will drink, or about your body, what you will wear. Is not life more than food, and the body more than clothing? . . . Therefore do not worry, saying, 'What will we eat?' or 'What will we drink?' or 'What will we wear?' For it is the Gentiles who strive for all these things; and indeed your heavenly Father knows that you need all these things." (Matt 6:25, 31–32)

Jesus exactly contrasts "anxiety" and "the father God" who knows all our needs. It is an elemental lack of trust in the creator God—elemental distrust that is the common human predicament but that is enhanced for us as children of the Enlightenment—that leads to *sabbath-negating anxiety*. Jesus invites his disciples into *anxiety-negating sabbath*, grounded in abundance, about which birds and flowers know, that refuses the scarcity imagined in our autonomy.

As a second text consider Mark 8:14–21 that occurs after Jesus has fed five thousand people (Mark 6:30–42) and four thousand people (Mark 8:1–9). Jesus instructs his disciples, but the narrative begins badly. They had forgotten their bread for the boat ride because they had not, even after all of the feeding miracles, connected the authority of Jesus (the creator God) with the abundance of bread. And so he quizzes them and rebukes them:

> And becoming aware of it, Jesus said to them, "Why are you talking about having no bread? Do you still not perceive or understand? Are

your hearts hardened? Do you have eyes, and fail to see? Do you have ears, and fail to hear? And do you not remember?" (Mark 8:17–18)

Of course, he gets no answers; like every embarrassed student, the best the disciples could do was to avoid eye contact. Like a good teacher eager for engagement, Jesus retreats to concrete operational questions. Those they can answer:

"When I broke the five loaves for the five thousand, how many baskets full of broken pieces did you collect?" They said to him, "Twelve." (Mark 8:19)

"And the seven for the four thousand, how many baskets full of broken pieces did you collect?" And they said to him, "Seven." (Mark 8:20)

They know the right answer to concrete questions: "Twelve," "seven!" They are good at numbers, but they have no clue that the numbers indicate abundance from God given through the Eucharistic verbs, "he took," "he blessed," "he broke," "he gave." There would be more than enough because in Jesus *the full functioning of Creation is restored*. And then in one of Jesus' saddest, most pathos-filled comments the narrative ends:

"Do you not yet understand?" (v. 21)

We are the ones who have understood about anxiety and sabbath, about work and rest, about the truth of the gospel being more powerful than our nightmares. This guarantee of abundance makes our anxiety unnecessary because it is a gift. We understand because we receive!

Chapter Nine

Just Like You . . . Forgiven!

The community of Israel, now bound in covenant to YHWH and now committed to sabbath, lingered at Sinai. But then, in Numbers 10:11, Israel left Sinai on its way to the land of promise. They imagined "milk and honey" as it had been promised, signs of a generous Creator. But what they got—for forty years—was quail and "a fine flaky substance" of which they said, "What is it?" (Exod 16:13–14). They imagined extravagance, and what they got was wilderness leanness. They did persist in the wilderness. After forty years, they arrived at the Jordan, at the very edge of the land promised to Abraham and Sarah. They were ready to leap the Jordan to get there, these land-hungry peasants, ready to swim the Jordan, these land-desperate desert people. But then they stopped at the Jordan River.

They stopped there longer than they intended because Moses had final instructions, long final instructions that we call the book of Deuteronomy. What Moses spoke about, on and on in a stylized harangue, was the "Canaanites." The land is filled with "Canaanites," and we cannot understand the crisis of land in that tradition unless we understand what Moses means by "Canaanites":

And they told him, "We came to the land to which you sent us; it flows with milk and honey, and this is its fruit. Yet the people who live in the land are strong, and the towns are fortified and very large; and besides, we saw the descendants of Anak there. The Amalekites live in the land of the Negeb; the Hittites, the Jebusites, and the Amorites live in the hill country; and the Canaanites live by the sea, and along the Jordan." (Num 13:27–29)

The Canaanites are formidable indeed. What must be understood, however, is that "Canaanite" is not an ethnic term, for it is likely that those called "Canaanite" are ethnically identical to those who became Israelites. The differences are not ethnic but political, economic, sociological, and eventually theological. The term "Canaanite" comes from the term "purple," and refers first of all to those who traded in purple dyes. Then the term comes to refer to all those who engaged in commerce who operated a money economy as distinct from peasants and nomads, pastoral and agricultural people. Eventually the term "Canaanite" comes to refer to those who have mastered the urban economy, built cities as centers of military and political power, and developed the sociological patterns that belong to urban life—social stratification, division of labor, and surplus value.[1] Moses, good sociologist that he was, was able to see that such complex social relationships that are generically labeled "Canaanite" are inimical to the covenant community with its passion for more-or-less egalitarian or communitarian relationships. Thus the Moses tradition—then extended by Elijah—is that there is a clash of social systems that is reflective of a clash of theological passions.[2]

Moses pauses at the Jordan River to instruct the covenant community that is pledged to egalitarianism, because he knows that the land under "Canaanite" aegis is enormously seductive to Israel; in its seduction it constitutes a threat to covenantal models of social relationships. In response to that anticipated seduction and threat, Moses offers several homiletical pieces, of which I cite four:

- In Deuteronomy 6, Moses warns that the advanced, affluent standard of living in Canaanite culture would produce amnesia in Israel about the past and indifference to the God of the exodus:

  When the LORD your God has brought you into the land that he swore to your ancestors, to Abraham, to Isaac, and to Jacob, to give you—a land with fine, large cities that you did not build, houses filled with all sorts of goods that you did not fill, hewn cisterns that you did not hew, vineyards and olive groves that you did not plant—and when you have eaten your fill, *take care that you do not forget the LORD*, who brought you out of the land of Egypt, out of the house of slavery. The LORD your God you shall fear; him you shall serve, and by his name alone you shall swear. Do not follow other gods, any of the gods of the peoples who are all around you, because the LORD your God, who is present with you, is a jealous God. The anger of the LORD your God would be kindled against you and he would destroy you from the face of the earth. (Deut 6:10–15, emphasis added)

This warning about "other gods," as is characteristic in Israel, is inescapable. The contract is at the same time a warning about other systems of social relationships that are inimical to YHWH.

- In Deuteronomy 7, Moses reminds Israel that its peculiar identity is a gift from YHWH, and maintenance of that identity is urgent:

  For you are a people holy to the LORD your God; the LORD your God has chosen you out of all the peoples on earth to be his people, his treasured possession.
      It was not because you were more numerous than any other people that the LORD set his heart on you and chose you—for you were the fewest of all peoples. It was because the LORD loved you and kept the oath that he swore to your ancestors, that the LORD has brought you out with a mighty hand, and redeemed you from the house of slavery, from the hand of Pharaoh king of Egypt. (Deut 7:6–8)

  That distinctiveness, moreover, required purgation of all advertising slogans and icons of the Canaanite social system that would seduce or challenge:

  But this is how you must deal with them: break down their altars, smash their pillars, hew down their sacred poles, and burn their idols with fire. (Deut 7:5)

- In Deuteronomy 8, the best known of these reflections, Moses is back to the danger of amnesia due to affluence:

  For the LORD your God is bringing you into a good land, a land with flowing streams, with springs and underground waters welling up in valleys and hills, a land of wheat and barley, of vines and fig trees and pomegranates, a land of olive trees and honey, a land where you may eat bread without scarcity, where you will lack nothing, a land whose stones are iron and from whose hills you may mine copper. You shall eat your fill and bless the LORD your God for the good land that he has given you.

Take care that you do not forget the LORD your God, by failing to keep his commandments, his ordinances, and his statutes, which I am commanding you today. When you have eaten your fill and have built fine houses and live in them, and when your herds and flocks have multiplied, and your silver and gold is multiplied, and all that you have is multiplied, then do not exalt yourself, forgetting the LORD your God, who brought you out of the land of Egypt, out of the house of slavery, who led you through the great and terrible wilderness, an arid wasteland with poisonous snakes and scorpions. He made water flow for you from flint rock, and fed you in the wilderness with manna that your ancestors did not know, to humble you and to test you, and in the end to do you good. Do not say to yourself, "My power and the might of my own hand have gotten me this wealth." But remember the LORD your God, for it is he who gives you power to get wealth, so that he may confirm his covenant that he swore to your ancestors, as he is doing today. (Deut 8:7–18)

Amnesia will cause Israelites to sign on to Canaanite perceptions of reality. Israel will forget that its life is a gift of the generous Creator and a miracle accomplished by a powerful redeemer; Israel will imagine it is autonomous and without accountability. And says Moses, "If you imagine that long enough, the covenantal option of neighborliness will disappear and all will become Canaanites":

If you do forget the LORD your God and follow other gods to serve and worship them, I solemnly warn you today that you shall surely perish. Like the nations that the LORD is destroying before you, so shall you perish, because you would not obey the voice of the LORD your God. (Deut 8:19–20)

• Finally, in Deuteronomy 10:12–22, Moses reflects on the God who is full of grace and truth. We have beheld his glory:

For the LORD your God is God of gods and Lord of lords, the great God, mighty and awesome. (Deut 10:17a)

But that glory is evidenced in graciousness:

> who is not partial and takes no bribe, who executes justice for the
> orphan and the widow, and who loves the strangers, providing
> them food and clothing. (Deut 10:17b–18)

With a recall to the exodus and the wonder of liberation from the
Pharaonic system of brick quotas, Israel as alternative community is
empowered to neighborly compassion:

> You shall also love the stranger, for you were strangers in the land of
> Egypt. You shall fear the LORD your God; him alone you shall wor-
> ship; to him you shall hold fast, and by his name you shall swear.
> (Deut 10:19–20)

The urging of Moses is that the radical neighborliness exhibited by YHWH
in the exodus as an alternative to Pharaoh should become the organizing
principle of Israel's life in the new land. The alternative of YHWH to
Pharaoh is to organize a society resistant to Canaanite seduction, and the
pivot point of it all is neighborliness, for neither Pharaoh in Egypt nor the
Canaanites has a clue about the neighbor. "Canaanites" characteristically
viewed the other as commodity, as threat, as rival, as competitor. It is only
YHWH, the God of neighborliness, who breaks the cycle of commodity
pressure for the sake of the neighborhood. Eventually we will see that sabbath is a decisive gesture in the breaking of that cycle. The seduction of
the land is that Israelites would join the "Canaanite" enterprise, that is,
the pursuit of commodity, the commitment to productivity, and the consequent inevitable erosion of the neighborly commitments of Sinai.

But Moses at the Jordan River not only issues a warning. He also, in
quite concrete ways, envisions that the "land of Canaan," the society given
over to commodity and productivity and anti-neighborly ways, can be
transformed. That is, market relations can be radically transposed into
neighborly relations by a different set of neighborly practices. Indeed the
"legal corpus" of Deuteronomy—half commandment and half sermonic
appeal—is committed to alternative social relationships. In quite concrete
ways, Israel is a "counter-society" that is in contrast to the remembered
political economy of Pharaoh and the experienced political economy of
Canaanite city-states:

- Moses proposed the dismantling of the economic arrangement of
  slavery by permitting village protection for runaway slaves:

Slaves who have escaped to you from their owners shall not be given back to them. They shall reside with you, in your midst, in any place they choose in any one of your towns, wherever they please; you shall not oppress them. (Deut 23:15–16)

- Moses seeks to protect the covenantal economy by prohibiting usury within the neighborly community, a practice much sanctioned belatedly in the Calvinist tradition:

  You shall not charge interest on loans to another Israelite, interest on money, interest on provisions, interest on anything that is lent. On loans to a foreigner you may charge interest, but on loans to another Israelite you may not charge interest, so that the LORD your God may bless you in all your undertakings in the land that you are about to enter and possess. (Deut 23:19–20)

- Moses prohibits taking as loan insurance the "means of production" from a worker that would deny the capacity to earn a living:

  No one shall take a mill or an upper millstone in pledge, for that would be taking a life in pledge. (Deut 24:6)

- Moses prohibits forcing anyone into economic bondage and reduction to slavery:

  If someone is caught kidnaping [*sic*] another Israelite, enslaving or selling the Israelite, then that kidnaper [*sic*] shall die. So you shall purge the evil from your midst. (Deut 24:7)

- Moses prohibits excessive collateral for a loan from a poor person, urging instead a regularly repeated neighborly gesture:

  When you make your neighbor a loan of any kind, you shall not go into the house to take the pledge. You shall wait outside, while the person to whom you are making the loan brings the pledge out to you. If the person is poor, you shall not sleep in the garment given you as the pledge. You shall give the pledge back by sunset, so that your neighbor may sleep in the cloak and bless you; and it will be to your credit before the LORD your God. (Deut 24:10–13)

- Moses prohibits the practice of withholding pay from poor laborers, of saying that "the check is in the mail":

  You shall not withhold the wages of poor and needy laborers, whether other Israelites or aliens who reside in your land in one of your towns. You shall pay them their wages daily before sunset, because they are poor and their livelihood depends on them; otherwise they might cry to the LORD against you, and you would incur guilt. (Deut 24:14–15)

- Moses focuses upon the characteristically poor and vulnerable in the community, urging that welfare provisions in an agricultural economy must be provided:

  You shall not deprive a *resident alien* or an *orphan* of justice; you shall not take a *widow's* garment in pledge. Remember that you were a slave in Egypt and the LORD your God redeemed you from there; therefore I command you to do this.

  When you reap your harvest in your field and forget a sheaf in the field, you shall not go back to get it; it shall be left for the *alien*, the *orphan*, and the *widow*, so that the LORD your God may bless you in all your undertakings. When you beat your olive trees, do not strip what is left; it shall be for the *alien*, the *orphan*, and the *widow*.

  When you gather the grapes of your vineyard, do not glean what is left; it shall be for the *alien*, the *orphan*, and the *widow*. Remember that you were a slave in the land of Egypt; therefore I am commanding you to do this. (Deut 24:17–22, emphasis added)

Frank Crüsemann discusses these laws under the rubric "The Social Safety Net: Toward Social Legitimization." He concludes:

  This whole inter-coordinated system of laws for social security springs from a fundamental deuteronomic idea: the freedom that has been experienced, which exodus and land represent and which is manifest in the freedom of the agricultural population, includes freedom from requirements of payment of tribute or compulsory labor (to the state). It is limited only by the double connection to the giver of freedom and to those who do not participate in freedom to the same degree. Guarantees of social security and survival are established for all problem groups and those might be threatened. Furthermore, this relationship is not portrayed as a moral appeal for charity, but as law. Only by passing on this freedom and wealth can the continuance of these gifts be secured.[3]

- Moses provides "cities of refuge" for accidental death, perhaps an easement against capital punishment:

  Now this is the case of a homicide who might flee there and live, that is, someone who has killed another person unintentionally when the two had not been at enmity before: Suppose someone goes into the forest with another to cut wood, and when one of them swings the ax to cut down a tree, the head slips from the handle and strikes the other person who then dies; the killer may flee to one of these cities and live. But if the distance is too great, the avenger of blood in hot anger might pursue and overtake and put the killer to death, although a death sentence was not deserved, since the two had not been at enmity before. Therefore I command you: You shall set apart three cities. (Deut 19:4–7)

- Moses limits corporal punishment in the interest of not humiliating the subject of punishment:

  Suppose two persons have a dispute and enter into litigation, and the judges decide between them, declaring one to be in the right and the other to be in the wrong. If the one in the wrong deserves to be flogged, the judge shall make that person lie down and be beaten in his presence with the number of lashes proportionate to the offense. Forty lashes may be given but not more; if more lashes than these are given, your neighbor will be degraded in your sight. (Deut 25:1–3)

- Moses provides honest trade provisions, so that the poor are not exploited:

  You shall not have in your bag two kinds of weights, large and small. You shall not have in your house two kinds of measures, large and small. You shall have only a full and honest weight; you shall have only a full and honest measure, so that your days may be long in the land that the LORD your God is giving you. For all who do such things, all who act dishonestly, are abhorrent to the LORD your God.   (Deut 25:13–16)

Now, of course, these laws are quite concrete and designed for a simple, face-to-face agricultural community. The sum of them, however, is a vision of a radically alternative society in which neighborly commitments supersede all the requirements of commodity and production and consumption. The news is that "Canaanite" society and its pattern of exploitative relationships can end, can be transformed into covenantal relationships that concern not only interpersonal interactions, but also institutional practices and policy commitments.

These two accent points, I believe, summarize the urgency of Moses at the Jordan River:

1. *The land is seductive* because it is organized in "Canaanite" ways that preclude serious neighborly interaction.

2. *The land is transformable*; that transformation is accomplished by daily concrete attentiveness to neighborly interaction that is not to be defined by the market. That is, Israelites are not to act in "Canaanite" ways, but in ways that derive from the passions of Sinai. Indeed, if Israel were to persist in "Canaanite" ways, to which it is susceptible in its amnesia, it will undo the covenant at Sinai. Eventually it will undo the emancipation from Egypt, and will find itself back in the grip of Pharaonic slavery. For in fact what the tradition of Deuteronomy terms "Canaanite" is in the end a replication of Pharaonic slavery. The consequence is that Israel must always again, in every circumstance, always again leave Egypt and commit to an alternative.

The dynamism of the book of Deuteronomy keeps the vision of an alternative society richly available. The book of Deuteronomy itself understands that the teaching of Moses is not an old, fixed, settled point, but is always a reiteration that is done with imaginative freedom in order to be pertinent to a new form of the issues of acquisitiveness versus neighborliness:

In the book of Deuteronomy itself, of course, the issue of acquisitiveness is set in the thirteenth century, just at the Jordan River, just at the edge of Canaan. The primal memory of the Bible is that Israel represents an alternative to Canaan.

As you may know, critical scholarship treats the book of Deuteronomy as a seventh-century document when Israel faced life in the midst of Assyrian hegemony. In that context, the advocacy of the tradition of Deuteronomy is that Israelites, especially under Josiah, should not give in to Assyrian definitions of reality as the king Ahaz had so readily done in 2 Kings 16.

But current ferment in critical study of the Old Testament may suggest that Deuteronomy is not from the seventh century. Rather it may be a document peculiarly suited to the reforms of Ezra and Nehemiah in the fifth century. Nehemiah's remarkable action in Nehemiah 5 has the fingerprints of Deuteronomy all over it. In that narrative account, rich Jews are taxing poor Jews to death:

> And there were those who said, "We are having to borrow money on our fields and vineyards to pay the king's tax. Now our flesh is the same as that of our kindred; our children are the same as their children; and yet we are forcing our sons and daughters to be slaves, and some of our daughters have been ravished; we are powerless, and our fields and vineyards now belong to others."(Neh 5:4–6)

Nehemiah responds to that exploitative economic transaction with powerful indignation:

> I was very angry when I heard their outcry and these complaints. After thinking it over, I brought charges against the nobles and the officials; I said to them, "You are all taking interest from your own people." And I called a great assembly to deal with them. (Neh 5:6–7)

And then, reformer that he is, Nehemiah proposes restorative action:

> Moreover I and my brothers and my servants are lending them money and grain. Let us stop this taking of interest. Restore to them, this very day, their fields, their vineyards, their olive orchards, and their houses, and the interest on money, grain, wine, and oil that you have been exacting from them. Then they said, "We will restore everything and demand nothing more from them. We will do as you say." And I called the priests, and made them take an oath to do as they had promised. (Neh 5:10–12)

This is a clear example of the way in which covenantal solidarity outflanks the raw power of economic transaction. Nehemiah's actions are in sync with Moses in Deuteronomy, and clearly reflect elemental Sinai commitments.

Thus the teaching of Deuteronomy pertains to the thirteenth century, to the seventh century, to the fifth century . . . or to *any* century. The book of Deuteronomy, moreover, is itself quite self-conscious in seeing that the issue of acquisitiveness practiced in amnesia versus neighborliness practiced in vigorous memory is everywhere a recurring issue. For that reason Deuteronomy is fundamentally a process of dynamic interpretation, always connecting the primal issues to the circumstance of the day. Thus:

- In Deuteronomy 1:5 the narrative reports:

  Beyond the Jordan in the land of Moab, Moses undertook to expound this law as follows: (Deut 1:5)

  The term "expound" is tricky, but clearly Moses did not merely reiterate the Torah of Sinai. Rather he interpreted it, thus making a stark covenantal ethic pertinent to an agricultural economy.
- In Deuteronomy 5:3, Moses acknowledges that the covenant which invites to an alternative society is not a one-time deal, but must always be articulated afresh:

  Not with our ancestors did the LORD make this covenant, but with us, who are all of us here alive today. (Deut 5:3)

  It must be done again in the seventh century, in the fifth century, in the time of Jesus who reinterprets Torah, and now, in this company, for our own time and place.
- That process of reinterpretation, further, is indicated in Deuteronomy 17:18 where it is said, according to the usual rendering,

  When he has taken the throne of his kingdom, he shall have a copy of this law written for him in the presence of the Levitical priests. (emphasis added)

The term "copy," as you may know, is in Greek *deuteros*, from which comes the term "Deuteronomy." But perhaps the term means "second" and thus "second edition" of the Torah, that is, not the Torah at Sinai, but now Torah in an agricultural community with a threat and a challenge to Canaanite acquisitiveness that was hardly on the screen at Sinai. In fact, Deuteronomy is a model for always producing "new versions" of Torah, and indeed, Jesus himself in his formulation, "You have heard it said of old . . . but I say to you," offers a new version of Torah that matters to the present crisis (see Matt 5:21, 27, 31, 33, 38, 43).

These hints of dynamism in Deuteronomy 1:5, 5:3, and 17:18, moreover, are given fuller exhibit in the work of Ezra, the primal scribal teacher of Judaism. In the founding moment of Judaism, it is said that as the assembly listened, the reading Levites,

> helped the people to understand the law, while the people remained in their places. So they read from the book, from the law of God, with interpretation. They gave the sense, so that the people understood the reading. (Neh 8:7–8)

The task of authorizing, empowering, and envisioning a community of neighborly practice as an alternative to acquisitiveness is an unending task in which we ourselves are engaged.

Now I have taken this long in preliminary matters to state three premises:

1. *The land of acquisitiveness is seductive* to those who are victims of amnesia.
2. *The land of acquisitiveness is transformable* into a land of neighborliness.
3. *The interpretive process is a dynamic one* whereby the constant issue of acquisitiveness versus neighborliness, Canaanite versus Israelite, life versus death, is a constant that takes many variable forms. We may see that defining issue given classic articulation in the hard-nosed summary of Moses:

> See, I have set before you today life and prosperity, death and adversity. If you obey the commandments of the LORD your God that I am commanding you today, by loving the LORD your God, walking in his ways, and observing his commandments, decrees, and ordinances, then you shall live and become numerous, and the LORD your God will bless you in the land that you are entering to possess. But if your heart turns away and you do

> not hear, but are led astray to bow down to other gods and serve them, I declare to you today that you shall perish; you shall not live long in the land that you are crossing the Jordan to enter and possess. I call heaven and earth to witness against you today that I have set before you life and death, blessings and curses. Choose life so that you and your descendants may live, loving the LORD your God, obeying him, and holding fast to him; for that means life to you and length of days, so that you may live in the land that the LORD swore to give to your ancestors, to Abraham, to Isaac, and to Jacob. (Deut 30:15–20)

To make the connection for our time and circumstance, all that is required is to see that death and adversity come from not obeying the commands of neighborliness, that is, by succumbing to the social vision of the Canaanites and, before the Canaanites, the social vision of Pharaoh. Alternative life and prosperity come from obedience to Torah commands, that is, to neighborly practice, especially toward widows, orphans, and immigrants.

To this end, Moses at the Jordan River, assuming a heavy dose of amnesia in the community, goes back to basics. He reiterates the Ten Commandments. Here is the introduction to the Decalogue:

> Moses convened all Israel, and said to them:
> Hear, O Israel, the statutes and ordinances that I am addressing to you today; you shall learn them and observe them diligently. The LORD our God made a covenant with us at Horeb. Not with our ancestors did the LORD make this covenant, but with us, who are all of us here alive today. The LORD spoke with you face to face at the mountain, out of the fire. (At that time I was standing between the LORD and you to declare to you the words of the LORD; for you were afraid because of the fire and did not go up the mountain.) (Deut 5:1–5)

In Deuteronomy 5:6–21 we get the full statement of Decalogue from Exodus 20. It is this statement that becomes the basis for all that follows in Deuteronomy concerning both seduction and alternative. As you may know, this recital of the Ten Commandments in this second (*deutero*) version is an exact reiteration from Exodus 20 at Sinai with only slight variation. There are, as at Sinai, the first three commands concerning *love of God* as the holy one who will have no competitor or be made "useful."

There are, as at Sinai, the last six commands on *love of neighbor* and the protection of social relationships that are so easy to distort and exploit. All is the same at the Jordan River for Moses as it was at Sinai . . . with one big exception, the exception that concerns us here.

In Deuteronomy 5:12–15, Moses again places at the center of the Decalogue the sabbath command. Now the lead imperative is not "remember" as at Sinai, but "keep" (*šmr*), a verb of more urgency that is consistent with the intense urgency of Deuteronomy. The command is the same. It concerns work stoppage:

> Observe the sabbath day and keep it holy, as the LORD your God commanded you. Six days you shall labor and do all your work. But the seventh day is a sabbath to the LORD your God. (Deut 5:12–14a)

As at Sinai, the command to work stoppage is comprehensive, including all members of the household of the stockholder, the lead male who is addressed.

But then, in most remarkable variation, Moses departs from a reiteration of the command at Sinai in two regards. First, after having mentioned "your male and female slave" in the inclusive list, he adds,

> so that your male and female slave may rest as well *as you.* (Deut 5:14c, emphasis added)

This may also be rendered, "be like you in rest." *Be like you!* Moses—and Israel with him—is accustomed to social contrasts, class and economic distinctions. They could remember back to Egypt wherein there was massive distinction between Egyptian power people and the slave community soon to become the people of Israel. They could remember that the privileged power people had short work hours, lots of leisure time, plenty of food, opportunity to bathe regularly and get your hair done, but the slaves worked all of the time, without leisure, had sparse food, and no baths. Indeed, they could remember that the Hebrew slave supervisors had accused Moses and Aaron of causing trouble:

> They said to them, "The LORD look upon you and judge! You have brought us into bad odor with Pharaoh and his officials, and have put a sword in their hand to kill us." (Exod 5:21)

They had called attention to slaves by seeking their freedom, and now it was said in the empire, "these people smell bad." They remembered these powerful social distinctions. And behind that they could remember the narrative of father Joseph that the Egyptians ate separate from Joseph and his brothers:

> They served him by himself, and them by themselves, and the Egyptians who ate with him by themselves, because the Egyptians could not eat with the Hebrews, for that is an abomination to the Egyptians. (Gen 43:32)

They could remember all of the ignominious social contrasts and recognized that the Israelites were always on the losing end, discriminated against by the Egyptians and by all those who held the upper hand. They understood that society based on productivity is always unequal:

> *Not all produce the same*, and the ones who produce more are privileged and end up with surplus value.
> *Not all own the same*, but the big producers always end up with the most property.
> *Not all consume the same*, because the ones who produce are treated with immense social entitlement.

And those who produce less and own less and consume less are devalued, devalued in the eyes of dominant society and, consequently, devalued in their own eyes. Those who produce the most and own the most and consume the most tend to be those who do not take sabbath, even though they could. They do not take sabbath because they are on the make . . . greedy, seeking more control, obsessed with more, because once the drive of producing, owning, and consuming becomes definitional, there is never enough yet. What an irony, those most able to keep sabbath do not do so. And then it follows, surely, that the ones on the bottom are not permitted sabbath. As productivity comes to obsess the haves, so the have-nots are defined by work and judged by society as lazy welfare cheats who want time off.

The interlocking relationship between the big-time producers who are mesmerized by production and the lowly workers who invisibly produce creates a social situation in which nobody is permitted sabbath. In such an environment defined by the practice of acquisitiveness, all parties to the social network are caught in a context of coercion that mandates always increasing production quotas, all of which echo the old imperial demand, "Make more bricks":

Then the Israelite supervisors came to Pharaoh and cried, "Why do you treat your servants like this? No straw is given to your servants, yet they say to us, 'Make bricks!' Look how your servants are beaten! You are unjust to your own people." He said, "You are lazy, lazy; that is why you say, 'Let us go and sacrifice to the LORD.' Go now, and work; for no straw shall be given you, but you shall still deliver the same number of bricks." The Israelite supervisors saw that they were in trouble when they were told, "You shall not lessen your daily number of bricks." (Exod 5:15–19)

Coercion becomes the order of the day.

All of that unbearable social reality is on the horizon of Moses at the Jordan. All of that acute social analysis operates for Moses at the Jordan. And then Moses takes a big breath, and asserts—quite unlike the words of Sinai—"Your male and female slave will be like you in their rest."

Sabbath breaks the great cycle of social contrasts and social differentiation. Sabbath rest—work stoppage—requires no expensive equipment as for polo or scuba diving or rappelling. Just stop. Just breathe. Just wait. Just rest. Just receive. Just receive life as a gift. And do so in an amazing equality, because as you look around, all manner of creatures—oxen and donkeys and livestock—and zebras and pandas and oak trees and thistle and kudzu break from the pattern of production. And now says Moses, "All manner of human creatures—landowners and slaves, urban elites and rural peasants, lords and handmaidens, ladies and eunuchs, all are invited to this exodus festival. *All rest. All break the pattern of production.* All declare, visibly and publicly, that life is not defined by meeting quotas."

I could think of two instances of breaking the vicious cycles and you may think of others:

1. In the old slave society of the South, the practice of a hoe-down mattered enormously. We may think of a hoe-down as down-and-dirty dancing and singing at the edge of being out of control. Well, yes, except quite likely "hoe-down" meant to put down the instruments of production (in that case, to chop cotton), which are at the same time insignia of coercion. The point is not to rest in order to chop cotton better. The point rather is to create time and space precisely for the humanness of restfulness outside the appetites of coercion that thin our humanness in fear and in fatigue.

2. A long time ago Elie Wiesel wrote a book entitled *The Jews of Silence*.[4] It concerned the oppressed Jewish community in Russia. That community lived in such fear that no member of it would even talk to Wiesel when

he was in Moscow, and then one night in Moscow, Wiesel was on the street next to the Kremlin. And there were Jews dancing in the street. It was *Simchah Torah*, the festival of the Joy of the Torah. He asked a young woman who was dancing why this exhibit of Jewish visibility in a matrix of such fear. She answered, "All year I am frightened as a Jew. Once a year, on this day, I will not be afraid. I will be a Jew and I will dance." She might have said, "I will dance like Miriam and the other women because I no longer submit to Pharaoh in Moscow."

Sabbath is the festival of egalitarianism that defies the coercion of dominant society. The first variation in the sabbath command in Deuteronomy from Sinai is the egalitarian "like you." The second variation is the motivation for the sabbath that has no parallel in the Sinai version:

> Remember that you were a slave in the land of Egypt, and the LORD your God brought you out from there with a mighty hand and an outstretched arm; therefore the LORD your God commanded you to keep the sabbath day. (Deut 5:15)

It's all exodus! Because exodus is the ultimate, defining, paradigmatic work stoppage in the memory and hope of Israel. YHWH permitted work stoppage in that most demanding of empires by making clear that the workforce belongs to YHWH and not to Pharaoh. In their book *Roll Jordan Roll* Genovese considered why slaves in the old South could get through the day without devouring insanity or hateful violence.[5] The answer suggested by their work is that every morning and night, before and after chopping cotton, the black preacher and the black mammy declared with authority, "Remember, you do not belong to whitey." So Moses in Egypt, so YHWH in every coercive setting in the world:

> You do not belong to whitey;
> You do not belong to Pharaoh;
> You do not belong to Canaanite city kings;
> You do not belong to the production system.

The exodus, perhaps you noticed, permeates Deuteronomy:

> Take care that you do not forget the LORD, *who brought you out of the land of Egypt, out of the house of slavery*. The LORD your God you shall fear; him you shall serve, and by his name alone you shall swear. Do not follow other gods, any of the gods of the peoples who are all around you. (Deut 6:12–14, emphasis added)

. . . .

It was because the L ord loved you and kept the oath that he swore to your ancestors, that the L ord has *brought you out with a mighty hand, and redeemed you from the house of slavery,* from the hand of Pharaoh king of Egypt. Know therefore that the L ord your God is God, the faithful God who maintains covenant loyalty with those who love him and keep his commandments, to a thousand generations. (Deut 7:8–9, emphasis added)

. . . .

When you have eaten your fill and have built fine houses and live in them, and when your herds and flocks have multiplied, and your silver and gold is multiplied, and all that you have is multiplied, then do not exalt yourself, forgetting the L ord your God, *who brought you out of the land of Egypt, out of the house of slavery,* who led you through the great and terrible wilderness, an arid wasteland with poisonous snakes and scorpions. He made water flow for you from flint rock, and fed you in the wilderness with manna that your ancestors did not know, to humble you and to test you, and in the end to do you good. (Deut 8:12–16, emphasis added)

. . . .

You shall also love the stranger, for *you were strangers in the land of Egypt.* (Deut 10:19, emphasis added)

Everywhere exodus! Everywhere work stoppage! Everywhere end of production schedules! Everywhere end of coercion! Everywhere rest for you and peasants and slaves and beavers and carrots and the sun and moon and stars. Everywhere exodus because the exodus God is yet saturating the world with emancipation from every coercion. And we who proclaim the good news must see if the news of emancipation from coercion is the deep truth of our own lives.

> *End of Pharaoh's economic requirements* because Pharaoh finally said to Moses:
>
> > Then he summoned Moses and Aaron in the night, and said, "Rise up, go away from my people, both you and the Israelites!

Go, worship the LORD, as you said. Take your flocks and your herds, as you said, and be gone. And bring a blessing on me too!" (Exod 12:31–32)

End of Canaanite exploitation, as Joshua rallied around the world trade center in Jericho with its secrets and its levers of manipulation and the walls came tumbling down by peasant resistance:

So the people shouted, and the trumpets were blown. As soon as the people heard the sound of the trumpets, they raised a great shout, and the wall fell down flat; so the people charged straight ahead into the city and captured it. (Josh 6:20)

End of punctilious moral requirements in a graciousness that invites companionship:

As he was setting out on a journey, a man ran up and knelt before him, and asked him, "Good Teacher, what must I do to inherit eternal life?" Jesus said to him, "Why do you call me good? No one is good but God alone. You know the commandments: 'You shall not murder; You shall not commit adultery; You shall not steal; You shall not bear false witness; You shall not defraud; Honor your father and mother.'" He said to him, "Teacher, I have kept all these since my youth." Jesus, looking at him, loved him and said, "You lack one thing; go, sell what you own, and give the money to the poor, and you will have treasure in heaven; then come, follow me." (Mark 10:17–21)

End of excessive church expectations because it is the creation and maintenance of a zone of noncoerced well-being that is at the heart of ministry. This is what the disciples found as they traveled with Jesus, and it is whatever every coerced producer in our congregation most wants.

End of coercive capitalist exploitation of having to get the job with the most money because we got into the best college because we had the best SAT scores because we went to the prep school because we started at the best lower grade school because we filled our dossier with soccer and summer camp and dance lessons and church and all manner of busyness.

End of commitment to acquisitiveness that wants only commodity that dehumanizes neighbor and dehumanizes self into fatigue and resentment. Imagine, an empire—a society, a church, a family, a self—committed to productivity and shutting it all down, thereby making production penultimate and the restful act of receptivity ultimate and defining among all the creatures.

This alternative offer of *restfulness*, alternative to coerciveness, does remarkable things for folk:

- It makes *art* possible, poetry, music, narratives.
- It makes *neighbor* visible, neighbor in need, neighbor in joy, neighbor in solidarity.
- It makes the *self* coherent, not divided in frantic, productive ways.
- It recognizes *God*, lover of our ourselves, central to the human project, not pushed aside in idolatrous pursuit of control.
- It enables us *not to worship other gods* and to violate the first three commandments.
- It makes it possible to *love neighbor* and not to covet neighbor's self.

So I propose that we take time enough to ponder our several coercions that cause clergy to violate sabbath. I presume that clergy violation of sabbath is not usually a part of the usual pursuit of commodity; our coercions are more hidden and perhaps more noble:

Perhaps it is the coercion of being good enough for the first child or the only child, the ones who flock to ministry. These are folk raised in homes with demanding expectations of both high performance and good moral standards. It is hard to be good enough, and that requires effort 24/7.

Perhaps it is, as in my case, the coercion of overcoming a low-level background of education, of demonstrating competence, a demonstration in good performance of sermons or journal articles or whatever, a demonstration that requires effort 24/7.

Perhaps it is a need to be loved and to merit approval, and since there is no unconditional grace given among us, certainly not in the church, the need to be loved and approved requires effort 24/7.

Perhaps it is the conviction that God has no hands but our hands, and one more effort "in the vineyard" will bring the kingdom close. And since on most days the kingdom does not seem to be coming any closer, the effort to do God's will requires effort 24/7.

Let us admit: Pharaoh takes many forms. Pharaoh as a hovering parent long since dead but hovering. Pharaoh as colleagues more competent than us who set the bar very high and who, by their very existence, summon us to greater excellence than we have yet reached. Pharaoh as approval giver who does not give it easily—and always reluctantly and grudgingly, so that we ourselves up the quota to satisfy performance. The church as Pharaoh who will never say, "Well done, enter into my rest." Rather it keeps available an endless list of duties, and we cast as the duty officer of every day.

We clergy who do 24/7 or who work less than that but refuse self-care or who take a day off but fill it with "programmed leisure"—we clergy who stay restless and unrested, we participate in the very society of productivity and acquisitiveness that the gospel aims to critique. We imagine that our initiative taking is what makes us effective pastors, and of course it is. But we model poorly the alternative of a God who does not coerce, for our busyness and our weariness and our many accomplishments can as well testify to idols made by our hands that have no power to save.

So imagine sabbath. Imagine sabbath as the breaking of the cycle of coercion. Imagine sabbath as the great day of equality when all of God's creatures sit quietly and wait and receive gifts of healing and nourishment and well-being. It is promised to us that this God of grace constitutes a summons to a different time management at the center of which stands restfulness. The great gods of coercion have been defeated! And we with Miriam stand at the edge of the waters of chaos and watch the agents of coercion tread water for a while and then bubble down into impotence with a loss of authority that need no longer be obeyed. Imagine how it felt to those women: no more brick quotas, no more gathering of straw, no quotas to meet, just to wait and to watch and to dance, knowing that the power of healing and saving and liberating goes on in our restfulness. The work of the creator-redeemer God gets done, even though that God of sabbath is like you at rest, unhurried and unharried.

Imagine the church as a sabbath-keeping community that is a drastic contrast to the world of productivity. Imagine that the peasants are waiting and watching for the seventh day, and we model it. Imagine that the big-time players who are coerced by their own success also wonder if there is an alternative, and imagine that clergy as leaders are to embody and model the reality of restfulness that is rooted in God's self-giving love, this God who is a lively, life-giving alternative to every Pharaoh.

We can see in ancient Israel that they were, as alternative to Pharaoh, so drawn to sabbath that they organized society according to what Patrick Miller terms "the sabbatic principle," an alternative to coercive acquisitiveness.[6]

Moses, in the book of Deuteronomy, articulated the commandment for the year of release, a provision that the poor could not be held in hostage to the acquisitive society. In an early version of the bankruptcy law, it is proposed that poor people will have their debts canceled at the end of seven years. There is no doubt that the fix on the seventh year is an extrapolation from the sabbath. More than that, the poor will not only have their debts canceled, but they will be given the economic wherewithal to reenter the economy with viability. In the words of Moses in Deuteronomy 15:1–18, we can tell that there was resistance to the requirement of the year of release because it could be immediately recognized that forgiveness of debts will disturb the grip of productivity. To that objection, Moses makes a characteristic plea:

> Remember that you were a slave in the land of Egypt, and the LORD your God redeemed you; for this reason I lay this command upon you today. (Deut 15:15)

It's all about exodus! Israel will be sabbatically generous toward poor neighbors if they remember their own emancipation from coercion, if they remember they came from nowhere, and all that they have is a gift. If, however, exodus emancipation is forgotten and we imagine autonomy and self-sufficiency, then the poor person is no longer a neighbor but a competitor who is entitled to nothing. Everything depends upon remembering our own liberation to new life without brick quotas.

And, of course, after that rendition of sabbath as generosity to the poor neighbor, Moses dreams bigger and teaches Jubilee, the readiness to give back what belongs to others after forty-nine years, the breaking of the pattern of greed (Lev 25). In that command, Moses even precludes a charge of interest (v. 37), and then concludes:

> I am the LORD your God, who brought you out of the land of Egypt,
> to give you the land of Canaan, to be your God. (Lev 25:38)

Moses ponders the economically dependent and then asserts that even they belong to YHWH and not to Pharaoh:

> For they are my servants, whom I brought out of the land of Egypt;
> they shall not be sold as slaves are sold. (Lev 25:42)

And the chapter finally concludes with yet one more exodus flourish:

For to me the people of Israel are servants; they are my servants whom I brought out from the land of Egypt: I am the LORD your God. (Lev 25:55)

In this threefold circle of emancipation—sabbath—year of release—Jubilee year—the cycle is broken! No one need any longer serve Pharaoh or Pharaonic demand. You can run the narrative of coercion sociologically and economically. Or you can line it out psychologically and emotionally. Or you could tell it ecclesiologically and in terms of our vocation. It is all the same. The power of death has been defeated! The power of life has created new life space! It is no wonder that the regime of Pharaoh shrivels and life dances. Life does not dance at achievement or accomplishment or possession. Life dances at gift. And that dance is the truth of our evangelical existence!

I conclude by carrying my exposition briefly toward the New Testament by reference to four texts in which *forgiveness* turns out to be the outcome of a life lived in restfulness:
1. In Luke 4:16–30, Jesus shows up at the synagogue in Nazareth. As you know, he reads from Isaiah 61:

> "The Spirit of the Lord is upon me,
>   because he has anointed me
>   to bring good news to the poor.
> He has sent me to proclaim release to the captives
>   and recovery of sight to the blind,
>   to let the oppressed go free,
> to proclaim the year of the Lord's favor."
> (Luke 4:18–19)

That text is a clear attestation to the Jubilee of the Old Testament. The "Year of the Lord's favor" is reference to Jubilee and looks back to Leviticus 25. Thus the text announces that the Spirit of God is on the loose with an extreme form of the sabbath principle to liberate people from all kinds of debts, to forgive all kinds of liabilities. Of course, reading from that scripture in the synagogue is unexceptional, until Jesus adds:

> "Today this scripture has been fulfilled in your hearing." (Luke 4:21)

That is, the person of Jesus is now the embodiment of Jubilee, of sabbath writ large. Jesus in Luke subverts the entire system of coercion upon which society operates. It is the sabbath rest of which Mary sings in anticipation of Jesus:

> "He has brought down the powerful from their thrones,
> and lifted up the lowly;
> he has filled the hungry with good things,
> and sent the rich away empty.
> He has helped his servant Israel,
> in remembrance of his mercy,
> according to the promise he made to our ancestors,
> to Abraham and to his descendants forever."
>
> (Luke 1:52–55)

It is no wonder that the crowd in the synagogue surged against him to drive him out of town. All the Pharaohs, ancient and contemporary, have recognized the sabbath (and Jubilee) as profoundly subversive and cannot tolerate such deconstructive action. So it is in terms of public reality and so in personal reality as well. The oppressive society and the coerced person cannot entertain the year or the day of the Lord's favor.

2. As you know, the petition for God's forgiveness in The Lord's Prayer understands that ready human forgiveness is the measure of divine forgiveness (Matt 6:12; Luke 11:4). It is the case, as Patrick Miller has shown, that forgiveness is rooted in economic transactions, and the forgiveness of debts is deeply rooted in the year of release and in the Jubilee Year, that is, in sabbath writ large.[7] Thus, as we pray for forgiveness, we in fact petition that God will break the vicious cycle of coercion that keeps us all in hock, that we may come to the seventh day free of debt and ready for restfulness. There is no doubt that much of our violation of sabbath rest is an endless attempt to come to terms with coercions in our lives, some of which are quite ancient and some of which are self-imposed, but all of which are powerful. That is why we must petition to have the cycle of restless indebtedness broken by the Lord of the sabbath.

3. In the eloquent ethical instruction of Paul in Romans 12, Paul anticipates that gospel people are those who have had the vicious cycles of anxiety and coercion broken and who are now in position to be free people. I cite only one antithesis in that admonition. The positive urging is to "extend hospitality to strangers" (v. 13). The negative that is precluded is vengeance:

> Beloved, never avenge yourselves, but leave room for the wrath of God; for it is written, "Vengeance is mine, I will repay, says the Lord."

No, "if your enemies are hungry, feed them; if they are thirsty, give them something to drink; for by doing this you will heap burning coals on their heads." Do not be overcome by evil, but overcome evil with good. (Rom 12:19–21)

The juxtaposition of "hospitality" and "vengeance" is a telling summary of what I have been saying. Vengeance is a practice that perceives others as threat or competitor or rival; the opposite is hospitality that sees the other as guest. On the one hand, it is clear that we live in an inordinately vengeful society, and the Christian community is called to counter that propensity with hospitality. On the other hand, if we ask what makes hospitality a possible practice, I submit that hospitality is possible for those who trust their creatureliness and who are not under compulsion, that is, those who practice sabbath. I have no doubt that sabbath rest can indeed break the cycle of vengefulness, precisely because it breaks the pattern of drivenness that eventuates in violence against the neighbor.

4. In Matthew 18:21–22, in the midst of teaching on church discipline, Peter asks Jesus about the number of times forgiveness should be practiced. Peter proposes the number seven, a good holy number that echoes the sabbath. Jesus' answer, however, is seventy times seven, a clear reference back to the curse of Lamech (Gen 4:23–24). And of course "seventy times seven" is not an exact number but means without limit, no curb on the capacity to forgive, no limit on the ability to break the vicious cycle of violence and indebtedness. This is sabbath writ large. The teaching of Jesus summons a church totally situated in the practice of forgiveness:

> Put away from you all bitterness and wrath and anger and wrangling and slander, together with all malice, and be kind to one another, tenderhearted, forgiving one another, as God in Christ has forgiven you. Therefore be imitators of God, as beloved children, and live in love, as Christ loved us and gave himself up for us, a fragrant offering and sacrifice to God. (Eph 4:31–5:2)

The church is a counter-movement in a society that is characteristically violent and unforgiving. I have no doubt that sabbath is the wedge that makes counter-community of this sort viable at all, disengagement from the brutality of acquisitiveness that seeks not to take but to give as the creator God has given life. If the church is to be such an alternative, then its leadership must model that alternative life, not in conspicuous performance, but in lives genuinely at rest. This alternative is choosable. Our mothers and fathers had to choose to leave Pharaoh's Egypt. The invitation to follow is always a choice, to follow the Lord of the sabbath. It is news and practice and possibility for which the world desperately waits. Imagine all of us, men and women, boys and girls, oxen and donkeys and radishes and porcupines and sun and moon and stars . . . all at rest, all forgiven, all at sabbath . . . just like us!

Chapter Ten

Bread

The Good Stuff on the Table

I wish to consider what it means to be involved in the complex web of activities that we may call biblical scholarship, or academic research, or ministry of proclamation, or the reflective Christian life. These matters are not easily separated, yet their mingling together is not well understood either. This reflection begins with two good pieces of advice from a friend to a preacher:

- Consider what ought to be on the table.
- Consider to whom we are accountable.

When I look at the table, do you know what I see? There, right in the center of the table, is bread. That is always what is on the table; for that reason I propose that the primal agenda of all of our work and research is bread—of course, bread variously understood and taken in many dimensions.

Bread is the central agenda of our faith and, therefore, of our work:

- Bread has to do with the entire ecosystem of creation, the management of water and soil to the breeding of good seed. So the Psalmist, after marveling at the miracle of ample water in the arid Near East, can exclaim:
  You cause the grass to grow for the cattle,
      and plants for people to use,
  to bring forth food from the earth,
      and wine to gladden the human heart,

oil to make the face shine,
and bread to strengthen the human heart.
(Ps 104:14–15)

- Bread has to do with the most elemental staple of all human diet, in every culture, for every economic class, the concrete guarantee that human life can be sustained, regardless of status or resources, aware that if not shared, human life is placed in jeopardy.
- Bread, the kind we watch being blessed and broken when we are gathered at communion table, is a sign that the most elemental stuff of the earth is infused with Holy Mystery, so our work is to see how the life-giving generosity of heaven is at work in the life-needing appetites of the earth, an issue peculiar for theological types like us.
- Bread, in the rougher language of the street, of course means "money," and by its reference we are introduced into the entire world of the economy, of credit and debt, of mortgages and interest rates, of spending and budgets and tax incentives and market management and the high cost of neighborliness.

Right there on the table, then, are

- *the issues of the life sciences,* and we ponder the ways in which the design for bread among us is not obviously "intelligent";
- *the social science issues* of how the common realities of the human community and the way that community is sustained as goods are shared;
- *the theological issues of holiness* in the very midst of creation; and
- *the economic issues* of personal well-being and advantage, community sustenance, and the issues of greed and finance for the human infrastructure.

These issues are all on the table, where we are given access to hear with some regularity, but nonetheless with the chill of newness, the primal verbs of faith, "to take, to bless, to break, to give again."

Seeing now the bread on the table before us, we must consider to whom are we accountable in the scholarly work of research.

- For *academics,* we are of course accountable to the larger academy that holds expectations for our disciplines. Now, concerning bread,

I imagine that the academy would focus on the organization of the bakery, how it is managed, the flow of wheat to the mill and then delivery to the bakery, better ovens, and issues of distribution, certification of health standards, budget arrangements, and concern for a fair margin of profit. Those pragmatic issues are important, and we engage them fully.

- But we meet because our common work has to do with more than the academy. We are rooted in our several *faith traditions* that go all the way back to the narrative of manna bread. We are aware, because of that rootage, that all bread is wonder bread, all bread is laden with sacramental significance; we live, finally, not in a world of the buying and selling of grain, but in a world where bread is a sign. The bread we bake and sell and consume signifies more than the academy will ever fully discern.

- It is a given that we are accountable to *the guild* and to *the church*, not only the church, but to very particular church traditions such as Calvinism or Anglicanism or whatever; we each therefore have our coded ways of bread, the personal and the communal, the pragmatic and the ideological, the nonnegotiable and that yet to be imagined in the intensity of our particular way of thinking.

- But after we have fully acknowledged guild and faith community, I suggest that our most intense and inescapable accountability is given to us by *the very bread itself.* Our research is answer to *the creator* who gives bread to the eater and seed to the sower, to *the savior* whom we confess inhabits the bread in ways we cannot articulate. And then this: bread is guarantee of life to *the neediest, the least, the last, the most precarious, the ones without leverage or claim or resource.* Our accountability is to them, for our best research remains haunted, after careers and dossiers and tenure and promotions and fellowships and publications. We are, in our research, most like the lepers in the narrative of 2 Kings 7 who find bread in the enemy camp and report the "gospel news" that will counter the famine (v. 9). The finding of bread is always gospel news, most especially to those beset by hunger.

The reason this constituency of lepers and other bread-seekers counts, long after guild and church are credited, is that a peculiar mystery about the bread has been entrusted to us. It is *the Friday mystery* that the bakeries owned by the empire cannot nourish us. It is *the Sunday mystery* that loaves do indeed abound, and we, in our research and in our faith, bear witness to the truth that the world and its bread are under alternative management. It is the beggars and the lepers who surround our work and who stand at the edge of our study, monitoring us, calling our most erudite research and our most esoteric investigations to stay connected to the holy gift and to the deep crisis. This is research that will stand behind our teaching, that will equip a new generation of leaders and provide resources for a world that is beyond all of our old categories. The gift of God and the voices of hunger that haunt us urge us beyond the established certitudes of our guilds and beyond the stabilities of old church truths. They push us, all of us, back to the fundamentals of daily bread that cannot be stored, lest it turns foul and breeds worms. There is urgency in our work because of the truth of the bread that is entrusted to us.

Academics, focused on their research, are not unlike the disciples of Jesus. In the Gospel of Mark, they had just witnessed the two feeding miracles, first of five thousand (Mark 6:30–44) and then four thousand (Mark 8:1–10); but in our reading for the day, the first thing we learn is that the disciples "had forgotten the bread." They were otherwise occupied and forgot that Jesus' community is in the bread business. Jesus warns his disciples: beware the leaven of the Pharisees and of Herod; beware the passions of the learned guilds and the powerful church, because you will get phony bread that will not nourish.

Then Jesus reprimands the disciples with a series of questions that require and receive no answer:

> Do you not perceive or understand?
> Are your hearts hardened?
> Do you have eyes and not see?
> Do you have ears and not hear?
> Do you not remember?

He immediately recognizes that these questions are too difficult for his concrete-operational followers, so he retreats to concrete-operational questions. He reviews the two feeding miracles and asks how much bread was left over. And they, in their eagerness, can answer those sorts of questions: "Twelve . . . Seven!" And then he speaks in weary exasperation to those who know the data but do not get the point. He utters what may be the saddest words in Scripture:

> Do you not yet understand?

Beyond our guilds and our particular communities of faith, Jesus invites the disciples to understand and engage the new governance of the bread that has been blessed, broken, and given . . . in abundance. It is enough for us now to understand two things that go back to our beginning:

- What is on the table for us is *bread*.
- Our accountability is to the haunting hands of hunger and to the one who blesses, breaks, and gives.

If we understand that, all our research will matter differently . . . for the age to come.

Chapter Eleven

Some Theses on the Bible in the Church

It is not always easy to see how the Bible figures in the liberal theological tradition and in the liberal churches. All of us are aware, of course, of how the Bible has become a vehicle or a weapon for ideology, and of how "mainline" liberal folk have often given up on the Bible and have chosen to stake our claims on other grounds.

As a teacher of the Old Testament, I of course take a dim view of simply handing the Bible over to any particular ideology, because the strangeness and the newness of the Bible do not honestly fit with any ideology, either red or blue.[1] I have been thinking about the ways in which the Bible is a critical alternative to the enmeshments in which we find ourselves in the church and in our society. It may well be that in the end I have not escaped these enmeshments, but in any case I offer a series of theses about the Bible in the church, specifically for those of us who assume and affirm more about the Bible than we most often make explicit.

1. *Everybody has a script.* People live their lives by a script that is sometimes explicit but more often implicit. That script may be one of the great metanarratives of Karl Marx or Adam Smith or Carl Jung or Sigmund Freud or Julius Wellhausen. Or it may be an unrecognized tribal mantra like, "My dad always said. . . ." It is the practice of the script that eventually evokes a self, as we get a self put down with some coherence and integrity into a script that yields something like a coherent identity. At the personal level it is the practice of the script that yields a sense of purpose, a notion of calling, a resource for security. And soon or late when one engages in psychotherapy, it most often has to do with the reexamination of the script, revision of the script, or the complete scuttling of the script in the embrace of a new script, a process that we call "conversion."

As the self is organized by script, so communities are formed and sustained by script: community leaders, moreover, know with some skill how to appeal to the script, often by allusion and code word, clear enough that the members of the scripted community can recognize and make response.

2. *We are scripted by a process of nurture, formation, and socialization that may go under the large rubric of liturgy.* Some of that liturgy is intentional work, and much of it is incidental; but all of it, especially for the young and especially for the family, is a modeling out of the way the world "really is." The script is inhaled along with every utterance and every gesture, because the script-bestowing community is engaged in the social construction of a distinct reality.[2] A case in point is the observation of my colleague Mark Douglas, that regular table prayers of thanksgiving are a primal way in which to challenge the market view of the supply and movement of valuable goods.[3]

3. *The dominant scripting of both selves and communities in our society, for both liberals and conservatives, is the script of therapeutic, technological, consumer militarism that permeates every dimension of our common life.* It is important in my judgment that that script be named; it is equally important to recognize that all of us, across the spectrum, are powerfully inducted into it; none of us a priori can claim high moral ground:

> I use the term "therapeutic" to refer to the common assumption that there is a product or a treatment or a process to counteract every ache and pain and discomfort and trouble, so that life may be lived without any inconvenience. If we consider, for example, the high use of drugs and the cosmetics industry, one may say that such an ersatz therapeutic view of the world is an offer of immortality, for there is somewhere an antidote to aging and ground for the maintenance of youth and beauty and living easily. Witness the ads!
>
> I use the term "technological," after Jacques Ellul, to refer to the assumption that everything can be fixed and made right according to human ingenuity; there is no issue too complex or too remote that will not have imposed upon it a solution from the global monopoly that specializes in imposition.
>
> I use in that script "consumerist," because we live in a culture that believes that the whole world and all of its resources are available to us without regard to the neighbor, with the assumption that more is better and with the proviso that "if you want it, you need it." Thus there is now an ad, "It is not something you don't need; it is just that you haven't thought of it."

> The militarism that pervades our society serves to protect and main-
> tain a monopoly that can deliver and guarantee all that is needed
> for therapeutic technological consumerism. That militarism occu-
> pies much of the church, much of the national budget, much of the
> research program of our universities, with a high degree of "excep-
> tionalism" that imagines that the United States is immune to the
> normal workings of the national economy. Witness the exemption
> of U.S. personnel from the aegis of the World Court with eco-
> nomic reprisals for those who do not agree to U.S. exceptionalism.

It is difficult indeed to imagine life in our society outside the reach of this
script that is everywhere reiterated and legitimated among us.

4. *That script*—enacted through advertising, propaganda, and ideology,
especially in the several liturgies of television—*promises to make us safe and
happy.* Thus, the therapeutic, technological, consumer militarism per-
vades our public life and promises us security and immunity from every
threat. And if we shall be safe, then we shall be happy; who could watch
the ads for cars and beers and deodorants and give thought to such matters as the trade deficit or the index of homelessness or the residue of anger
and insanity left by the war or violence to the environment? This script,
with its illusion of safety and happiness, invites life in a bubble that is
absent of critical reflection.

5. *That script has failed.* I understand that this is indeed a mouthful
and is not the conclusion that all would draw. It is, however, a lesson
to be learned by the nations over and over again that military consumerism never makes safe. It was a lesson learned recently in the Soviet
Union. It was a lesson learned by the apartheid regime in South Africa.
It is a lesson learned by every great military power that security offered
is provision and contains within it the seeds of its own destruction. It is
clear to all but the right-wing radio talk people and the sponsoring neo-
conservatives that the reach of the American military in global ambition
has served only to destabilize and to produce new and deep threats to our
society. The charade of a national security state has left us completely
vulnerable to the whim of the very enemies that our security posture
has itself evoked. A byproduct of such attempts at security, moreover,
has served in astonishing ways to evoke acrimony in the body politic
that makes our democratic decision-making processes nearly unwork-
able. Even without reference to the study of the rise and fall of the great
powers by Paul Kennedy,[4] one can reach in more deeply to the wisdom
of Isaiah:

For thus said the Lord GOD, the Holy One of Israel:
In returning and rest you shall be saved;
  in quietness and in trust shall be your strength.
But you refused and said,
"No! We will flee upon horses"—
  therefore you shall flee!
and, "We will ride upon swift steeds"—
  therefore your pursuers shall be swift!
A thousand shall flee at the threat of one,
  at the threat of five you shall flee,
until you are left
  like a flagstaff on the top of a mountain,
  like a signal on a hill.
                                        (Isa 30:15–17)

And when we are frightened enough, we will live under the old curse of
anxiety that is voiced in Leviticus:

> And as for those of you who survive, I will send faintness into their
> hearts in the lands of their enemies; the sound of a driven leaf shall
> put them to flight, and they shall flee as one flees from the sword, and
> they shall fall though no one pursues. They shall stumble over one
> another, as if to escape a sword, though no one pursues; and you shall
> have no power to stand against your enemies. (Lev 26:36–37)

And if not safe, then this script cannot make us happy, for it is clear that
we have among us an irreducible index of unhappiness. Even the right
wing, in control of the government as I write this, can offer a daily recital
of unhappiness, which in fact is a silent acknowledgment that the script is
not really working to the full benefit of its primary beneficiaries. *That
script is guaranteed,* so the evidence would suggest, *to produce new depths of
insecurity and new waves of unhappiness.* And in response to new depths of
insecurity and new waves of unhappiness, we find only a greater resolve
to close the deal according to the script that produces ever new waves and
new depths. Somebody has to say this!

   6. *Health depends, for society and for members of it, on disengagement from and
relinquishment of that script.* This is a truth that is exceedingly difficult to utter,
and even more difficult to imagine acting upon across the sociopolitical
spectrum. All of us, liberals and conservatives, are so inured to the dominant
script that it is all but impossible to entertain the thought that we would dis-

engage or relinquish. We resist the thought of such disengagement and at best are profoundly ambiguous. This script has been an established truth since early days when we all learned to place our hands over our hearts and salute the flag. We did so in innocence, not imagining that the flag would become an icon of aggressive military policy and rapacious economic ambition. And beside that, we are ambiguous because the script does deliver! We are indeed well off, comfortable, and by any standards better off than most of the world can imagine. We are ambiguous because we know better than to trust our privileged status, and yet if we move our heads slightly away from such a recognition, we fall back into the easier conviction that this is our birthright and our entitlement, and we do not want to reconsider.

7. *It is the task of the church and its ministry to de-script from that powerful script* that dominates even though it is mostly unnamed and unchallenged. It is the task of the church to bear witness to the failure of that script and to relinquish the world evoked by that script that no longer exists and that indeed never did exist. Such witness has been the work of the biblical tradition since the initial task of Moses and the subsequent work of the Deuteronomists, the prophets, and the scribes. When inured to the script, departure from it is scarcely imaginable. That, of course, is what Moses had to do in Egypt in the slave camp. He had to make the case that the Pharaonic arrangement of brickyard quotas was not the true destiny of the Israelite community, but that its destiny called it to otherwise. In the text, we can see that such a de-scripting is a risky calling with endless challenges to his leadership and with recurring proposals for a return to that exploitative Egyptian arrangement (Exod 16:3; Num 11:4–6). Later the Jerusalem establishment was caught in its own illusion of security; the prophets repeatedly urged Israel to leave off the illusion of entitlement and to face the reality of covenantal requirements. And of course Jesus delineated a regime change in Mark 1:14–15 in nothing less than a call to de-script from Rome and from what had become an exploitative religious system.

8. The task of de-scripting, relinquishment, and disengagement is undertaken through *the steady, patient, intentional articulation of an alternative script that we testify will indeed make us safe and joyous.* I do not want to be misunderstood. This is not the stark confrontational urging of a young man who champions the "prophetic." For I know almost no Christian congregation—well, a few—where we can assert that the dominant script has failed. No, this is, rather, the sense of an old man—after many years of hard psychotherapy—who has come to understand that the availability of a new script invites, seduces, teases, requires the abandonment of an old script that is deathly.

I bother with this argument because I believe we have become so jaded in the church—most particularly in the liberal church—that we have forgotten what has been entrusted to us. We have forgotten that the script entrusted to us is really an alternative and not an echo. Liberals tend to get so engaged in the issue of the day, urgent and important as those issues are, that we forget that behind such issues is a metanarrative that is not about social passion but about the world being beyond our control. The claim of that alternative script is that there is at work among us a Truth that makes us safe, that makes us free, that makes us joyous in a way that the comfort and ease of the consumer economy cannot even imagine. I say that it is the steady, patient, intentional articulation of this counter-script that is our main chance for disengagement and relinquishment. Of course, it would make an important difference if the church were candid in its acknowledgment that that is the work to which we are called and in which we are engaged. The offer of the alternative script is an invitation to repentance down to the root of the matter.

9. *That alternative script as an offer of a counter-metanarrative—counter to the script of therapeutic technological consumer militarism—is rooted in the Bible and enacted through the tradition of the church.* Liberals must do all that we want about social analysis and social science, and that is all to the good. But too many among us have become embarrassed about that ancient script, too aware of the ideological failures that are present in the script, too ready to hand it over to the waiting arms of the dominant ideology; we have to some great extent given up on the hard work of hearing and speaking the alternative that is in the script. Karl Barth's famous formula about "the strange new world within the Bible" is on target.[5] In that essay, Barth understands well that we cannot find in the Bible many of the things for which we look. But what is there, he understands, is an alternative world; it is an alternative network of symbols and signs that are stitched together that yield a coherence that subverts and keeps us always on edge about the newness that keeps welling up.

10. *That alternative script has as its defining factor the Key Character in all holiness, the God of the Bible who is variously Lord and Savior of Israel, Creator of heaven and earth, and as fleshed in Jesus, we name as Father, Son and Holy Spirit.* The script is about God, about a particular God whose name we know, whose story we tell. The historians of Israelite religion have traced all of the borrowing and appropriations from ancient Near Eastern culture and religion and have in general concluded that for all the borrowings and appropriations, there is something inexplicable and underived, something originary in the God of Israel who blew over waters of disor-

der, to summon Abraham and Sarah abruptly, and who came in a burning bush to give Moses an unbearable assignment.[6]

All of us have been through and still live in the crisis of the Enlightenment; we find God generically to be an embarrassment whom we siphon off into intimate family life because we cannot imagine generically that God might be present in the public domain. We fear to be frontal because we do not want to sound like silly supernaturalists; we hedge and duck and then wonder why on Easter the assertion of the resurrection is without context, and we are, in such an Easter assertion, more awkward than grace-filled. But the script entrusted to us knows all about such awkwardness. Paul, even among his "enlightened" colleagues, refused awkwardness, voiced the script, and emptied prisons. Thus, while we guard against silly supernaturalism, we may from this script join issue with the ideology of the day, for the dominant script of therapeutic technological consumer militarism is not godless or atheistic. Rather, it distorts and offers among us a god who has no power to save.

To try to answer to atheism is an intellectual embarrassment. But as Michael J. Buckley has made clear, our own awkward theological embarrassment has made atheism possible.[7] But no church or minister who challenges the dominant script meets atheism. Rather we meet idolatry; the issue can thus be joined because the argument is more about a powerless god than about godless power. We make the claim from Easter on back about the power of God—of this God—to give life in a world of death.

11. *The script of this God of power and life is not monolithic, one-dimensional, or seamless, and we should not pretend that we have such an easy case to make.* The script is flawed in many ways of which we are now aware concerning violence and discrimination according to race and gender and even class. It is all there in patriarchal bias.

> The script is ragged and disparate, because it is crafted over time by many committees. The ongoing disputatious work of committees such as JEDP, and such sources as the Jesus Seminar constituted by Paul and Mark and Q and Matthew and Luke and even Johannine voices. They all have had a say in the articulation of this disjunctive offer.
>
> But the primary reason that the text is not monolithic, one-dimensional, or seamless is not the flaws of which we are now aware and not the disputed work of the tradition. The point to notice is that the script is not monolithic, seamless, or one-dimensional because the Key Character takes up a great deal of

space. That Key Character is elusive, as Job found, irascible in freedom, and pathos-filled in sovereignty, one who trafficks often in hiddenness and violence. This God does not fit much of our theological preference and certainly does not conform to any of our bourgeois reductionism.

But that is precisely the point. This God is the one who keeps life ragged and open, who refuses domestication but who will not let our lives be domesticated either. Long before the Department of Homeland Security and its color-coded alert levels, this God has kept life at orange alert, precisely because newness will surge that is threatening to all of our arrangements. The church and particularly the lectionary committee have tried to make this God user-friendly. But this God is filled with the kinds of disjunctions that are deeply offensive to the dominant narrative of military consumerism.

I cite only one example. The God of the Bible cannot seem to remember whether God has been through clinical pastoral education or not. In Job 38–41, God seems to have learned nothing about sensitivity, for Job relates in great detail his anguish and pain and bewilderment, and YHWH responds, "Let me tell you about my crocodile." Any supervisor would write on YHWH's verbatim, "You couldn't stand the pain and you changed the subject." On the other hand in Isaiah 41:14, Israel has complained about feeling like a worm. Here YHWH shows acute pastoral sensitivity and says to self-deprecating Israel, "Fear not, worm." YHWH stays with the subject and does not try to talk Israel out of its diminished self-perception. But we never know for sure. We never know, and we imagine a community of faith gathered around this Character in the script, open, at risk, venturesome, and refusing to be mascots for dominant society and for the illusions of a dominant script.

12. *The ragged disjunctive quality of the counter-script to which we testify cannot be smoothed out and made seamless, as both historical-critical study and doctoral reductionism have tried to do.* Every such smoothing out betrays the Key Character. When the script is smoothed out, it becomes flattened, domesticate itd, and uninteresting. More than that, it too easily becomes a neat, weak echo of the dominant script. The way to co-opt the biblical script for any dominant ideology is to flatten and domesticate it so that the Key Character is made into a flat patron of conventional truth. So it is with the script of therapeutic technological consumer militarism. It requires a God who can entitle and guarantee. The script in which we are so much inured is all about certitude, privilege, and entitlement. But the

script entitled to the church and its ministry is not about certitude, privilege, or entitlement. Indeed, I read recently the helpful insight that any religious claim that generates entitlement is sure to be idolatrous. Care must be taken that our testimony to God concerns God as a true, elusive, irascible self even in the face of our privileged entitlements.

13. *The ragged, disputatious character of the counter-script to which we testify is so disputed and polyvalent that its adherents are always tempted to quarrel among themselves.* Polyvalence, the fact that the Bible has God speak in different voices, invites us to choose the part we happen to like. Thus we quibble about whether he said "poor" or "poor in spirit." We solemnly vote about whether we stand in Leviticus wherein holiness has to do with sexual regulation or that we stand in Deuteronomy where holiness has to do with concern for justice for widows, orphans, and immigrants. This God has spoken differently at different times in a dynamic traditioning process; as a consequence there is always something for everyone. Every position we take is readily countered with some other part of the script.

The quarrels we undertake are not only sometimes vicious; they are also convenient because the quarrels detract us from the main claims of the text, and so debilitate the force of the text. Of course it matters what the church decides about sexuality, but in the long run that skirmish or a dozen like it are as nothing before the truth that the therapeutic technological military consumerism cannot deliver or keep its promises. All of us—conservatives who are attentive to what the Bible says about sexuality and indifferent about the Bible on economics, and liberals who mumble about what the Bible says on sex but major in economics—all of us stand under the awareness that the primary commitments of our society amount to a choice of a path of death. The quarrels we undertake must be kept in perspective, because none of those quarrels occupy this Holy Character unduly. What counts is that we were not there at the outset of Creation, and we will not be there at the curfew; our life between the outset and the curfew is the gift of the One who calls us not to assault neighbor but to be on our way in wonder, love, and praise.

14. *The entry point into the counter-script is baptism.* Surely it follows that the church must recover the generativity of baptism. The entry point into the dominant script is perhaps the first lavish baby shower with more accoutrements than any baby ever needed, or the first cell phone, or the registration for the draft, or whatever. But baptism, a bold counter-act, is entry into a stream of promise that is free but not cheap. In the ancient liturgy, still sounded where we are not too sweetly bourgeois, we say, "Do you renounce Satan and all his works?" We do not explicate that phrase,

and we let everyone imagine as they will. No doubt "Satan and all his works" is taken by some to be Muslims and by some to be homosexuals, but we at least leave open the thought that Satan acts subtly and by indirection, perhaps by including us in a dominant narrative that promises us security and happiness that cannot be delivered. And so we ask, by inference, "Do you renounce the dominant script?" The issue cannot be put directly; it is, however, latent in this thick moment of holy vows as we watch the splash of the holy water and hear the uncompromising name of the irascible Maker of promises. Baptism creates an alternative context for praise and preaching and for missional action. No wonder the church has little additional energy when it has not made clear that this is indeed an alternative world assigned by sacrament.

15. *The nurture, formation, and socialization into the counter-script with this elusive, irascible Key Character at its center constitute the work of ministry.* All those called in the Bible are inducted into this task, and it is not different now. I say this because I think I know very many ministers who are filled with despair, who are exhausted from too many tasks, who are riding it out in cynicism, or who work ad hoc without much focus on coherence. Ministry in our society is, at best, acutely difficult and problematic; it is more so to the point of being unbearable where there is no large, comprehensive sense of purpose.

We may specialize in and develop various skills and arts in ministry, each of which is urgently important. Thus we value and require preaching, liturgy, education, social action, counseling, administration, stewardship, evangelism, and all the rest. These, however, are not ends in themselves. They are instruments in nurture, formation, and socialization into an alternative scripting of reality. Nurture is aimed at the embrace of the new script and relinquishment of the old script. Formation is aimed at receiving and living into an alternative reality and disengagement from the old. Socialization is entering into another world that comes by "switching stories."[8] Each practice of ministry is to "improve our baptism" wherein we live with increasing singularity in this alternative script.

16. *Ministry is conducted in the awareness that most of us are deeply ambiguous about this alternative script.* We do not want to choose decisively between the dominant script of therapeutic technological consumer militarism and the counter-script of the elusive, irascible God. Most of us vacillate or mumble in our ambivalence. This ambivalence takes a conservative form of attentiveness to personal and familial stuff with the public sphere left to the ideology of the market. This ambivalence takes a liberal form with a subjective consciousness so that there is an urbane,

ironic filter between what we say and what we mean. The ambivalence touches every church member, liberal and conservative, and engrosses every minister of whatever ilk.

We are characteristically double-minded, standing between two scripts the way Elijah found Israel standing between Baal and YHWH. And we know what happens in our double-mindedness:

> "No one can serve two masters; for a slave will either hate the one and love the other, or be devoted to the one and despise the other. You cannot serve God and wealth." (Matt 6:24)

We are filled with anxiety:

> "Therefore I tell you, do not worry about your life, what you will eat or what you will drink, or about your body, what you will wear. Is not life more than food, and the body more than clothing?" (Matt 6:25)

It is the anxiety about our double-mindedness that becomes the grist of ministry that makes us fearful and strident and adversarial. It is our anxiety that causes us to enlist as red or blue ministers in red or blue churches. It is our anxiety that precludes the ease of sabbath, the dalliance of birds, the leisure time of lilies:

> Look at the birds of the air; they neither sow nor reap nor gather into barns, and yet your heavenly Father feeds them. Are you not of more value than they? (Matt 6:26)

There is, of course, an antidote, even if it is given in patriarchal form:

> For it is the Gentiles who strive for all these things; and indeed your heavenly Father knows that you need all these things. (Matt 6:32)

And we are left, post-anxiety, with only God's realm and God's righteousness.

17. *The good news, I judge, is that our ambivalence as we stand between scripts is precisely the primal venue for the work of God's spirit.* I know God's spirit will work where it will and accomplish its purposes (John 3:8). But humanly speaking, it is our ambivalence where the spirit can most readily stir and make new, and empower to new possibilities. When we cover over and deny our ambivalence, our faith grows hard and we find ourselves committed with ideological passion and without the grace to rethink.

So I propose: One of the great and crucial tasks of ministry is to name and exposit the deep ambiguity that besets us, and to create a venue for waiting for God's newness among us. This work is not to put people in crisis. The work is to name the crisis that people are already in, the very crisis that evokes resistance and hostility when it is surfaced and named.

- God may yet lead us anew where liberals and conservatives can disrupt the shrillness long enough to admit that variously we are frightened by alternative patterns of sexuality. We do not want to kill all gays as the book of Leviticus surely teaches, but we are in fact uneasy about changes that seem so total among us.
- God may yet lead us anew when conservatives and liberals can interrupt our passion for consumer goods and lower taxes long enough to admit that we believe all other neighbors should be cared for, even with taxes. We have a passion for social programs, and we are nonetheless aware of being taxed excessively and it causes us alarm.
- God may yet lead us so that liberals and conservatives can stop the loudness to know that the divestment that costs us nothing is too easy, toward Israel or the Palestinians; the core divestment to which we are first called comes closer to our own entitlements. The spirit has always been, for the church and beyond the church, "a way out of no way."

The church and its pastors await the gift of newness from the spirit. One of the ways in which the church and its pastors do that is that they consistently give voice and visibility to our common ambivalence whereby we are in a place for re-choosing, for re-choosing beyond all of our old, jaded options. The spirit is wind and not wall. It is possibility and not coercion. It is opportunity and not threat. And when we do wall and coercion and threat, we only imitate and replicate the dominant narrative of consumer militarism. Ours, however, is an alternative not only in outcome but also in mode. The wind, so the script says, is about

new creation
new freedom from slavery
being born again

All of that is less likely behind the barricades of certitude that require us to deny so much about ourselves. Ministry is for truth-telling about the shape we are in, all of us together. And that truth-telling makes us free.

18. *Ministry, and mission beyond ministry, is to manage that inescapable ambivalence that is the human predicament in faithful, generative ways*—management not as manipulation toward preferred ends, but management for truth-telling, waiting, and receiving newness. The work is the slow, steady work of ministry among liberals and conservatives so that we, personally and communally, are in the process of renouncing old scripts of death and entering new scripts of life. The hallmark of the church is not certitude; it is openness to the spirit. In the book of Acts, after the apostles preach the gospel of Jesus Christ with all the certitude they could muster, there was still a waiting and a big leap beyond themselves. Moving beyond ourselves is only made possible by the spirit. It is for sure that none of us goes beyond ourselves when we sit close in the dominant script. It is equally for sure that movement beyond ourselves in the church is not possible when the church script only imitates the dominant script. Signs of the kingdom and its newness characteristically happen when we are empowered beyond ourselves. Imagine ministry, close to the God who is beyond all our preferences, sharing in the possibility of newness.

19. *If what I have said is true, then it follows that the work of ministry is crucial, pivotal, and indispensable; as in every society, so in our society.* The cruciality of this ministry is not that the church may prosper. It is that the world may live (and not die) and rejoice (and not cower). The reason this ministry is so crucial is that for the most part there are none except the church in its better days—and the synagogue and the mosque on their better days—to mediate irascible holiness as newness, to evoke consequent ambivalence, to manage that ambivalence toward newness, and then to wait. The dominant script of therapeutic technological consumer militarism does none of that:

- *It does not mediate* irascible holiness or acknowledge it.
- *It does not evoke* or acknowledge consequent ambivalence.
- *It cannot manage* ambivalence toward newness.
- *It does not wait.*

Ministry, with all the cost and joy of discipleship, is urgent among us, as urgent as it is wondrous and difficult and amazing and disconcerting. It is indeed a treasure in earthen vessels.

My purpose is for us to reflect on what has been entrusted to us. Some of you will slot what I have said, after George Lindbeck and Stanley Hauerwas, as a "sectarian hermeneutic." But I have no interest in that per se. Some of you will take my words as a grinding of a liberal axe, but I have no interest in that here. I am a teacher of the Bible, and I think we are in a moment of recovery about the Bible. The Bible has mostly been lost to conservative ideology and liberal indifference. But not now.

Now is the time for our expectations of the church to grow. We must expect of the church

- that it continue to tell the truth about the great issues of the day,
- that it continue the wonderful gossip about the little network that we are, and
- that it continue to pull us toward strange voices that are beyond our own.

We need to expect this of the church, and all the more of ourselves. This is not just so that we can continue to entertain each other with these voices of truth and gossip, but because there is a latent audience beyond the conventional church of a quite different, quite new positioning about American exceptionalism, about democratic capitalism, about globalization and all the rest. And the question now haunts, across the spectrum, about how to submit these great worldly realities to the holy God. And so, I ask you, ponder with me what we are doing when the leader says,

The word of the Lord.

And we answer mostly out of habit,

Thanks be to God.

Thanks be to God indeed!

Notes

Chapter 2—Weeping and Hoping in Jerusalem

1. Meg Greenfield, *Washington* (New York: Public Affairs, 2001).
2. On the ordering of political and economic power in the Canaanite city-states, see Norman K. Gottwald, "Early Israel and the Canaanite Socio-economic System," in *Palestine in Transition: The Emergence of Ancient Israel*, ed. David Noel Freedman and David Frank Graf (Sheffield: Almond Press, 1983) 25–37. In more recent scholarship, the idea of "urban elites" has become something of a slogan that contrasts "high theology" and "folk religion." See the polemical use of the label by William G. Dever, *Did God Have a Wife? Archaeology and Folk Religion in Ancient Israel* (Grand Rapids: Eerdmans, 2005). In a more reasoned way, Rainer Albertz, *A History of Israelite Religion in the Old Testament Period*, vol. 2, *From the Exile to the Maccabees* (Louisville, KY: Westminster John Knox Press, 1994) 497, can refer to "the upper class."
3. James C. Scott, *Domination and the Arts of Resistance: Hidden Transcripts* (New Haven, CT: Yale University Press, 1990), and *Weapons of the Weak: Everyday Forms of Peasant Resistance* (New Haven, CT: Yale University Press, 1985). The rhetoric of Josh 1 in this regard is telling, for it is an advocacy for the Torah, but the rhetoric makes the Torah sounds like military power. Thus, the Torah is offered as a "weapon" for the Israelites who in the narrative are "weak."
4. See Walter Brueggemann, *Solomon: Israel's Ironic Icon of Human Achievement* (Columbia: University of South Carolina Press, 2005).
5. Ibid., 87–103.
6. On the theological agenda of these psalms, see Ben C. Ollenburger, *Zion the City of the Great King: A Theological Symbol of the Jerusalem Cult* (JSOTSup 41; Sheffield: Sheffield Academic Press, 1987).

Chapter 4—A Welcome for the Others

1. On the theological force and contemporary power of the book of Lamentations, see Kathleen M. O'Connor, *Lamentations and the Tears of the World* (Maryknoll, NY: Orbis Books, 2002).

2. For a relentless polemic against "urban elites," ancient and contemporary, see William G. Dever, *Did God Have a Wife? Archaeology and Folk Religion in Ancient Israel* (Grand Rapids: Eerdmans, 2005).

3. On Isaiah 56–66, see Elizabeth Achtemeier, *The Community and Message of Isaiah 56–66* (Minneapolis: Augsburg Publishing House, 1982); Paul D. Hanson, *The Dawn of Apocalyptic: The Historical and Sociological Roots of Jewish Apocalyptic Eschatology* (Philadelphia: Fortress Press, 1975); and Otto Ploeger, *Theocracy and Eschatology* (Richmond, VA: John Knox Press, 1968).

4. See Daniel Smith-Christopher, *A Biblical Theology of Exile* (OBT; Minneapolis: Fortress Press, 2002).

5. There were apparently several waves of return as reflected variously in Haggai and Zechariah, Third Isaiah, and Ezra and Nehemiah. It is not easy to reconstruct the history of these several movements, but there can be no doubt of successive movements of return to Jerusalem.

6. On the ethnic self-awareness of the community of restoration, see Theodore E. Mullen, *Narrative History and Ethnic Boundaries: The Deuteronomistic Historian and the Creation of Israelite National Identity* (Atlanta: Scholars Press, 1993), and *Ethnic Myths and Pentateuchal Foundations: A New Approach to the Formation of the Pentateuch* (Atlanta: Scholars Press, 1997).

7. See Frederick Gaiser, "A New Word on Homosexuality? Isaiah 56:1–8 as Case Study," *Word & World 14* (Summer 1994) 280–93.

8. See Jeffries M. Hamilton, *Social Justice and Deuteronomy: The Case of Deuteronomy 15* (SBL Dissertation Series 136; Atlanta: Scholars Press, 1992).

9. See the recent discussions of Harold V. Bennett, *Injustice Made Legal: Deuteronomic Law and the Plight of Widows, Strangers, and Orphans in Ancient Israel* (Grand Rapids: Eerdmans, 2002), and Enrique Nardoni, *Rise Up, O Judge: A Study of Justice in the Biblical World* (Peabody, MA: Hendrickson Publishers, 2004).

10. Karl Barth, *Prayer*, 50th anniversary ed. (Louisville, KY: Westminster John Knox Press, 2002) 78, and the citation to *Church Dogmatics III/3*.

11. See George Stroup, *Before God* (Grand Rapids: Eerdmans, 2004).

12. On the "new catholicity," see Justo L. Gonzalez, *The Changing Shape of Church History* (St. Louis: Chalice Press, 2002) chap. 5.

Chapter 5—The Fearful Thirst for Dialogue

1. George Steiner, *Real Presences* (Chicago: University of Chicago Press, 1989) 225.

2. See Walter Brueggemann, "Voice as Counter to Violence," *Calvin Theological Journal 36*, no. 1 (April 2001) 22–33.

3. On God's role in the daring dialogue of the book of Job, see Samuel E. Balentine, "'What Are Human Beings, That You Make So Much of Them?' Divine Disclosure from the Whirlwind: 'Look at Behemoth,'" *God in the Fray: A Tribute to Walter Brueggemann*, ed. Tod Linafelt and Timothy K. Beal (Minneapolis: Fortress Press, 1998) 259–78.

4. See Susan A. Handelman, *The Slayers of Moses: The Emergence of Rabbinic Interpretation in Modern Literary Theory* (Albany: SUNY Press, 1982), and John Joseph Cuddihy, *Ordeal of Civility: Freud, Levi-Straus, and the Jewish Struggle with Modernity* (New York: Basic Books, 1974).

5. This is a reiteration of the same term from v. 21.

6. On the many voices of the self, see Roy Schafer, *Retelling a Life: Narration and Dialogue in Psychoanalysis* (New York: Basic Books, 1992), especially chap. 2. It is clear that the recovery of "many voices" in current psychoanalytic theory and practice replicates what the Psalter knows and reflects.
7. The "then" is clear in NRSV translation; the point is not so clear or dramatic in the Hebrew. I take the translation, however, to rightly reflect the force and intent of the rhetoric.
8. Claus Westermann, *The Praise of God in the Psalms* (Richmond, VA: John Knox Press, 1965) 25–30, has given classic formulation to the judgment that praise is a more faithful and noble act toward God than is thanks, and that thanks is a lesser and potentially more self-interested act. See the counter opinion of Harvey H. Guthrie Jr., *Theology as Thanksgiving: From Israel's Psalms to the Church's Eucharist* (New York: Seabury Press, 1981).
9. Fredrik Lindstrom, *Suffering and Sin: Interpretations of Illness in the Individual Complaint Psalms* (Coniectanea Biblica Old Testament Series 37; Stockholm: Almqvist & Wiksell International, 1994).
10. Ellen Davis, "Exploding the Limits: Form and Function in Psalm 22," *JSOT* 53 (March 1992) 93–105.

Chapter 6—Can We Hope? Can Hope Be Divided?

1. Karl Barth, "The Strange New World within the Bible," in *The Word of God and the Word of Man* (New York: Harper & Brothers, 1957) 28–50.
2. Gerhard von Rad, *Studies in Deuteronomy* (SBT 9; Chicago: Henry Regnery Company, 1953).
3. See Jacques Ellul, *The Technological Society* (New York: Knopf, 1964).
4. Karl Barth, *Church Dogmatics: The Doctrine of Creation III/2* (Edinburgh: T & T Clark, 1961) 597–98.
5. Ibid., 608, 609, 611.
6. Ibid., 613, 615.
7. Ibid., 615.
8. Ibid., 613.
9. Martin Buber, *Moses: The Revelation and the Covenant* (Atlantic Highlands, NJ: Humanities Press International, 1988), 52.
10. Samuel Terrien, *The Elusive Presence: Toward a New Biblical Theology* (New York: Harper & Row, 1978), 119.
11. James C. Scott, *Weapons of the Weak: Everyday Forms of Peasant Resistance* (New Haven, CT: Yale University Press, 1985), and *Domination and the Arts of Resistance: Hidden Transcripts* (New Haven, CT: Yale University Press, 1990).
12. Albrecht Alt, *Essays in Old Testament History and Religion* (Oxford: Blackwell, 1966) 1–77; Gerhard von Rad, *The Problem of the Hexateuch and Other Essays* (New York: McGraw-Hill, 1966) 1–78; and Jürgen Moltmann, *Theology of Hope: On the Ground and the Implications of a Christian Eschatology* (New York: Harper & Row, 1967).
13. See John J. Collins, *The Apocalyptic Imagination: An Introduction to the Jewish Matrix of Christianity* (New York: Crossroad, 1987).
14. See Brevard S. Childs, *Struggle to Understand Isaiah as Christian Scripture: A Hermeneutical Study* (Grand Rapids: Eerdmans, 2004).

15. R. W. L. Moberly, *The Old Testament of the Old Testament: Patriarchal Narratives and Mosaic Yahwism* (OBT; Minneapolis: Fortress Press, 1992).

16. See the critical discussion of R. Kendall Soulen, *The God of Israel and Christian Theology* (Minneapolis: Fortress Press, 1996).

17. David Novak, *Jewish-Christian Dialogue: A Jewish Justification* (Oxford: Oxford University Press, 1989) 156.

18. Tim LaHaye and Jerry B. Jenkins, *Left Behind: Ilumia Edition* (Wheaton, IL: Tyndale House Publishers, 2002).

19. Alan E. Lewis, *Between Cross and Resurrection: A Theology of Holy Saturday* (Grand Rapids: Eerdmans, 2000); see Walter Brueggemann, "Reading from the Day 'In Between,'" in *A Shadow of Glory: Reading the New Testament after the Holocaust*, ed. Tod Linafelt (London: Routledge, 2002) 105–16.

20. Steiner, *Real Presences*, 232.

21. Eberhard Busch, *Karl Barth and the Pietists: The Young Karl Barth's Critique of Pietism and Its Response* (Downers Grove, IL: InterVarsity Press, 2004) 289.

Chapter 7—Spirit-Led Imagination: Reality Practiced in a Sub-Version

1. On "miracle," see the stunning phrase of Buber, *Moses*, 75, that miracle "can be defined at its starting point as an abiding astonishment."

2. Thanksgiving characteristically entailed both an utterance of gratitude and a material offering or, as we might say in Christian tradition, both "Word and sacrament." On the material offering, see Lev 7:11–18 and Ps 116:12–19. On the theology of such action, see Guthrie, *Theology as Thanksgiving*.

3. See the discussion of I. John Hesselink, "Karl Barth on Prayer," in Karl Barth, *Prayer*, 50th anniversary ed., ed. Donald E. Saliers (Louisville, KY: Westminster John Knox Press, 2002) 75–84, and his references to Barth, *Church Dogmatics III/3*.

4. Westermann, *The Praise of God in the Psalms*; see also Patrick D. Miller, *They Cried to the Lord: The Form and Theology of Biblical Prayer* (Minneapolis: Fortress Press, 1994) chap. 3.

5. See the exposition of "the cry" in Israel's faith by James L. Kugel, *The God of Old: Inside the Lost World of the Bible* (London: Free Press, 2003) chap. 5.

6. On the contemporary dominant version of reality and its capacity for self-maintenance, see Charles Reich, *Opposing the System* (New York: Crown, 1995).

Chapter 8—You Cannot Fool Your *Nephesh*

1. See Patrick D. Miller Jr., "The Human Sabbath: A Study in Deuteronomic Theology," *The Princeton Seminary Bulletin* 6, no. 2 (new series; 1985) 81–97.

2. Peter J. Kearney, "Creation and Liturgy: The P Redaction of Exod 25–40," *ZAW* 89 (1977) 375–87; Joseph Blenkinsopp, *Prophecy and Canon: A Contribution to the Study of Jewish Origins* (Notre Dame, IN: University of Notre Dame Press, 1977), 54–69.

3. Mark Slouka, "Quitting the Paint Factory," *Harper's Magazine* (November 2004) 57–65.

4. Ibid., 61.

5. Ibid., 64.

6. Ibid., 65.

Chapter 9—Just Like You . . . Forgiven!

1. See *Palestine in Transition: The Emergence of Ancient Israel*, ed. David Noel Freedman and David Frank Graf (Sheffield: The Almond Press, 1983).

2. Older scholarship, typified by G. Ernest Wright, *The Old Testament Against Its Environment* (SBT 2; London: SCM Press, 1950), sought to make the contrast between Canaanites and Israelites total. More recent scholarship has given much greater nuance to the contrast and shown that the likeness between the two and the kindred reality behind the contrasts. Nonetheless, as Norman Gottwald, *The Tribes of Yahweh: A Sociology of the Religion of Liberated Israel, 1250–1050 B.C.* (Maryknoll, NY: Orbis Books, 1979), has argued in a more nuanced way, conflict and tension are reflected in the text. Even the more recent accent on "folk religion" does not completely negate the sense of conflict and contrast.

3. Frank Crüsemann, *The Torah: Theology and Social History of Old Testament Law* (Edinburgh: T. & T. Clark, 1996) 224, 234.

4. Elie Wiesel, *The Jews of Silence: A Personal Report on Soviet Jewry* (New York: Holt, Rinehart, and Winston, 1966).

5. Eugene D. Genovese, *Roll Jordan Roll: The World the Slaves Made* (New York: Pantheon Books, 1974).

6. Patrick D. Miller Jr., "The Human Sabbath: A Study in Deuteronomic Theology," *The Princeton Seminary Bulletin* 6, no. 2 (New Series 1985) 81–97.

7. Patrick D. Miller, "Exposition of Luke 4:16–21," *Interpretation* 29 (October 1975) 417–21.

Chapter 11—Some Theses on the Bible in the Church

1. The language of "strange and new" is that of Karl Barth, "The Strange New World within the Bible," in *The Word of God and Word of* Man (New York: Harper & Brothers, 1957) 28–50. It is clear in the current conflicts in the church that too many folk claim to know fully the mind of God and do not credit the fact that the Bible is always "strange and new" and does not conform to our ideological categories. When that strangeness and newness are disregarded, we may be sure to be on the way to idolatry.

2. On "social construction" from a sociological perspective, see Peter L. Berger and Thomas Luckmann, *The Social Construction of Reality: A Treatise in the Sociology of Knowledge* (Anchor Books; Garden City: Doubleday, 1967). For such an act of theological imagination, see Garrett Green, *Imagining God: Theology and the Religious Imagination* (San Francisco: Harper & Row, 1989).

3. Mark Douglas, *Confessing Christ in the 21st Century* (New York: Rowman & Littlefield, 2005) 235–39.

4. Paul M. Kennedy, *The Rise and Fall of the Great Powers: Economic Change and Military Conflict from 1500 to 2000* (New York: Random House, 1987).

5. Barth, "The Strange New World within the Bible," 28–50.

6. On the interplay between Israel's faith and the cultural environment of the ancient Near East, see Rainer Albertz, *A History of Israelite Religion in the Old Testament Periods, Volumes I and II* (OTL; Louisville, KY: Westminster John Knox Press, 1994); Patrick D. Miller, *The Religion of Ancient* Israel (Library of Ancient Israel: Louisville, KY: Westminster John Knox Press, 2000); and Philip F. Esler, ed., *Ancient Israel: The Old Testament in Its Social Context* (Minneapolis: Fortress Press, 2006).

7. Michael J. Buckley, *At the Origins of Modern Atheism* (New Haven, CT: Yale University Press, 1987).

8. The phrase is from Berger and Luckmann, *Social Construction of Reality*, 157.

Index of Ancient Sources

Index of Names and Authors